Joseph Cobbinah

Barriers to Community Participation and Rural Development

D1806387

Joseph Cobbinah

Barriers to Community Participation and Rural Development

The hidden secrets in community participation

LAP LAMBERT Academic Publishing

Impressum / Imprint
Bibliografische Information der Deutschen Nationalbibliothek: Die Deutsche Nationalbibliothek verzeichnet diese Publikation in der Deutschen Nationalbibliografie; detaillierte bibliografische Daten sind im Internet über http://dnb.d-nb.de abrufbar.
Alle in diesem Buch genannten Marken und Produktnamen unterliegen warenzeichen-, marken- oder patentrechtlichem Schutz bzw. sind Warenzeichen oder eingetragene Warenzeichen der jeweiligen Inhaber. Die Wiedergabe von Marken, Produktnamen, Gebrauchsnamen, Handelsnamen, Warenbezeichnungen u.s.w. in diesem Werk berechtigt auch ohne besondere Kennzeichnung nicht zu der Annahme, dass solche Namen im Sinne der Warenzeichen- und Markenschutzgesetzgebung als frei zu betrachten wären und daher von jedermann benutzt werden dürften.

Bibliographic information published by the Deutsche Nationalbibliothek: The Deutsche Nationalbibliothek lists this publication in the Deutsche Nationalbibliografie; detailed bibliographic data are available in the Internet at http://dnb.d-nb.de.
Any brand names and product names mentioned in this book are subject to trademark, brand or patent protection and are trademarks or registered trademarks of their respective holders. The use of brand names, product names, common names, trade names, product descriptions etc. even without a particular marking in this works is in no way to be construed to mean that such names may be regarded as unrestricted in respect of trademark and brand protection legislation and could thus be used by anyone.

Coverbild / Cover image: www.ingimage.com

Verlag / Publisher:
LAP LAMBERT Academic Publishing
ist ein Imprint der / is a trademark of
AV Akademikerverlag GmbH & Co. KG
Heinrich-Böcking-Str. 6-8, 66121 Saarbrücken, Deutschland / Germany
Email: info@lap-publishing.com

Herstellung: siehe letzte Seite /
Printed at: see last page
ISBN: 978-3-659-28163-1

Zugl. / Approved by: Bradford, University of Bradford, Dissertation, 2011

Dedication

To my beloved father Joseph Cobbinah Anyimah for his living memory

Acknowledgement

I wish to express my sincere gratitude to a number of individuals who in diverse ways contributed towards the completion of this thesis.

My sincere gratitude goes to my supervisor Dr Behrooz Morvaridi, who went through the pain of guiding me to successfully complete this work. His useful criticisms, comments and suggestions made it possible for me to bring this work to its final completion. I will never forget the numerous letters he wrote to support me, while soliciting for funds and regularizing my stay in the United Kingdom to complete my studies.

I wish also to register my sincere thanks to some individuals who in various ways contributed in bringing this work to its final stage. My sincere thanks go to Ms Patricia Kom Ngong, a very special friend who supported me during the final stages of my work. Her immense assistance made it possible for me to finish this thesis. She will never be forgotten.

I will like to thank the following individuals who in diverse ways contributed towards my success. Paul Cobbinah, Harley Anane, Desmond Nkrumah and few individuals whose names cannot be mentioned, but in one way or the other contributed towards the completion of this work. May the Lord richly bless them.

Finally, my sincere thanks go to the Almighty God, whose guidance and mercies followed me throughout my life in the City of Bradford to successfully complete my studies. At long last, it is finished.

JEC

Bradford, 2011

2

Table of Content

ABBREVIATIONS USED IN THE STUDY

ADRA	Adventist Development Relief Agency
AFRC	Armed Forces Redemption Council
CBO	Community Based Organisation
CBOs	Community Based Organisations
CDEC	Co-operation for the Development of Emerging Country
CDR	Committee for the Defence of the Revolution
CPP	Convention People's Party
CSO	Civil Society Organisation
CSOs	Civil Society Organisations
DA	District Assembly
DAC	District Assembly Concept
DACF	District Assembly Common Fund
DCD	Department of Community Development
DCE	District Chief Executive
DSW	Department of Social Welfare
31stDWM	31st December Women's Movement
ERP	Economic Recovery Programme
GPRS	Ghana Poverty Reduction Strategy
HIPC	Highly Indebted Poor Countries
HIPCF	Highly Indebted Poor Country's Fund

4

IMF	International Monetary Fund
INTRAC	International NGO Training and Research Centre
ISSER	Institute of Statistical Social and Economic Research
MESW	Ministry of Employment and Social Welfare
MLGRD	Ministry of Local Government and Rural Development
MLGRDE	Ministry of Local Government, Rural Development and Environment
MoA	Ministry of Agriculture
MRD	Ministry of Rural Development
NCD	National Commission for Democracy
NCWD	National Council of Women and Development
NDC	National Democratic Congress
NED	Nzema East District
NGOs	Non Governmental Organisations
NNGOs	Northern Non-Governmental Organisation
NPP	New Patriotic Party
NRC	National Redemption Council
PLA	Participatory Centre Learning Action
PNDC	Provisional National Defence Council
PPRIS	President's Poverty Reduction Initiative Strategy
PRA	Participatory Rural Appraisal

PRSP	Poverty Reduction Strategy Papers
RRA	Rapid Rural Appraisal
SAP	Structural Adjustment Programme
SNGOs	Southern Non-Governmental Organisation
TDC	Town Development Committee
TTC	Teacher Training College
UC	Unit Committee
UCM	Unit Committee Members
UNDP	United Nations Development Programme
UNECA	United Nations Economic Commission for Africa
UNECLA	United Nations Economic Commission for Latin America
US	United States
USAID	United States Agency for International Development
WB	World Bank
WST	World System Theory

Chapter One

Introduction

1.1 Background to the Study

Participation in rural 'development is conventionally represented as emerging out of the recognition of the short comings of top-down development approaches' (Cooke and Kothari, 2007:5). However it has become increasingly clearer that community participation will help 'increase the involvement of socially and economically marginalised people in decision making' that affects their lives (Guijt, 1998 cited in Cooke and Kothari, 2007:5), but some critics also argue that the enormous limitations of the application of the concept make participatory practice very difficult and complex. It is therefore argued that participatory practice has to be re-examined and the 'methodological tools used, for example in Participation Rural Appraisal (PRA) and those that pay more attention to the theoretical, political and conceptual limitations of participation' also looked at (Cooke and Kothari, 2007:5). While the management and control of development resources still remain in the hands of facilitators and funding agencies (Mohan, 2002 and Sahley and Pratt, 2003), Cooke and Kothari (2007) also ask how many questions have to be asked before it is observed that the concept of participation starts display paradoxes and snarl-ups.

The concept of participation therefore became part of Ghana's democratic and development agenda in the late 1980s when the District Assembly Concept (DAC) became fully operational as a result of the introduction of a government decentralisation programme which was introduced during that period. It was aimed at involving the people at grassroots level in development decision-making and also giving them the opportunity to get involved in day-to-day policy formulation and implementation of programmes that affect their lives. Community participation in development activities has been the central focus of the

7

development agenda for past and present governments in Ghana since independence. However, the main focus has been on agriculture, especially in crop production for local industries and for export. Holistic involvement of community members in development decision-making had been patchy until the late 1980s when the then - Provisional National Defence Council (PNDC) government introduced political decentralisation as part of the political reforms and grassroots participation in development decision-making. Even then, the emphasis had been political rather than development. Arguably some critics stressed that it was the PNDC government's strategy to cling permanently onto power by using people from the grass-roots (Dzorgbo, 2001). This makes the concept of participation have more of a political orientation than community and social development.

Before the establishment of the DAC in the late 1980s public decision-making especially at the grassroots level, never formed part of the government's development agenda. Development policies and programmes were designed or formulated by the central government in Accra. Modifications to such policies were made at the regional offices by the Regional Ministers and Coordinating Directors and were implemented at the district level under the auspices of the then District Secretaries and the District Coordinating Directors. Implementation of development programmes was carried out by people hired by the district. However in the late 1980s when the district assembly concept (DAC) became operational, the government white paper stipulated that decision-making was to be made at the local level to involve local people (Constitution of Ghana, 1992). The Local Government Information Digest (1991) however stipulated that decision-making at the grassroots level was still limited only to the assembly members who were representatives in the assembly.

The involvement of civil society organisations (CSOs) and people at the grass root level also helps to enhance participatory practice in development activities at the local level. The assemblies were involved in development activities within the various communities; though their agenda never included active community participation in the day-to-day development decision-making in the rural communities. The assemblies in collaboration with the assembly members, take decisions on behalf of the community members. In the early 1980s, the neo-liberal development agenda that advocated involvement of the private sector and CSOs began to feature in Ghana's development agenda. The neo-liberalism development paradigm has also suffered a lot of set-backs and criticism, but in spite of that the absence of any alternative development approach has made organisations and institutions in Ghana to adopt it as their main agenda for development. This has encouraged the involvement of CSOs and enhanced their level of participation to community development activities. It opened doors for other development partners and paved the way for the evolution of many NGOs in the country. The objectives of most of these NGOs were towards capacity building and empowerment of women, to make them proactive in rural communities so that they could take full control of their lives and improve their livelihoods.

LaFord (1995) has argued that in the 1980s international donor agencies began questioning their investment in supporting development activities to improve the lives of the rural poor by asking these three questions: - why do many projects fail to survive after initial investment? What happens after the expenditure of the donor's money? How could development projects be sustained? As we begin to look for answers to those questions, LaFord, (1995) further argued that, while many countries in the developing world continue to struggle to keep their services running with their limited resources, unstable economies and galloping inflation continue to hamper their development efforts while external support continue to dwindle. Though some critics argue that participation slows down the development process (Chambers, 1983; 1997 and Korten 1996, cited in Open University, 2001) and others also argued that development objectives would be difficult to achieve if beneficiaries were not placed first in participatory decision-making and overall management remained in the hands of facilitators.

1.2 Statement of the Problem

Ghana's political decentralisation system, which was launched in the late 1980s, had its focus at the grass-roots level. The aim of the programme was mainly to encourage people at the grass-roots to become proactive so that they could participate actively in political decision-making. However the adoption of participatory practice in recent development practice was a way of encouraging those people to influence development decision-making and take control of and management responsibilities for resources within their communities (Cooke and Kothari, 2007). The involvement of the local people would also empower them to demand better accountability and ensure transparency in every development activity in their communities. Besides, through participation development institutions, governmental and non-governmental organisations (NGOs) would be able to involve beneficiaries in their development practice to promote and achieve sustainable development objectives (Francis, 2002; Desai, 2002; Kotze and Kellerman, 2003).

Community participation has been embraced by funding agencies and CSOs, because they argue that it is through participation that rural community members would be able to become part of the intervention and contribute to its improvement (Cooke and Kothari, 2007). Besides some critics also view participation as a way of transferring control of

10

resources and power to community members, because they argued that 'local knowledge reflects local power' (Mosse, 2007:19). Yet other critics argue that participation is a threat to facilitators' control of resources and management of intervention, because it empowers the local people to enable them take responsibilities and control (Roche in Open University, 2001). It thus become comprehensible for facilitators to hold on to and control resources and power because they 'still face other pressures to get things done and other measures of efficiency than those provided by measures of participation' (Mosse, 2007:24). Besides participation is still constrained by bureaucratic agenda that have to be met by institutions that apply the concept of participation (Mosse cited in Cooke and Kothari, 2007).

In Nzema East District (NED), NGOs that undertake development rely on external project officers in the management of intervention. Notwithstanding that community participation forms part of their development agenda as a way of empowering the community members to become proactive in their development efforts; active participation seems difficult to achieve in practice. So how long will development organisations, government development institutions and departments continue to manage projects and make them sustainable? To what extent 'have participatory methods driven out others which have advantage that participation cannot provide' or 'do group dynamics lead to participatory decisions that reinforce interest of the already powerful' (Cooke and Kothari, 2007:8)?

These are some of the questions that are commonly asked to ascertain the degree of effectiveness, inefficiencies, complexities and contradictions in participatory practice. Therefore the paradoxes and constraints that hinder the effective application of participatory practice still remain an issue that needs to be investigated. Whether community participation is effective and could help to improve the lives of rural communities or enhance their control and management of development resources still needs

11

to be empirically investigated (Cleaver, 2001; LaFord, 1995). It is against this background that a piece of empirical research to ascertain the paradoxes and snarl-ups that hinder effective application of the concept of participation has become important.

1.3 Significance of the Study

The concept of participation has been a development application tool to involve people at the grass-roots level in development policy formulation and practice. In spite of its use for over four decades, there are still some bottlenecks that hinder the effective and smooth application of the concept and some contradictions that have been led to dilemmas for the people who are supposed to benefit from participatory practice. This study would help development organisations/institutions that apply the concept to understand some of the major snarl-ups and contradictions that influence effective application of the concept. It would also enlighten organisations/institutions that engage the people at the grass-roots level on how they could re-design their policies and programmes when they engage in participatory activities. In addition it would serve as a basis for development policy formulation and help development facilitators to understand rural people in their own world as they involve them in development activities. Finally it would identify new areas for future development research to improve not only participatory practice, but also development practice.

1.4 Aim, Objectives and Research Questions

Aim of the Study – The study is aimed at investigating the nature of barriers that affect and hinder effective participatory practice and rural development. Many factors constrain rural people's participation in development activities in their communities. For instance, time limitations for development facilitators, the family commitment of women; lack of

12

opportunity for women to freely express their opinion, the *blue print* approach to development practice (Mosse, 2007), which does not pave the way for adequate participation, gender bias and a lack of institutional preparedness to include community knowledge. All these factors militate against effective and active community participation.

Research Objectives – The objectives of the study is to understand the nature of barriers that hinder effective participatory practice. However, in the broader sense, the investigation will help achieve the following research objectives;

- To examine the nature of rural development interventions in selected villages in NED and assess the nature of community participation

- To understand how the DA and NGOs adopt participatory approach to engage people in development activities

- To ascertain the barriers that hinder rural people becoming involved in participatory practice in their communities.

- To examine the inconsistencies in participatory practice and the dilemmas that face rural people

- To find ways of addressing participatory problems which arise when rural community members are engaged in the management of development interventions

- To ascertain ways in which development interventions could be made sustainable through participatory practice, in order to bring improvements to the lives of rural people.

Achievement of the research objectives will help provide answers to the research questions that underpin the overall investigation. Attention will therefore be focused on the *nature* of participation and the numerous constraints associated with its application.

The Research Questions – Previous studies have shown that development organisations encourage community participation, yet they consider the involvement of community members a challenge to their control of power and the management of resources (Roche in Open University, 2001). It however, become clear that, externally imposed ideas and the over reliance of expert knowledge which seem not to improve participatory practice became evident since the 1980s, that, participation was not only showing no result, but also having no significant impact in lives of community members they serve (Cooke and Kothari, 2007). This reflects Mosse's (2007) observation that, in spite of the general assumption that participation defines the success of the intervention, donor nations and funding bodies maintain that holistic participation, which leads to transfer of power to beneficiaries – in order to encourage them to participate actively and on equal terms with development facilitators - is heavily resisted (Pretty, 2003). Eman (1991) argued that, unless management performance is seriously addressed and participation become effective, donor support for grassroots interventions will be seriously reduce and community support will be weakened.

The aforementioned arguments identify the nature of questions that became relevant for the investigation.

- *What is the extent of participation of the people in rural communities in the development activities?*

A lot of research has been conducted into participation and the involvement of rural community members in development decision-making, but the extent to which local people must be involved, in order to become active and proactive participants, remains unclear. Information is scarce on how people *should* participate, the complexities involved in participatory practice, and the obstacles and difficulties related to participatory practice. It

14

will examine how the DA and NGOs apply the concept in the villages; for example, *who* are involved, *why* are they involved and *how* are they involved in participatory practice. In addition to that people in rural communities differ in their expectations and aspirations (Penrose, 2000). Achieving these various objectives will require the involvement of those who will benefit from the programme in policy formulation, decision-making and implementation of their ideas - rather than imposing the *outsiders'* ideas and opinions that would weaken local support and trust (Chambers, 1997; Robinson et al, 2000). This study is never intended to investigate only the nature of participatory practice in development activities in the villages of the district but rather, it intends to investigate the constraints and the inconsistencies that make the application of the participatory approach difficult. Thus the question asked is;

- *What barriers affect and hinder the active participation of rural people and how could these be addressed?*

It is evident that variation of management style, language and cultural barriers, and the use of external knowledge to manage development interventions also weaken community trust in development facilitators (Penrose, 2000). However, while there is good evidence that community participation helps improve the management of rural development interventions, there are also studies that draw different conclusions and raise new questions about the problems and barriers associated with participatory approach. How many rural areas have developed in one generation, cannot be ascertained by empirical evidence and whether participatory activities are really improving rural communities, also remains an illusion (Burkey, 1993 and Clever, 2001).

Korten's observation also shows that rural life is constantly changing and development objectives are becoming more complex. With ever-changing socio-economic factors, effective management that brings harmony to rural communities is vital in order to enhance community cohesion (Korten in Open University, 2002). Paradoxically, even the World Bank advocates for participation in development practice yet leaves major decisions about development activities to be made by external experts, and even the parameters of participation is determined by external agencies and development facilitators (Datta, 2003). So the effective participation of community members that will address those obstacles and inconsistencies to make participatory practice effective and people at the grassroots proactive in community development brings some significance to this study.

1.5 Delimitation of the Study

The research was carried out to cover only the Nzema East District (NED) of the western region of Ghana. The study did not cover all the 138 districts, but one was selected from one of the thirteen (13) districts of the Western Region. The decision to carry out the investigation in NED was due to the fact that, since the introduction of the DAC in the late 1980s as a result of the government decentralisation programme, community participation in development activities has either been partial or non-existent. Some political critics still argue that the introduction of the unit committees in every village/town at the district level throughout the country has helped to enhance the level of community participation, although the problems that are hindering the effective application of community participation in development still remain unclear to development organisations and even government development institutions.

The study was limited to NED because it was aimed at exploring the nature of community participation in the district and ascertaining how people at the grass-root level are being involved in the decision-making process. Looking at the number of districts and the time available for the study, it became necessary to limit the study to only one district so that a comprehensive and detailed investigation could be carried out. NED is one of the most deprived districts in the region. However in spite of the government decentralisation concept, which some experts claim has brought governance to the grass-roots level enabling the local people to make their views heard or make contributions towards the assembly development efforts, the district still lag behind many others even within the region. Ranging from low school turnout to high levels of employment, the problems in the district make it an ideal area for research study to help evaluate the situation so that recommendations could be put forward for the formulation and improvement of future development policy. A couple of NGOs have been making some significant efforts to help the people in the district to improve their way of life, yet the level of progress is relatively slow. The introduction of the government's district assembly common fund, which most districts were taking advantage of to improve their communities, has made little impact in the life of the people and the nature of development in NED. Besides, the researcher was familiar with the area and the location of respondents, thus making it a bit easier to identify the key informants for the study.

1.6 Research Contribution to Knowledge

A successful completion of the study would be a significant contribution to the field of development studies and to organisations and institutions that actively engage rural people in participatory activities. The study has provided the basis for development organisations to assess the nature of the complexities and constraints that exist in participatory practice. It became evident from the literature search that there are many types of participation but the definitions of forms of participation still remain very implicit, while information on the

17

concept is either patchy or unclear. Whilst the typology continues to elongate as a result of different interpretations and application of the concept, little is said on forms. This study has very explicitly created the distinction between the concepts of form and type of participation, which hitherto has been very difficult to comprehend. It also explained when and how development organisations e.g. NGOs have to apply those two terminologies in participatory practice.

Previous research has revealed some of the paradoxes and snarl-ups that make participatory practice very difficult. This study has gone further to identify new paradoxes and constraints that have been overlooked or seem difficult for organisations to appreciate as key issues that hinder participatory practice. The findings revealed some of the major snarl-ups affecting and hindering participatory practice. The use of juju and witchcraft by some of the people in the rural communities scare most people especially the women and youths and even some men, involved in participatory practice. These, among others, have limited effective application of the concept of participation. The study calls this *institutional limit* in participatory practice. Chapter 8 of this thesis gives a more detailed account of what is meant by institutional limit.

Briefly, threats, intimidations and the use of juju and witchcraft are some of the factors that are weakening participatory practice in the communities where the investigation was carried out. The study has therefore made it clear that development institutions, organisations and beneficiaries should take a closer look at these problems when they employ the principles of participation to achieve their development objectives. As a further contribution to knowledge, this research is the first to be carried out in the NED of Ghana that looks at participatory practice and the management of rural development. Development studies discourse will now contain empirical information from NED about participatory practice as the thesis gets into the public domain.

1.7 Structure of the Thesis

The thesis has been divided into nine main chapters. It begins with the introduction of which this sub-section forms part. The introduction is followed by the conceptual framework which forms Chapters Two and Three. The literature review illustrates how the relevant themes have been reviewed to interlink with other concepts that have been used and included in the study. It identifies the concept of participation and how development institutions apply it when they engage rural community members in their work. It takes into consideration other concepts such as CSOs, power relations, empowerment, capacity building and partnership. These concepts are examined by detailing how they are applied in development practice. The second chapter also looks at how CSOs and NGOs apply the concept in development practice. While Chapter Three examines how participation has been applied in Ghana's local governance through its district assembly concept since its introduction in the late 1980s. This chapter examines the development trend adopted by various governments in Ghana from independence to the present.

Chapter Four examines the research methodology and the motivation of the study. It looks at the research design which examined the philosophical underpinnings of the study (which includes interpretivist and constructionist perspectives). This is followed by the research profile in Chapter Five, which explains the socio-economic activities of the villages in the district that were involved in the study. Chapters, Six, Seven and Eight look at the research findings and discuss the results. Chapter Six and Seven illustrate decision-making at the local level and examines how the effectiveness of participatory practice, while looking at some of the paradoxes and how they affect effective development management. The seventh chapter examines some of the paradoxes encountered when NGOs engage the local people in development activities. Chapter Eight looks at some of the snarl-ups in participatory practice and the dilemmas facing rural people as they become engaged with development activities, be they institutional-driven or community-initiated. The final chapter (Chapter Nine) revisits the objectives of the study to ascertain how the achievement those objectives would help in the formulation of new policies in development practice. The section revisits the key findings and reflects on how the study has contributed to the body of knowledge through recommendations and policy formulation for future practice. Finally new areas for future research are suggested.

Chapter Two

Civil Society Organisations and NGOs in Community Participation: A Conceptual Framework

2.1 Introduction

This chapter looks at the concept of participation and how it is applied in community development. It examines the origin of civil society and the debate surrounding its application in the past and its relevance in today's world and how it influences development policy and practice. Activities of Civil Society Organisation (CSOs) and NGOs will be explicitly examined in terms of their engagement with rural community members in development work. The concept of power and power relations will also be examined in detailed to assess how it affects development practice. This chapter will also examine how neo-liberal development theory has shaped development thinking through integration of community members in rural development activities. Ways in which NGOs apply the concept of participation in community development will also be examined. The chapter will lastly look at the link between participation, empowerment, capacity building and partnership and how these concepts could be integrated to help improve community members' involvement in development activities.

2.2 Civil Society Organisation and Community Development

2.2.1 Understanding Civil Society Organization

According to Hooker and Locke the civil society organisation (CSO) debate entered the European political discourse in the sixteenth and seventeenth centuries (Hall and Trentmann, 2005). However, the concept of CSO, can trace its true origin from European thinkers who argued for protecting the 'interest of those living in a civilised political

21

community' through the creation of a state to serve the community's interest (Rooy, 1998:7). The term 'civil society' comes from the Latin word '*civilis societas*'. The term evolved in the late seventeenth and early eighteenth centuries and was associated with the 'thinking and ideologies of John Locke, an English philosopher who set out the distinction between a state of nature – which included absolute monarchy – and civil society/political formed by social contract', and of Thomas Hobbes and Kant (Francis, 2002:72; Hooker, 2005:30).

In the nineteenth and the early twentieth centuries, the concept of CSO was used to describe the common and unitary social desires that embraced 'the protection of different ethical or normative nations against a drift of flattening uniformity' (Hall and Trentmann, 2005:14). Hall and Trentmann further argued that towards the end of the twentieth century, the concept began to move towards the centre stage of political discourse because it was understood as a problem identified in the political society and social formation of a number of nations. The works of Francis, Hall and Trentmann show that towards the later part of the second millennium, the concept of CSO begun to triumph, with a comprehensive and remarkable revival in the late 1970s onwards as a result of the backdrop of totalitarian experience in Europe, dictatorship in Latin America and communism in Asia as well as the 'failure of earlier development decades, to global political events in the 1990s and to the domestic concerns of industrialized countries' (Francis, 2002; Hall and Trentmann, 2005:1, 3).

CSO has been in the development discourses since and has been a conceptualised issue in the development debate in the last century (Whaites, 2000). However besides, the controversies the concept of CSO has brought divergent views about which organisations are supposed to be engulfed within its perimeters. Recent development discourse has embraced the concept but further research was being done into its operations and continued to give different definitions and interpretations, thus making the meaning and interpretation of CSO broad and blurred. Interestingly the growing numbers of organisations that call themselves a CSO has also contributed to the difficulties that face development activists in coming to a clear comprehension of the concept.

According to Scholte, CSOs are usually made up of individuals who through their concerted efforts either by voluntary or deliberate action bring about social construction or reconstruction (Scholte, 1999). Hall and Trentmann (2005) on their part also view CSO as a concept that is embedded in the power which is entrusted in an organisation and it is used activities of those individuals, but through consciousness and independence could act with freewill. Individuals in a CSO act according to the conscience of others who might be the influential body behind the ideologies of the organisation. The deliberations of such individuals or groups of individuals could be influenced by the philosophy and principles underpinning the establishment of the CSO. Interestingly, individuals may be in a CSO, although the ideology of the organisation may represent that of a few and influential individuals who formed the organisation; though the ideology of these influential individuals may be in resonance with that of the main organisation. Hall and Trentmann, (2005) pointed out that CSOs give people a sense of thinking beyond the state or community, but it does not mean that commentators are blind to the fact that they form an integral component of civil society.

CSO has been defined as organised activities by individuals or organisations that may try to influence a policy or may use their influence to improve the activities of a society but such organisations are not part of government or business. By their nature of operations, CSOs

23

are commonly referred to as organisations in the third sector[1] (Trivedy and Acharya, 1996; Scholte, 1999; Weinberger, 2000; Clarke, 2002). According to Francis CSOs are organisations that function between the state and the private sector (Francis, 2002). They include a wide range of non-governmental and non-for-profit organisations that operate in the public interest, while at the same time express the interests and values of their members or organization based on ethical, cultural, political, religious or philanthropic considerations (World Bank, 2005). The state is known as the first sector[2], while the commercial marketplace is the second or private sector (Trivedy and Acharya, 1996; Scholte, 1999).

CSOs can neither be state-run nor operate under market forces. CSOs may include; churches, educational institutions, professional bodies like the bar associations, workers and trade unions, farmers' and fishermen's associations, consumer protection bodies, the media, commentators, traditional leaders, environmental associations, human right groups, community-based organisations, indigenous peoples organisations, NGOs, cultural associations, youth clubs, ethnic associations, etc (Trivedy and Acharya, 1996; Jorgensen, 1996; Scholte, 1999; Long, 2001; Winter, 2001; Whaites, 2002; Francis, 2002; World Bank, 2005). Though the examples above are regarded as CSOs some critics such as Francis (2002) argue that it is wrong to generalise that organisations like funeral associations or trade unions are all CSOs, because the contributions of some of these organisations may remain very doubtful and sometimes their philosophies may not reflect the whole organisation or community. The philosophy of such organizations may reflect views from some few influential members of the organization. Even though the ideology of the CSO may exist, it is sometimes influenced by a few individuals who may also use their

---

[1] The third sector here is being referred to as the organisations that are not state owned and also not belong to the private sector which may have profit generation orientation though some individuals may have their own of such organisations.

[2] The first sector does not mean it entered the development discourse first but to show it is a form of division among these three different groups

24

expertise to push their own ideas forward or make their views dominate the overall ideology of the organisation. In some cases, it may be for their own selfish interest, but in the name of the CSO. .

2.2.2 Civil Society Organizations and Community Development

Over the years CSOs have contributed either directly or indirectly towards the development of a number of communities most especially in the developing world. Depending on their orientation and ideology, CSOs have many objectives and aims, though most of their objectives are towards the improvement of the lives of the people they serve, through advocacy, social development and empowerment. In community development CSOs activities can be classified according to the nature of their operations and their stated objectives. Jorgensen, (1996) puts CSOs into three main categories, based on their area of operation and the nature of their activities. The first category is grassroots organisations, whose operations may be limited to local communities. Those that have their operations limited to particular district and have little coverage at the national level are often referred to as middle range CSOs. The third category is those that operate at the national level - they operate at the national and even the international levels and may even have some global influence. Different CSOs may have some common agenda/objectives but can still vary in terms of their sociological, political or ideological orientation. Those in advocacy, rural community development and relief supply in disasters and war zone areas, are often classified as NGOs; nevertheless their aspirations and philosophical orientation may also differ remarkably.

Civil society organisations give room for debate about the direction a particular society or organisation follows. It gives people the opportunity to influence the activities of government and business (Jorgensen, 1996). According to Leftwich (1995) and Jorgensen (1996), CSOs can exercise pressure on governments in decision-making or in the amendment of government policies and programmes and may help strengthen the democratic principles of a state. This falls in line with the observation by Francis that they serve as a 'useful construct for orienting and advancing a range of policies and operational initiatives', decongesting government control and enhancing public consultation and service delivery (Francis, 2002:73). He further argues that CSOs respond to the anxieties of their societies and serve as advocates for the people in areas where the government is rolling back its objectives in meeting the needs of her citizens, while some use their influence to re-shape government activities.

Scholte and Weinberger have argued that, by definition and orientation, CSOs do not organise their activities to maximise profits nor use their activities to earn a living for their members (Scholte, 1999; Weinberger, 2000). However, other critics also argue that the lack of project generation by CSOs is untrue and remain debatable. Studies conducted by Yunus, the Open University and Thomas and Allen indicate that some CSOs operating as micro-credit financial institutions have developed into bigger commercial banks through profit generation (Yunus, 1997; Open University, 2000; Thomas and Allen, 2000). They cited BancoSol in Bolivia and Grameen Bank in Bangladesh as examples of organisations that have developed through profit generation. Weinberger, (2000) has argued that though such organisations have developed into mainstream banks, as already pointed out above that, by their nature, orientation and establishment, the focus of CSOs is mainly on human development and community improvement. Weinberger added that the profits they generate from their activities are used for further development activities and address issues that are

26

centred on social development for the benefit of needy individuals but not for the benefit of members of the organization.

2.2.3 Development Organisations and Institutions: Conflicting Concepts

Having looked at the concept of CSO, and how they influence community development, we will turn our attention to examine in more detail the concept of an organisation and how it differs from an institution with respect to the way they involve people at the grassroots level in development practice. I will begin by asking, what are organisations and how do they differ from institutions? The terms organisation and institution are similar but not synonymous. Interpretation of the concepts by development practitioners and organisations seem confusing and blurred. According to North, Fowler and others an organisation is made up of a group of individuals who come together to work towards a common goal (North, 1990; Fowler et al in Open University, 2002). Their activities are not spontaneous, but rather they are planned and somewhat controlled (Tellegen and Wolsink, 1998). They involve people from different backgrounds and philosophies. Examples of such organisations are churches, NGOs, funeral associations, fishermen groups, farmers associations.

An institution as explained by Knight (1992), is made up of members, with shared beliefs or knowledge and have rules that governs their operations and activities. There are rules, norms and (sometimes) a code of practice that govern the mode of operation of members within an institution, and the members are expected to have a certain standard of knowledge. In some cases specific qualifications are a pre-requisite for one to become a member of an institution. Knight argued that unlike organisations, some requirements are needed for individuals to become members of an institution. For instance one may have to

27

sit a standard examination in order to become a member of an institution; this is true of example colleges of surgeons, institutes of bankers, bar associations, hospitals, etc.

Fowler et al have argued that by their nature and operations both organisations and institutions overlap (Fowler et al cited in Open University, 2002). They explained that some organisations exhibit some functions similar to those of institutions, yet by orientation the two are not the same. Some NGOs are organisations because most do not have a code of ethics while their members may have divergent views, aspirations, qualifications and ideology; though the members work towards a common goal. Agencies like the IMF or the World Bank working on behalf of a particular government or even the United Nations when implementing certain agendas and programmes work within the parameters or code of conduct of the agency and are classified as financial institutions. The focus of both development institutions and organisations is geared towards socio-economic development of the people they serve, so the meanings of the two terms is a bit confusing, blurred and tend to overlap.

2.2.4 NGOs as Civil Society Organisations

NGOs are forms of CSO whose main activities are concentrated on community improvement, poverty alleviation, advocacies, capacity building and community empowerment. Over the years NGOs activities have gone beyond above and beyond these parameters. The term NGO is used to cover a host of organisations, ranging from relief organisations to service provisioning. Christian Aid, CARE International, Save the Children, environmental conservations groups such as Friends of the Earth, wildlife conservation groups and self-help groups such as funeral associations, welfare

28

organisations, farmers and fishermen's associations, etc are all classified as NGOs (Lane, 1995; Moyo, 2000; Mawdsley et al, 2002).

The activities of NGOs can be traced back into the late 1940s, immediately after the Second World War; as explained by Winter (2001) and Desai (2002b). The evolution of NGOs came at a time that some CSOs felt that they could alleviate the suffering of those affected by the war in Europe and other parts of the world; and assist countries that were experiencing economic slowdown as a result of the war. Long (2001), Desai, (2002b), Francis (2002), Nelson (2002) and others have argued that the activities of NGOs have grown beyond only welfare provisioning, especially since the late 1980s and early 1990s. In the developing world, some areas where government resources cannot reach as a result of lack of funds and the donor support is not forthcoming, the assistance from NGOs has been very significant.

NGOs are mostly self-governing, not-for-profit or voluntary development 'organisations that are geared to improving the quality of life of disadvantaged people' or organisations not benefiting directly from government development initiatives (Vakil, 1997:2060; Long, 2002). In some cases, they work on behalf of a government, though not under direct control of any government department. Their agendas are based on the philosophical orientation that underpins the establishment of the organisation. Long (2002) enumerated some of the activities of NGOs as - service delivery to poor individuals or communities; support work such as capacity building, technical assistance and funding to communities, advocacy of the neglected, the marginalized and women amongst others. In some countries, NGOs act as government's quangoes and work on their behalf in some kind of service delivery, while others may distance themselves and run their activities in parallel to those of the state (Thomas and Allen, 2000; Desai, 2002b; Clark, 2002; Nelson, 2002). However, some

29

critics have also argued that although NGOs are considered to be effective organisations that deliver public services as pointed out by Long, the operation of some NGOs are socially and politically marginalised (Desai, 2002b; Francis, 2002), because they oppose some government's action plans and policies.

Lane (1995:184) has categorized NGOs into four types, 'welfare and relief, modernisation, community development and institution building'. The relief and welfare NGOs focus their efforts on assisting people affected by wars, drought, earthquakes, flood and other natural disasters and in conflict situations. The remaining three categories have been grouped under the term development NGOs. The work of these NGOs is primarily to help promote and improve the lives of people through community and institutional development techniques; empowerment and capacity building which could enable people to meet their own development aspirations and give them a way to improve their livelihoods.

Types and Characteristics of NGOs: Variations in community needs and diversification of the development agendas of NGOs have increased the dichotomy of NGOs operating in the world today. Luong and Weinthal (1999) have noted that the inability of some countries to meet the development needs of their citizens, has created gaps which many NGOs are seeking to fill, although a reasonable number of them do not have clear development objectives. There are many NGOs operating today and their activities can be based on their geographical location, their level of operation, philosophical underpinnings behind their establishment or their orientation (Mayo, 2000; Kamat, 2002). Tables 2.1 and 2.2 clearly illustrate the type and characteristics of NGOs and their modes of operations.

Table 2.1 Typology of NGOs and their areas of operations

Types of NGOs	Origin and Areas of Operation
Northern	Mostly from the developed countries render most of their services in the developing world.
Southern	These are NGOs that are in the developing countries. They are often formed through local initiatives and their operations are at the regional and national levels. They may render their activities at village level and may liaise between donor nations and northern NGOs.
Community-based/ Indigenous/Grassroots	Such NGOs are mostly promoted by government ministries, church groups or community mobilisation groups. They operate at the grass-roots level and mostly in the village.

Sources: Hudock, (1999), Moyo, (2000).

The main focus of some NGOs is on rural community development (Ellis, 2000). Arguably NGOs are cost effective, adaptable to the local environment, very innovative and understand the local situation, as a result, government departments, and international development institutions seek the help of NGOs to spend resources on their behalf (Thomas and Allen, 2000; Desai, 2002b).

Table 2.2 Characteristics of NGOs and their performance

Characteristic of NGOs	Activities
Service Providers	They provide training services, capacity building, consultancy, research, etc., at the community level, and engage in service delivery for the needy, such as refugees, flood victims, etc.
Intermediary	They liaise with funding agencies and assist grassroots organisations in securing funds and other assistance for development activities.
Advocacy	They serve as advocates for the underprivileged, disadvantaged, widows, street children, etc,
Relief	They provide relief supplies to communities or countries affected by flood, earth quakes, famine, disease outbreaks, etc. Technical assistance in a form of training, fundraising strategies, proposal writing, to make local organisations to run their own activities and make them self-reliant.

Source: Hudock, (1999), Moyo, (2000)

This form of trust enhances the synergy between northern NGOs and southern or community-based NGOs in the execution of development activities. The over reliance of some governments on NGOs to spend money on their behalf gives such NGOs influence on government policy formulation and implementation. Farrington et al (1993) confirm that NGOs are the vehicle through which policies of development intervention could be implemented at the grassroots level.

The flexibility of the policies and programmes of NGOs, their ability to work directly with the rural poor and within rural and risky conditions, make them preferable to government development departments (Lane, 1995; Long, 2001). Yet some critics still argue that NGOs are just *gap-filling* organisations (Thomas and Allen, 2000; Desai, 2002b), though they can follow non-conventional policies and operate in areas that most government departments find it difficult to operate. NGOs would not offer 'rapid solution to a scale of global poverty or even alleviate it sufficiently to ensure relative social stability' (Pearce, 2001:21; 2004). However Thomas and Allen (2000) conclude that in spite of the hype about the work some NGOs are claiming to be doing towards the improvement of the lives of the rural poor, neglected and marginalised, NGOs will never change the world. Attention will now be turned to a critical evaluation of the concept of participation in order to ascertain how it has influenced development practice over the last four decades.

2.3. Overview of Participation

In the 1980s, development institutions, NGOs and governments departments began to examine why after more than thirty years of conventional and technocratic forms of development approaches, communities were not benefiting from development interventions while at the same time a number of projects that were already in place were failing (Wright and Nelson, 1995:3; Michener, 1998). Studies conducted by Feeney showed that many communities were deteriorating, while many people were struggling to make a living as a result of a lack of government support and 'ill-conceived, internationally financed infrastructure projects' being implemented in their communities (Feeney, 1998:10). According to Kotze and Kellerman, (1997) and Francis, (2002), the deteriorating nature of various rural communities has been due to a lack of integration of rural people's knowledge and ideas and limited opportunities for them to participate in development policy formulation that has are led to continuous and unsustainable failures in development processes. Though 'public works agencies view participation as a means to reduce operations and maintenance cost' and enhance community 'patronage and reputation' in projects (Mosse (2007:29), critics likes Schneider and Libercier, (1995) also argue that some people are still excluded and are not even considered in development decision-making.

2.3.1 Origin of Participation.

The concept of participation entered the development discourse in the 1960s as a development tool to improve the lives of rural people (Chambers, 1983; 1997, Francis, 2002). However according to Francis (2002) the concept originated from two main roots. The first ideology came from a Latin American thinker who argued that communities could eliminate their poverty, if views and opinions about ways of doing so could be solicited from those in poverty, the second came from American organisational management thinking, which argued that organisations could work effectively and make more profit if the workers were able to participate in the day-to-day decision-making of the organisation and in policy formulation and implementation.

Chambers (1983; 1997) Kotze and Kellerman, (1997) and Francis (2002) have argued that participation became very relevant in the 1960s as a tool to improve the lives of rural and deprived communities. That is, it allows community members to participate in development activities in the communities through decision-making, policy formulation and implementation of development programmes. Usage of the concept of participation begun when some development activists in a rural development appraisal workshop – which was organised by the Institute of Development Studies (IDS) of the University of Sussex was called rapid rural appraisal (RRA) (Bergdall, 1993; Chambers, 1997). Since then the principle of RRA has begun to gain recognition and acceptance by many institutions and countries that aim at developing the life of their rural communities through appraisal workshops. It became a principle used to assess better ways that facilitators could learn about the conditions and lives of rural people and integrate those ideas into their development agenda (Chambers, 1997; McGee, 2002). As McGee (2002) explained RRA has some power limitations. Development facilitation and decision-making were limited to a few influential individuals so concerns were raised about its short comings and the search participatory approaches continued.

The shift in the development paradigm led to participatory rural appraisal (PRA) which some critics argued evolved from RRA, but was aimed at addressing some of the weaknesses identified in RRA (Chambers, 1994b; Kabutha and Ford, 1988 cited in Chambers, 1997). The ultimate aim of PRA 'was intended to enable poor people to define the sort of development they aspired to, and become empowered through the very methods and processes of PRA' (McGee, 2002:100). PRA was to address the conflict of power and power relations that showed the weakness of RRA, so that it could give local people the opportunity to actively participate in their development work, becoming empowered and

34

very proactive. However, McGee further explained that although development policy analysis has shown that local knowledge is valued and helps in the formulation and modification of development policy and decisions, it suffers a lot of set-backs and resistance because it help to empower the marginalised social groups at the same time as it disempowers those in control.

In the last three decades PRA has added momentum to rural people's involvement in decision-making, use of community knowledge and engagement to improve development practice (Blackburn and Holland, 1998). In Tanzania, the United Nations Economic Commission for Africa (UNECA) organised a conference, that aimed at broadening the concept of participatory development through economic growth, good governance and popular participation (Nelson and Wright, 1995). However, the UNECA approach never permitted the poor people to assess their situation and find solution (Chambers, 1992; 1995), but emphasis on promotion of community involvement towards economic growth and effective system of governance. Development institutions and organisations interpretation of the concept of participation by development institutions and organisations continued to change, while rural peoples' understanding of the concept also became diverse. This led to different ways of defining and interpreting the concept of participation.

2.3.2 Defining Participation

Development activists, research institutions, development organisations and facilitators of development organisations have tried to explained ways in which the concept of participation could enhance the effectiveness of community development, especially at the grass-root level. The application of the concept has also led to the emergence of various definitions and interpretations of participation, but ways in which development organisations or institutions define the concept still differ remarkably. It is, however, argued that different interpretations of the concept and answers to questions such as who should participate, how should participation be practiced, when should participation be necessary, who should be the beneficiary of participation and in whose interest is participation, continue to dominate the interpretation of the concept of participation (Chambers, 1997; Agarwal, 2001; Open University, 2001; Datta, 2003; Clemente, 2003).

Feeney (1998:10) defined participation as 'an opportunity for citizens and public and private organisations to express their opinions on general policy goals or to have their priorities and needs integrated into decisions made about specific projects and programmes'. According to Desai, the United Nations defines participation as the sharing of ideas by people towards the benefits of development, activities, making an active contribution to the development process and being involved in decision-making at all levels of society (Desai, 2002a). The World Bank Participatory Learning Group (WBPLG) views participation in terms of stakeholders influence and their shared goals. It defined participation as a process through which stakeholders influence and share control over development initiatives, decisions and resources which affect them (Nelson and Wright, 1995; McGee, 2002). However, in the contrarily Oakley argued that participation should be a form of voluntary contributions made by people who might be involved in public programmes which are geared towards national, regional or community level development but they are not supposed to make any contribution through decision-making or influence any policy formulation or implementation (Hilhorst, 2003). Oakley's understanding shows that participation should be passive, where individuals become just representatives rather than active members in the participatory process.

Unlike the World Bank (WB), Oakley's argument presupposes that participation has to be voluntary, but the WB definition does not go far enough to encourage the inclusion of community members in decision-making or their influence on development policy formulation. To influence development policy and practice means people should have the opportunity to participate on equal terms in order to influence the development plan. Besides, the WB definition never considered devolution of power, which could help community members to participate on equal terms with development facilitators' and other stakeholders. It does not explicitly make provision for the inclusion of women in decision-making although there has been an outcry for organisations to review their policies on the inclusion of women in development policy formulation and implementation (Morvaridi, 1994; Agarwal, 2001). Mosse (2001) has argued that participation should embrace the total inclusion of men and women in the decision making process to bring about maximization of development benefits. This could bring about better design of development programmes that could in turn, lead to a more effective and sustainable process, because women have been suppressed in expressing their views on development.

Arguably some development organisations do not support participation that would give community members the opportunity to influence an already-formulated development plan, because they argue that may lead to deviation from an existing development agenda developed by donors or external organisations (Open University, 2001). This makes some organisations resist participation by local people in decision-making. Francis (2002) has argued that participation should not be limited to only facilitators or be influenced by outsiders; rather, it should involve devolution of power, so that those at the community level can be empowered and become active participants in decision-making and influence

37

development policies, bringing positive change to the lives of the people they are meant to serve.

The various definitions of participation still seem broad, diverse and contradictory yet the issue of when to participate, what sort of participation is appropriate and at what stage is participation necessary still remain unresolved this makes it difficult for development organisations to clearly define participation (Lane, 1995; Clemente, 2003). The broad objectives of development organisations and the different expectations of beneficiaries also make it relatively difficult for one particular definition to be considered appropriate. The unequal distribution of power and resources, the lack of participation by community members in decision-making, the various typologies of participation and unclear definitions of participation still remain unresolved thus making the meaning of participation confusing and contradictory (Dixon, 1990).

2.3.3 Types and Forms of Participation

Participation can be viewed in terms of *types* - the characteristic role participants play in the development process (see Arnstein, 1969; Pretty, 1995; Cornwall, 1995; Agarwal, 2001; Parkes and Panelli, 2001 and others), and in terms of *forms* - the degree of their involvement (Blackburn et al, 2002). Ways in which the term is used also leave people in a state of bewilderment and confusion as to how communities should be involved and how development organisations engage individuals (Lane, 1995; Guijt and Shah, 1998). But it is argued that the objectives of development interventions, the expectation of community members and the agendas of funding agencies make individuals perform different roles in development activities thus widening the ways in which individuals participate. For instance the World Bank (WB) considers information sharing, consultation, collaboration

38

and empowerment as ways of engaging community members in participatory practice (World Bank, 2004). Critics like Arnstein (1969), Cornwall, (1995) and Parkes and Panelli, (2001) also argue that coercing, enticing, co-learning and coaching are ways by which individuals could be engaged in participatory practice.

Types of Participation: There are several ways in which development organisations that adopt participatory principles involve community members in activities. The typologies are many but critics like Arnstein (1969), Pretty (1995), Cornwall (1995),

Tab. 2.3 Typology of Participation

Type of Participation	Characteristics and Roles of Participants
Manipulation	Members may represent some communities but not are elected and may not possess the power to influence policy formulation.
Passive	People may participate in meetings but may not contribute or speak. They may just be representatives.
Consultative	Participants may be asked to give their opinion but not to influence decisions.
Material incentives	Members may contribute resources eg. labour, money, materials, land, etc just to accomplish objectives.
Normal	Being part of a group or in membership.
Activity-specific	Members are made to perform specific tasks, eg planning or implementation.
Active	Members may be allowed to express opinion and partake in activities whether solicited or not and they do so with free will.
Interactive	Partake in decision-making or may be given the chance to influence policy either as individuals or in groups.
Self- mobilization	People participate by taking the initiative independently to influence institutional activities.
Functional	Members participate to meet some objectives, which may be decision-making or policy implementation.
Coercing	Where one powerful group may force the less powerful to accept their views or their ideology is imposed upon the less powerful through simple engagement.
Informing	Where information or ideas are transferred from top-down and there is no knowledge-sharing or joint decision-making.
Enticing	This involves various groups making decisions but the powerful use incentives to entice the less powerful so as to impose their ideology on them.
Co-learning	The sharing of knowledge and ideas between insiders and outsiders to formulate new ideas and policies through joint decisions and

	action plans in a form of learning exercise.
Co-acting	The mobilization of local knowledge through insiders' initiatives in the setting of agenda without outsiders' influence and initiatives. In this type both power and decision-making remain within the control of the local people.

Source: Arnstein (1969), Pretty (1995), Cornwall (1995), Agarwal (2001) and .Parkes and Panelli (2001)

Agarwal (2001), and Parkes and Panelli (2001) have argued that they are aimed at accomplishing the objectives of development interventions effectively and in a cost-effective way, and with the aim of community members or beneficiaries taking full control of development (Nelson and Wright, 1995; Francis, 2000; McGee, 2002). Table 2.1 above shows the typology of participation and a summary of the characteristic features. It illustrates the modalities of engaging individuals in participatory activities. Sahley and Pretty, (1995) have argued that in spite of the various types of participation application still differs among development organisations and institutions that apply the concept. Chambers, (1983; 1997), Sahley and Pretty (1995) and others have argued that participation should target the marginalized, women and the voiceless in every development process and at all stages of the development process; but this would seem difficult for organisations to implement, taking into consideration the time needed to involve the marginalized groups who may not be ready or willing to participate, coupled with timescales that may make it difficult, for some people to participate at every stage of the process. For instance some critics may ask, what work can a sick or disabled person do when labour is needed as part of the participatory activity? Are the sick and the disabled even willing to participate in every decision-making? Why should they participate? Is their participation relevant? Or are they supposed to participate only in decision-making? If a particular intervention needs continuous monitoring, how many rural women would have time to attend such activities, when they are always busy going about their daily lives or trying to make ends meet? Some critics like Clemente (2003) asked, who decides who should participate and when is it appropriate for community members to participate?

Lack of participation cannot always be blamed on development organisations because apart from the need to meet donors' deadlines, rapid inflationary rates in some developing countries leave organisations with no option other than to involve only those who can accomplish the development objectives within the requisite time frame. If community participation is to benefit the poor, the marginalized and women, then the policies governing such programmes have to be reviewed to enable these marginalized groups to play active roles in the formulation and implementation of development policies and programmes. Whatever role communities or beneficiaries are supposed to play must be made explicit, so that they will know why and when to participate and the form of participation that is appropriate

Forms of Participation: One of the contested concepts in development discourse is forms of participation. In his contribution to the book *'People's Participation: Challenges Ahead'*, Chambers (1998) asked whether the reality of those in the *upper* level whose decision have been dominating participatory decision-making or those at the *lower* level, who are suppose to benefit from development, should count. Whether it is the uppers or the lowers levels whose reality should count in participatory decision-making will also depend on the forms of participatory activity used and how well they are engaged in participatory practice. Participation has partially been divided into two main forms: *broader* and *narrow*, but whether narrow or broader also depends on the number of individuals involved and the roles they play in the participatory process (Johnston and Kilby, 1995; Blackburn et al, 2002).

Broader participation is the engagement of individuals in every aspect of the development process (Burkey, 1993; Blackburn et al, 2002), whether it is the initial design, planning, implementation, evaluation or auditing of the development process. Broader participation is often argued as a way of scaling-up participation to involve a greater number of individuals (Blackburn et al, 2002). It is also referred to as *widening participation*. A greater number of individuals are encouraged to partake in the process, irrespective of whether they are active or passive participants. In other words the participants are not deeply involved in their activities. Their involvement is in almost every aspect of the development process because the aim is to engage as many people as possible, so that every stage of the development process may involve some members in one way or another (Johnston and Kilby, 1995; Sahley and Pratt, 2003) no matter what type of activities they undertake and the nature of the contributions they make towards the development process.

Involving as many people as possible in every stage of the development process is an approach that Blackburn et al (2002) also call *scaling-up participation*. In this case individuals may just be representatives and may not enforce any decisions or influence any policy (Blunt and Jones, 1992). However, it creates the opportunity for individuals to partake in most stages and places them in a position to contribute to the process and to implement change if necessary. Studies done by Clemente (2003) and Sahley and Pratt (2003) indicated that such contributions could include active involvement of members in decision-making, allocation of resources and in controlling and managing development funds. This aspect of participation is what Roche argues has been very difficult for many organisations to accept, because they believe active community participation may threaten their control and management of financial resources, so many NGOs have tried over the years to resist (Roche cited in Open University, 2001).

42

Blackburn et al (2002) view *narrow participation* as looking at the active involvement of individuals in a particular stage of the development process. Participants in this form of participation are supposed to have equal powers to make deliberations associated with the day-to-day decision-making in the development process (Blunt and Jone, 1992; Sahley and Pretty, 1995). They argued that the members should be able to play their role in the development process. This form of participation enhances the active involvement of the members in areas such as financial management, rather than just providing cheap labour during the implementation stage, which is what most organisations term as participation. NGOs by virtue of their limited financial resources and inability to hire labour, tend to involve community members in the provision of free labour and term it participation (Burkey, 1993; Sahley and Pretty, 1995).

Some critics like Chambers (1994a), Schneider and Libercier (1995) and others have argued that this form of participatory activity should involve many people, but the attitude of some development organisations makes it difficult for such public engagement to become difficult. The participants have to be encouraged to make contributions towards the formulation of development policy and their views must be well integrated into the development decision-making rather than being dictated by development facilitators (Blackburn and Holland, 1998). This supports the thinking of Chambers (1997) and Blackburn and Holland (1998) that community members must be given the opportunity to control their own development and manage their own resources or else the concept of participation will achieve little result.

43

2.4 Power and Power Relations in Community Participation

The application of participation in community development has a lot of conflicting issues relating to power: who exercises power, who should transfer it and who needs to be empowered. Empowerment has come as a result of some stakeholders' excessive use of power, denial of power to others, control of development resources and reluctance to relinquish power to the less powerful. To examine power and power relations in more detail we will first look at the concepts of power and empowerment and their effect on community development and participatory practice.

2.4.1 The Concept of Power and Participation

Power is an and electrical current that controls the activities of every organisation and society (Fulop and Linstead, 2004; Mosse, 2004). Elias Canetti, a Nobel Prize winner who wrote the book *Crowds and Revolution*, defined power as the 'expression of order through command' (Fulop and Linstead, 2004:200). It is a form of force that is acted upon a recipient to enable him/her to behave in an acceptable and appropriate manner. Leurs argued that in development policy and practice power is the ability to influence policy formulation and to make decisions about others while at the same time maintaining and controlling resources (Leurs, 1998).

According to Dugan the feminist scholars look at power in three different forms: power over, power to and power with (Dugan, 2003). Blunt and Jones (1992), Dugan (2003) and Fulop and Linstead (2004) also categorise the use of power into five (5) different types: coercive, reward, expert, legitimate and referent power.. They explained the application and use of force based on what is to be achieved and what type of influence the user intends to have. They argued that *coercive power* is used by individuals to make others act against

44

their will or in fear of negative consequences or punishments – e.g. that exercised over prisoners to obtain information. The use of benefit to entice individuals to act in certain ways – e.g. that is the force exercised by school teachers over school pupils is termed *reward power*. *Expert power* is used by those with expert knowledge on those who lack such knowledge or expertise in a form of advocacy or assistance - e.g. lawyers, consultants, the clergy or physicians. *Legitimate power* is exercised by those mandated by law to exercise some form of authority over individuals or to act on behalf of their organisation, institution, region or nation. *Referent power* is normally possessed by those who are sometimes classified as having charisma. These individuals use their power to draw support and following, irrespective of the type of ideology they pursue.

The use of power over people in communities and organisations has a dramatic effect on the activities of the individuals and also influences the benefits that people in such communities may derive (Mosse, 2004). Observation made by Nelson and Wright (1995) showed that the issue of power has been in development discourse and debate among organisations, government institutions and even within communities where power relations have greater influence. However, while the debate remains ongoing, individuals and organisations that exercise power also interpret the concept differently because of how they use the concept of participation (Fulop and Linstead, 2004). Nelson and Wright (1995) argued however that the concept becomes complete when empowerment, participation and partnership are integrated.

One way of making participation work is by addressing how power is exercised between and within institutions (Lane, 1995; Schneider and Libercier, 1995). Distributing power to the powerless and the question of who should relinquish power has been another issue of debate in the development discourse (Mosse, 2004). The difficult challenge facing development organisations is how to transfer power, who should transfer power and to whom should the power be transferred? Nelson and Wright believe that answers to these questions will enable community members to gain recognition and experience equal treatment as partners in a development process so that they could have continuous access to and control of resources and also influence decision-making (Nelson and Wright, 1995)?

Nelson and Wright (1995); Chambers (1997) and Lukes (2005) ask how the bureaucrats and development facilitators at the helm of affairs can transfer power to the poor when they are not flexible, remain in control, are still participating and are not ready to create space for others to participate. Development facilitators would have to transfer power if they want community members to benefit from participatory practice, but to transfer power is one of the difficulties facing organisations today, most especially where control of financial resources is concerned (Open University, 2001). The debate about the application of power in participatory practice becomes more explicit when individuals and organizations fight for empowerment. To develop and promote social change, McGee (2002) and Alsop and Norton (2004) have argued that power differentiation between individuals and within organisations has to be addressed, if participation is to bring benefits to stakeholders and also help address the power relations that affect participatory process.

2.4.2 Power Relations in Participation: Does It Really Matter?

Understanding of the concept of power and empowerment raises questions about power relations in participatory practice, but does it really matter if development practitioners use their power to control resources and influence decision-making in participatory activities? Or does it matter if outspoken individuals with expert knowledge and ideas influence development decision-making for the benefit of everybody? Why has power relations

46

become a contested issue in the development debate and in participatory practice especially in rural development? To answer these questions, we will critically evaluate the effect of power relations on decision-making and whether it really matters in participatory practice. Disempowering the powerful in order to empower the less powerful is a way through which the conflict of power and the relations of power between individuals and within organisations comes under scrutiny.

Studies carried out by Gaventa and Valderrama (1999) suggest that community participation is about power and how it is exercised by different social actors in the spaces created for interactions between community members and development facilitators in development. Chambers (1997) and McEwan (2002) asked who voices a community's development needs, how do participants or beneficiaries voice their concerns, whose voices are included in decision-making, what power relations are involved, what social structures shape development and who creates those structures. Control of the structures and processes for participation defining actors, agenda and procedures - is usually in the hands of NGOs and other development organisations which can create barriers to effective participation (Gaventa and Valderrama, 1999). For instance, gender differentiations, religious affiliations, cultural backgrounds and social stratification are just some of the complexities which make it difficult for the ideological approach to tackle the controversies surrounding power and power relations within communities and organizations (Johnson and Mayoux, 1998).

The debate still remain on-going about the need to make community participation part of every development agenda and become a criterion for release of development funds (Killick, 2002), yet the issue of power sharing to make community members participate on equal terms in decision-making and to enable them have control over development resources still remain a difficult problem for a number of development organisations and institutions. This has raised eyebrows amongst community members and development practitioners as to who should control resources for development interventions; hitherto this has been under the control of development organisations facilitators. Some critics also argue that control of resources by beneficiaries, with the aim of transferring control and power, will be uncompromising, complicated and difficult to achieve (Drinkwater, 2003). Paradoxically, some development facilitators 'feel threatened by sharing power', so they try to resist power transfer which it is argued slows down the process of participatory activities and development practice (Clemente, 2003:44). This raises the question of whether the issue of power relations really matters in participatory practice and must therefore be critically evaluated and justified.

The issue of who should control development resources and the resources to be controlled still remains in the development debate because many agencies that advocate for participatory practice in development interventions still show some degree to relinquish control (Mohan, 2002; Fulop and Linstead, 2004). Those who possess power act and get things done in their own way (Chambers, 1997). This according to Dixon (1990:58) makes' the structures that lie behind the inequitable distribution of power and resources' become neglected and has been happening for years. Development organisations advocate for participation and empowerment during the development campaign but they find it difficult to relinquish power. White has observed that NGOs claim to empower the disadvantaged through participatory activities which also helps them to win the support of interest groups yet they still hold firmly onto power (White, 2000).

Power struggle, which surrounds control of resources for development interventions, still remains a problem for development organisations and other stakeholders. This emphasises

Desai's (2002a:118) argument that resources for development remain scarce, yet 'pressures for their allocation to various interest groups have progressively increased, but the poor who do not have either socioeconomic or political power do not generally gain access to the decision-making processes and hence are unable to influence them'. The pervasive effects of power relations within institutions and between communities and organisations has to be understood and addressed before participation can be effective (James, 2001). The transfer of power that could bring about empowerment means the powerful will have to be disempowered before the power relations within organisations become balanced.

2.4.3 How Do Power Relations Affect and Shape Participatory Practice?

A development organisation that adopts the concept of participation has its fundamental basics centred on power relations within the communities it serves (Nelson and Wright, 1995). How do power relations affect and shape the way participation is applied in development practice? According to Kontinen, the dynamics of power and power relations remains a key aspect of most communication in the development process and shapes relationships amongst individuals in organisations (Kontinen, 2005). However, Desai (2002a) has observed that a shift of the development paradigm has also shifted the argument of participation towards empowerment and is gradually leading to the transfer management responsibilities and control over resources to the powerless. That is, making the powerless able to 'affect the organisation's decisions and influence its actions' through decision making (Rieger and Wong-Rieger, 1990:104). The power relationship that exists between and within organisations and how power has to be transferred has also brought about institutional and social conflict between the powerful, that Chambers calls the 'uppers' (e.g. the NGOs and other CSOs), who are always in control of development

49

resources and the less privileged 'lowers', the rural poor and who are intended to benefit from the interventions (Chambers, 1983; 1997; Mohan, 2002).

Development agencies desire to empower the rural poor and make them proactive through participatory activities (White, 2000), but there is some scepticism among NGOs and development facilitators about when empowerment truly occurs, due to the power shift that may result. Community participation brings sustainability in development interventions and leads to the establishment of ownership of the intervention, but some critics also argue that such an assumption is naïve because there is no detailed empirical evidence indicating that participation brings empowerment to rural people (Kellerman, 1997; Thomas and Allen, 2000; Cleaver, 2001). This is because the power relations between development institutions or organisations and community members and the question of how power has to be transferred are not properly addressed in a way that would increase the level and effectiveness of participation in rural development activities (Schonwalder, 1997 cited in Gaventa and Valderrama, 1999).

There is a general perception amongst development organisations and even community members as to who, in what way and how participation must be practised (Desai, 2002a)? Pretty seems not to share this sentiment, but rather argues that development organisations should look at how participants would be empowered as they engage community members in a participatory process (Pretty, 1995). Hill (1997) and Francis (2002) have also noted that the engagement of community members will not only empower them but would help to sustain the development intervention. According to Johnson and Mayoux (1998), active community participation will never address the changes in the structures and policies that shape development policy and practice; furthermore, it will not even affect the power relations that hinder effective community involvement.

Knowledge is power and it is an asset in development (Chambers, 1983, 1997; Foucault cited in Lukes, 2005). Chambers (1983) has observed that it has been universally accepted that outsiders' knowledge is superior to local, indigenous and rural knowledge, and this biased notion has remained in development policy and practice. However the acquisition of such knowledge is only possible formal education, which rural people lack, and sometimes may not get due to deprivation. Formal education should not be the only route to acquiring development knowledge, informal education is another way by which local people could share information and acquire some basic skills for life. Education sensitizes communities about rights, responsibilities and opportunities; it aligns government's programmes to the needs of communities; it makes local institutions more responsible and accountable; it helps community members to liaise with governments in making their programmes more effective in meeting the needs of communities; it helps in building capacity and empowers rural people (Clark, 2002 and Sahley and Pratt, 2003). However, people can communities could be sensitised in an informal way to become proactive and make a contribution to their communities.

Chambers (1983) and Rooy (1998) have observed that, nowadays, the wealthier are those who have knowledge and therefore possess power, which is used to influence the direction in which information should flow and to control the social structures that shape the people's lives. Chambers calls them 'uppers', who exercise their power and impose their ideas and knowledge on the lowers who are usually the rural poor (Chambers, 1983; 1997). Making the conflict of power and power relations in participatory practice redress participatory problems seems far from reality. Therefore, so long as the flow of the funds remains unidirectional, power will definitely continue to flow in the same direction, thus making the poor to become recipients of outsiders knowledge rather making them decision makers and able to apply their local knowledge to improve their lives. Power and power relations are among some of the issues that control and shape participatory practice and have become of the dilemmas that face rural people, because those that advocate participatory practice also fear the lose of power and control over resources.

2.5 Limitations of Participation: The Missing Link

The concept of participation has registered some successes within communities and organisations that apply it in development practice, but critics like Chambers (1997), Mosse (2004; 2007) and others, have argued that for over three decades, there are still many set-backs, biases and limitations that continue to hamper the effectiveness of participatory practice. Paradoxically, while efforts are being made by development organisations and facilitators to address those bottlenecks, the missing links in participation seem to be neglected or have not been dealt with in recent development studies discourses. Issues such as societal norms, cultural practices, tribal and inter-tribal conflicts, among others, still remain very predominant and persist in most African societies, but absent in most development and community participatory literature. In many African societies, norms and some cultural practices either directly or indirectly prevent some individuals to participate in community decision-making and participatory activities, yet development literature seem to neglect such issues that effect participatory decision-making.

It is however important to note that, development discourse that explains how such societal norms and cultural practices affect local people active participation remain absent. Some critics like Nelson and Wright (1995) and McGee (2002) have pointed out that, issues such as lack of transfer of power from development facilitators to local people, external influence on development policy formulation, control of development resources by development organisations, among others, still affect effective participatory practice, but little is said about norms and cultural practices, that in many cases affect and prevent local people, mostly in many African societies to participate in community development decision-making. This supports Dwyer's (2002) observation, about ethnicity, which influences social cohesion. Like ethnicity, social norm is another concept that also promotes social cohesion, but Dwyer still argues that some development programmes that are influenced by some ethnic groups within the political spectrum take decisions and influence development policy formulation. Unfortunately, little is written on ethnicity, social norms, the use of magical powers such as witchcraft and juju, that has been predominant in most African societies and are used to exercise authority and influence participatory decision-making and policy formulation.

Overcoming some of these bottlenecks will not bring better development but as Hettne argued, it is one of the 'essential precondition for harmonious development' (Hettne, 1995 cited in Dwyer, 2002:460). Hettne further noted that understanding the ethnodevelopment helps development organisations to appreciate devolution of power within the local communities which forms the basis of development. This supports Dwyer's (2002) argument that when it became evident for instance that people were not benefiting from development policy due to ethnicity issues, as it is in some parts of the world today, affirmative action become necessary. In a situation whereby ethical, cultural and social problems are not well understood and made explicit in development literature, development organisations acceptance of such knowledge so as to reorient and streamline development policy and programmes, so as to integrate them into current development programmes become very difficult.

It became evident in the current development debate that, there is a gap between recent development discourses which place greater emphasis on socio-economic and political

53

issues, rather than issues such as social norms and negative cultural practices that hamper effective participation. This therefore makes the study very relevant to help identify some of the bottlenecks in participatory practice in the developing world, more especially in the African perspectives. This draws attention not only to the need for a careful analysis and evaluation of affirmative action towards disadvantaged groups, but also to the need to reorient recent development policy to accommodate issues such as societal norms, cultural practices that remain issues and realities in rural communities to and help to reshape development policy and practice. It will not only benefit practitioners of development, but rather enhance effective community participation in development policy and practice.

2.6 Participatory Paradox: The Dilemma of the Rural Poor

The dilemma facing the rural poor is whether to participate, and become proactive in development practice or be represented by the elite within their communities. Studies have shown that development organisations want the rural poor to participate actively in every development activity, but actually transferring power and making them active participants seems difficult for the organisations. As development organisations encourage active community participation in development practice, they also jealously protect their position of power so as to continue to remain in control of development resources. Some critics argue that the increasing control of resources by development organisations and whether power should be transferred to community members to make them active participants has been very difficult for development organisations to accept (Stiefel in Desai, 2002a; Fulop and Linstead, 2004).

Arguably, the pressure under which development workers find themselves to 'keep up the momentum to meet expenditure targets and to maximise quantifiable achievements' may lead them to give priority to familiar, conventional programmes over innovative initiatives

54

where approval may be uncertain or delayed (Mosse, 2007:24). Unclear interpretations of the term participation and contradictions in the use of the concept, put community members in a dilemma; whether to participate or be represented and in what aspects are they are supposed to participate? Sometimes organisations engage community members in participatory practice when the process is actually just representation. NGOs invite community members to meetings, make them provide labour during projects implementations, or get them to sit on committees and witness development decision-making yet the term 'participation' is used (Chambers, 1983; Burkey, 1993; Chambers, 1997; Cresswell, 1997; Guijt and Shah, 1998).

The difficulties involved in promoting effective rural development through participatory practice are enormous for development organisations working with rural people yet there is little effort from development organisations to eliminate the biases that weaken the ineffectiveness of participatory practice (Chambers, 1983; 1997; Kumar, 2002). Lane (1995) observed in his work that the elites who that work with the people and organisation at the grassroots often use their influence to control and make decisions for the whole community under the pretext of participation. Yet the underlining assumption is that, by allowing a few individuals to represent them community members will consider this as participation. Because the organisations have little time to execute development projects, holistic involvement of community members who may not initially be interested in participating seems far from reality.

To reach the poorest people participatory practice, Weinberger (2001) argued that the policies governing development will have to be redesigned in favour of the target groups, so that they become proactive and feel part of the process. It is, however, argued that, with over three decades of participatory practice in development policy and practice, institutions like the WB still control major decisions in such activities (Datta, 2003). Datta also observed that the dilemma facing community members is whether they are to participate or be represented by members in their communities in decision-making. Therefore, a lack of opportunities for the poor to participate and time limitations on delivery weaken the effectiveness of participatory practice and community support, and also hinder sustainability of development activities in such rural communities. For instance, a lack of adequate funding for development interventions makes development organisations adopt a participatory approach because it gives them the opportunity of getting cheap labour to execute their interventions (Hildyard, et al, 2001; Sahley and Pratt, 2003).

The concept of participation has been limited to organisations that rely on the services of local people for labour to accomplish development goals especially when there are no adequate financial resources to hire labour. This confirm the views of Burkey (1993), Cosway and Anankum (1996) and Pearson (2000) about how development organisations view participation. They argued that most development organisations look at participatory engagement a contribution of labour. For instance, women are not considered to be active participants in development activities because they are regarded as less effective or not physically strong. Consequently most women represent their households in decision-making and do not actively participate.

Arguably people who are made to participate in community development activities are those who have the confidence to speak to strangers or have time to spare; they may also be the 'elite' - mostly teachers or school leavers who might be idling in the communities (sometimes with no jobs) - or the elders (Mosse cited in Chambers, 1997). The involvement of such people in development activities is what most organisations call participation, because the time needed to accomplish the interventions and the rapid inflation of costs in

56

some countries in the developing world do not allow those Chambers calls the neglected, the marginalised and especially women who are always occupied with family responsibilities to participate and make a contribution to development work.

In Bangladesh, for instance, an NGO used to run a micro-credit scheme considered its weekly loan repayment meetings attended by borrower as participation (Sahley and Pratt, 2003). According to the report, those who spoke at such meetings were men representing their wives whose domestic commitments never permitted them to attend such meetings. Is participation attendance at meetings or talking on behalf of others? Who should participate, the beneficiaries, their representatives or those who have time to spare on behalf of a member or a partner? Whether to participate or to become a representative in development activity still remains the dilemma of rural community members. Until a new development paradigm emerges, participation will continue to dominate development policy and practice.

Kumar (2002) has also argued that there are many impediments and paradoxes that make participatory practice very difficult and confusing. He stated the following as some of the impediments that militate against the application of the principle.

- Participation may lead to delay and slow down the development process, which could affect the financial targets of a project especially in countries where inflation is very rapid or the economy is unstable

- Accepting the principle would lead to the involvement of human resources since many people within the community have to be involved, thus making it relatively expensive and cumbersome

- Since participation could lead to empowerment others must relinquish power which is very difficult for those in control to accept

57

- It raises many people's expectations and awareness, which could be very difficult to realise. If objectives are not accomplished many more people become disappointed

Considering the aforementioned problems, one could argue that participation becomes 'more illusory than real' or 'rhetoric rather than a reality' (Kumar, 2002:28). The concept of participation appears excellent on paper, but in practice the application becomes relatively difficult not only for the organisation that advocates participatory practice but also within communities whose members are engaged in participatory practice.

2.7 Neo-liberal Development Theory and Community Participation

2.7.1 Neo-liberal Development Theory: Another Paradigm Shift

Criticism over the years about the failure of previous development theories to address the problems of a lack of economic and social development in many developing world countries necessitated a further search for new development theories (Simon and Marman, 2002; Kessey, 2004). The search for new theories therefore shifted the development paradigm, which led to new ways and practices of development in order to address the lack of development in many countries. Dixon (1990) observed that, while some communities were not benefiting from development programmes, in some areas development was not only taking a long time to reach the poor who desperately need development. To address those bottlenecks identified in development practice, the search for new theories continued, which made the reformation of theories such as modernisation development theory[3] very

---

[3] Hettne, (2002:7) argued that the modernisation theorists development should be 'sociological and political in nature' and under-development was therefore classified between the rich and poor nations. The theory aimed at getting the poor nations to imitate the development efforts and programmes of their richer counterparts, which was aimed at helping to bridge the gap between the rich and poor nations in terms of development.

necessary because it was seen to have failed to bring improvement to countries that adopted or pursued it (Kothari and Minogue, 2002).

According to Hettne, modernisation and structuralism[4] theories were noted to have made developing countries to be over-reliant on developed nations and they became an impediment to development in many third world countries (Hettne, 2002). Countries that followed the world system theory[5] (WST), for instance, were supposed to be developed under conditions that were 'primarily shaped by economic process and interrelationships operating at the global scale' (Klak, 2002:107). According to Klak, individual nations would not succeed unless connected to that system. That is, it would be relatively difficult for nations that remained outside regional economic blocks to become successful or economically independent because the world economic system was interconnected. Klak observed that countries that followed WST also never made real improvement. Critics like Kessay (2004) believed that the failure of various development theories to address the problems of countries in the developing world both socially and economically, necessitated a further search for new development theories. The neo-liberal development theory evolved with the hope of addressing the failures of past development practices, though it had a capitalist ingredient.

The economic stagnation and market failure (Haque, 1999) noticed in some countries around the developing world during the 1970s also contributed to the continuous search for theories to curb the increasing economic imbalance. For instance, the *basic needs* approach

---

[4] The structuralism theorists argued that 'disparities between the core and periphery' resulted from the 'world trade and terms of trade; in short, the world economy was competitive and the colonial or ex-colonial periphery as producers and exporters of primary products was disadvantaged' (Clarke, 2002:92-93). According to the structuralists, countries that opted for modernisation were to do so without competition (Kay cited in Clarke, 2002).
[5] Klak (2002) explained that the WST was also another form of development paradigm shift. It aimed at addressing some of the problems of underdevelopment in the world, but failed

59

which according, to some critics was aimed at addressing some of the inequalities and social deprivation that faced many people due to past economic failures also failed (International Labour Organisation, 1976 and Streeten, 1979 cited in Haque, 1999). Other critics also argued that the involvement of the state in the 'economy was held to be inefficient, bureaucratic and an unnecessary drain on public resources' (Simon, 2002:87). The capitalist economic strategies which were left behind by the colonialists made the developing countries producers and exporters of only primary products, which further worsened their economic situation and deepened poverty (Clarke, 2002). The new development thinking and the paradigm shift made countries reconsider the 'state-centred' approach to development and move towards a 'market-driven' development perspective. They therefore welcomed the neo-liberal development agenda because it had economic impact which brought improvement in some communities (Haque, 1999:199). That is, it enhances market competition and increases economic growth to attract direct and foreign investment. The neo-liberal ideology was promoted as a development perspective that strengthens and reinforces the free market, promotes competition and limit state control and intervention (King, 1987 and Toye, 1991 cited in Haque, 1999).

With an over-emphasis on market mechanism, to enhance economic growth and improve peoples' social lives, development practitioners begun to embrace the neo-liberalism development paradigm as a dominant force in development thinking in the 1980s, aiming to curb the stagnation of development in many countries in the developing world (Thomas 2000a; 2000b). The evolution of new approaches to development, the paradigm shift in development policy and practice, and the 'search for new theoretical conceptualisations of development' has been mirrored by changes in the practice of development in the field (Potter, 2002:61). Besides the controversy surrounding the nature of development, how it has occurred in the past, current trends in development and how it should be pursued to help communities which hitherto have not benefited much from development, strategies to achieve their full share of development have also increased the momentum and theoretical perspectives of development policy and practice (Hettne, 2002; Potter, 2002).

The neo-liberal development theory which has gained recognition in the recent decades due to its successes not only focuses primarily on economic growth (Kothari and Minogue, 2002; Kihika, 2009), but is rather aimed at addressing the social inequalities and deprivation in today's world. The neo-liberals argue that social improvement could be enhanced through market forces (Espinal, 1992 cited in Haque, 1999). However Harrison has a different view, he argues that reformation of market failures alone cannot guarantee improved social conditions and reduced economic deprivation (Harrison, 2005 cited in Kihika, 2009).

It is therefore argued that the neo-liberal development agenda focuses more on economic emancipation than addressing the social problems that face many people in the Third World countries. According to Harrison the neo-liberal development paradigm was implemented with an economic standpoint, though it was aimed at improving social welfare services to benefit the majority that live in poverty. So countries that embraced neo-liberal thinking accepted and introduced market-friendly policies to curb the increasing poverty and misery in their countries. Some of the indicators of the ideology were promotion of public-private partnerships and participation of NGOs and other CSOs towards implementation of some of the agendas.

It has been observed that neo-liberal development theory has registered some success in a number of countries. The success has brought significant improvement, social progress and poverty reduction in some communities in the developing world (Kothari and Minogue,

61

2002), thus making the neo-liberal development agenda a triumph over other development perspectives from the 1980s. Paradoxically, Hewitt appears to have a different perspective. He argued that the neo-liberal free market alone has not brought development universally, though it remains a credible development force (Hewitt, 2000). Cammack explained that the neo-liberal orthodoxy became 'faithful to the disciplines required for capitalist accumulation on a global scale' and the generation of 'legitimizing ideology that obscures the presence of those disciplines at its core' (Cammack, 2002:157). From classical to post-Keynesian economics, neo-liberal development ideology is one of the development theories that was viewed as an optimally efficient means of enhancing economic growth through market competitiveness, capital accumulation and as a means to address market failures (Haque, 1999; Kihika, 2009), because it became evident that many past development theories had failed to address the development problems facing many countries.

Critics like McGrew (2000:349), Thomas (2000b), Cammack (2002) and others also argued that the collapsed of the Berlin Wall, which led to the unification of East and West Germany the disintegration of the Soviet Union and the triumph of capitalism over socialism towards the end of the twentieth century further signified the dominance of the neo-liberalism development paradigm as the most viable development path. This also confirmed the argument of Francis Fukuyama of the US State Department in the late 1980s that 'the fusing of liberal democracy and industrial capitalism now represented the only viable basis for modern human society' (Thomas, 2000a:9). However, in a free market economy it is unlikely that mobilisation of public resources to support health, education or housing policies to improve people's way of life would not make capitalism a viable alternative for development.

The doctrines of neo-liberal development compelled nations to enter into privatization of state-owned enterprises and industries introduce of subsidies on agricultural products and withdrawals from state monopolies in service provision (Haque, 1999). Simon (2002) observed that the withdrawal of some states from some service provision was demonstrated in the selling-off 'loss-making and inefficient public enterprises and Parastatal Corporation'. In countries like Ghana, Nigeria and many other African countries, the withdrawal of state welfare provision increased under the neo-liberal agenda (Walton and Seddon, 1994). Devaluation of currencies, introduction of monetary systems and removal of food subsidies were all embraced after adoption of the neo-liberalism development agenda (Kihika, 2009). Some schools of thought also argue that the pursuit of the neo-liberal development orthodoxy by some African countries was to increase their commitment to their foreign donors and made them continue as regular aid recipients.

2.7.2 Neo-liberalism and Community Participation: Searching for Answers

Over the years development discourses have embraced new theories and new techniques of development practice. Some of these new theories have reflected and embraced popular concepts like community participation, empowerment, social capital and capacity building (Miraftab, 2004). The search for new development theories were all aimed at looking for new ways of improving the socio-economic lives of the people, mostly those in the developing world. The question that still remains unanswered is with the emergence of such new theories and development strategies, where has it gone wrong? The neo-liberal development agenda has been adopted by many countries in the developing world since the late 1980s, but poverty, malnutrition, under-nutrition, unemployment and infrastructure breakdown, to mention just a few, still persist (Mbaku, 2004: Kihika, 2009). Some development discourses indicate that the neo-liberal agenda has become a dominant force

63

in development practice, but the argument that continues to be debated in development circles is whether it is properly addressing the economic and social problems facing the poorer majority living in the developing world. If so, where are the answers to the major and increasing problems that still prevail in countries around the developing world?

'Earlier criticism of the state's role in development questioning whether the conditions existed for third world states to operate effectively' would help improve the developmental efforts of those countries (Batley, 2002:137). Those critics questioned the position of the structuralism theory[6] and its ineffectiveness in the development of those countries, and the neo-liberal free market approach to economic improvement and community development which was noted to be a credible development alternative (Thomas, 2000b). The 'immediate roots of the neo-liberal revival lay in the financial crisis' which followed the massive rise in oil prices and a huge debt crisis in many countries in the South in the early 1970s (Batley, 2002:137; Simon, 2002). The situation brought serious global economic recession, which affected a number of countries around the world. However, in spite of the economic recession felt in most countries, it is still argued that neo-liberalism ideology has brought about successful development in many countries today (McGrew, 2000). This has been due to the open and competitive nature of the market.

The neo-liberal development agenda also embraced some concepts like community participation, empowerment, capacity building, social capital and partnership, which have entered development practice and have become some of the tools and building-blocks of

---

[6] According to Clarke the structuralism theory looks at the 'disparities between the core and periphery' which result from the 'world trade and terms of trade; in short, the world economy was competitive and the colonial or ex-colonial periphery as producers and exporters of primary products was disadvantaged' (Clarke, 2002:92-93). The structuralists noted that Latin American countries aimed at industrialisation but did so without competition. The structuralism ideology was in direct resonance with the neo-liberal development paradigm which focuses on competitiveness of various agents in development whether private or public sector

the neo-liberal governance of the IMF and WB (Miraftab, 2004). Datta (2003) stresses that the integration of those tools was to make the local people very proactive and capable of taking control of their own lives, and be able to manage resources and development in their communities. Intensification of development activities by NGOs and other CSOs in a participatory manner, also begun to feature prominently in a number of developing countries during the neo-liberal development era. This was because the WB and IMF preferred the involvement of the private sector and CSOs to government monopolisation of development, which was believed to be leaving a number of communities behind. As Miraftab (2004) puts it, it makes the state to role back in it control mechanism. This is in line with Long's observation and thinking, that if NGOs in the north and indigenous ones work in synergy and in a participatory manner in client countries it will improve the lives of the local people more especially the poor and marginalized people (Long, 2001).

The neo-liberal development theory embraces the inclusion of CSOs, the private sector and other stakeholders in promoting development. Yet critics like Brett have argued that it leaves the provision of goods and services to the free market and limits the role of the state to only the maintenance of law and order, and provision of a secure environment to promote development (Brett, 2002). This weakens the power of the state and takes control away from the central government. Brett's observation supports Thomas (2000b) argument that the policing role of the state makes the environment suitable for development and should therefore be paramount to enhance more accountable and effective development programmes. The government's enabling role, as explained by Hewitt (2002) and Desai (2002), also makes the environment more favourable for an efficient market and increased economic growth. .

In the 1980s, the neo-liberal development paradigm, which became active and was supposed to be the panacea to the problem of unsustainable development in most third world countries began to soften towards the end of the 1990s (Hewitt, 2000). There was some scepticism about the agenda, because it brought about division and demoralisation of the economic liberals (Cammack, 2002). The work of Pearce (2004:5) clearly illustrates these problems, that 'global poverty and inequality have grown in many parts of the world under the neo-liberal agenda' due to the trade liberalisation, privatisation and labour market reforms. This observation was noted in a UNDP development report (Batley, 2002). The commitment to practice the neo-liberal development agenda manifested itself when the IMF and the WB introduced the structural adjustment programme (SAP) in some developing countries, to reduce government expenditure in public service delivery, economic control and to promote liberalisation of trade (Manor, 1991 cited in Haque, 1999; Simon, 2002). However, the acceptance of SAP weakened state control and economic management, thus leaving the state with little economic power and control.

The introduction of SAP opened the market to global competitiveness and reduced government intervention and management (McGrew, 2000, Batley, 2002). McGrew and Batley further argued that SAP constrained the effectiveness of development strategies that were pursued by some governments and never brought any significant improvement in the lives of the citizens of countries that pursued it. Kihika (2009) noted that the neo-liberal development agenda introduced by the IMF and WB also brought huge problems for many countries in the developing world. Privatization of some of the welfare services and market reforms to promote competition and address economic failures, which were introduced under the SAP, never registered any economic improvement. Countries that pursued the SAP still have the majority of their citizens languishing in poverty and unemployment.

It is, however, argued that the neo-liberal development theory, which some critics contended had registered certain successes in the past later came under scrutiny and consideration (Hewitt, 2000; Kihika, 2009). According to Kihika (2009) it created a form of separation which she called 'economic apartheid where a small number in the advanced world live the life of surplus consumption' while the majority mostly in the developing world still languish in poverty, misery and deprivation; many do not have access to the basic necessities to make a good living. She argued that the growing social inequalities and deprivation resulted from the neo-liberal development orthodoxy because it could not address the unequal distribution of wealth and economic growth that formed it's foundation. In sub-Sahara African, for instance, many countries have not made any headway in overcoming their huge problems, while a lot of them are still struggling to provide social services for their citizens (Kihika, 2009). Poverty still remains a problem, unemployment in most rural areas has brought about rural-urban migration which has worsened the already aggravated urban unemployment problem in many countries. We cannot continue to praise the neo-liberal development paradigm in the face of these huge failures (Tucker, 1999 cited in Kihika, 2009).

Soederberg and de la Barra have argued that the neo-liberal ideology has failed to achieve its expected objectives because it was formulated from afar and the principles underlining its application are incompatible with local conditions (Soederberg, 2004; de la Barra, 2006 cited in Kihika, 2009). The rapid growth of NGOs in the 1980s and the involvement of CSOs in development was in line with the WB and IMF system of governance for countries in the developing world this advocates a public/private sector partnership system of engagement to help ease the burden on governments that were struggling to extend their meagre development budgets to reach all their citizens. However, there was no significant

67

improvement in the lives of the huge disadvantaged populations that did not benefit from their governments' development programmes. Recent development policies, have been politicized and have not brought any hope for the marginalized and impoverished in society (Kihika, 2009). Is it the same old wine in a new bottle, because new development theories are not helping the poor? Or is it the weaknesses of the development theory that are not helping to provide answers to the development problems facing the poor?

It is, however, agued that for over three decades of neo-liberal capitalist development, many areas of the world are worse off than they were three decades ago (Simon, 1997; Tucker, 1999 cited in Kihika, 2009). In spite of the hype being created about neo-liberal development theory - that it remains dominant in development practice because it has registered significant successes in some communities - poverty in many parts of the developing world continues to increase while most economies still remain fragile. So, where are the answers to those problems arising since the introduction of neo-liberal orthodoxy? Harrison (2005) concludes that the neo-liberal development paradigm therefore remains unfit to address the current problems or to bring the economic improvement and social prosperity needed by the majority in the developing world that are still languishing in poverty and economic misery.

2.8 Participation and Empowerment: The Act of Control

The concept of community participation and how community members are involved in decision-making has been looked at by Desai (2002a) in three different ways; power, influence and taking part. To participate is to take part in an activity, which means one will have the ability to influence they process. The extent to which an individual can influence a development process will depend on the power the individual possesses. To participate fully there should be power sharing between individuals to enable them to influence development policy and decision-making on equal terms. Participation has become another form of struggle where the powerful fight to retain their privilege to control resources and exercise those rights over the less powerful (Mohan, 2002). Thus, an opportunity to participate and become empowered gives an individual the opportunity to exercise control over the use of resources. The control of development resources is one of the major problems facing development organizations, community members, development workers and other stakeholders.

The better a groups position in the control of resources, the greater their bargaining power and the better the opportunity members have to make their voices heard and the more likely their decisions and views will be taken into consideration in the formulation and implementation of development policy. Observations made by Hildyard et al (2001) show that participatory decision-making is gradually becoming effective and has become a way through which the local people can get their voices heard, though it could be achieved if they have equal bargaining power like every stakeholder. In other words participation helps stakeholders to understand the power relations and how facilitators could exercise their power as they engage community members in development decision-making and other activities.

2.8.1 Community Participation and Empowerment

Empowering individuals, a community or an organisation means making them capable of doing something that hitherto they could not (Anwar, 2003; Lukes, 2005). How do power relations between clients and agencies, donors and recipients affect participatory activities? Development organisations and individuals cannot consider empowerment without looking at how to relinquish some of their own power to the less powerful. Leurs (1998) and Mosse

(2004) argued that to be disempowered and give others power, might involve some power struggle over control of resources and the exercise of authority over others, an aspect that a number of donor agencies and development organisations oppose.

Disempowering facilitators in order to empower rural community members seems extremely hard for the facilitators who hitherto have been in control of power. Power is jealously protected and all efforts to get those holding on to it, to relinquish it and empower others (especially community members) are vigorously resisted by those who Burkey (1993) and Anwar (2003) describe as losers of empowerment. How can community members participate effectively if development facilitators still continue to play their traditional roles? Effectiveness of participation will depend on how members are empowered to take up the challenge and become responsible for their lives. Foucault and Lukes believe that where there is always excessive use of power, there is always resistance from those lower down; this will lead to a breakdown of authority and an open power struggle (Foucault cited in Fulop and Linstead, 2004; Lukes, 2005).

The World Bank's Empowerment Team which undertook a study on the measurement of empowerment in five different countries, looked at empowerment as the 'increasing capacity of individuals or a group to make choices and to transform those into desired actions and outcomes' (Holland and Brook, 2004; 94; Alsop and Norton, 2004). This is described as a right-based approach to development that depends on people's equality of access to entitlements, which it becomes the state's responsibility to develop, advance, protect and promote (Alsop and Norton, 2004). The World Bank (2002) views empowerment as an expansion of assets and a concept that broadens the participatory capabilities of the poor, by equipping them with the authority to negotiate, influence policy, control resources and to hold institutions accountable for their actions. It indicates further

70

that to empower, institutional barriers that prevent poor people from acting effectively have to be removed. This will broaden their access to information and increase their ability to take advantage of the available opportunities.

Empowerment comes as a result of disempowerment of others which leads to devolution of power and institutional transformation. Thomas (2000b) believes this could be done through the activities of development organisations in rural communities. Empowerment is a desirable process by which individuals, including the poorest of the poor, will be able to take direct control over their lives once empowered, they become agents of their own development, improving and taking full control of their own lives. Bush and Folger look at how restoration of individuals' ownership, values and strength enable them handle life situations (Bush and Folger, cited in Dugan, 2003). That is, it becomes an enabling process that helps people to understand the realities of life, allowing them to design strategies to rectify and improve their way of life (Gajanayake and Gajanayake, 1993).

To make participation work, is a means of helping people to gain power and use it to influence decision-making that may result from power transfer from individual, organisation or institutional (Burkey, 1993; Pretty, 2003). Gill (2006:212) argues that, it is very limited to view empowerment as means of 'giving authority power and expecting responsibility in return', because it will mean delegation of decision-making responsibility, rather than true empowerment. Empowerment is about setting your own goals, using your own initiative to work towards achieving those goals, that is valued by the community or organisation (Gill, 2006). However, Clemente (2003), Malik (2003) and Pretty (2003) have argued that the fear of losing power, in other words to empower others, is still strong in some organisations and still remains a challenge to many that practice a participatory approach.

Participation enhances an individual's empowerment but Burkey (1993) holds a different view. Burkey views empowerment as a concept that challenges the forces that seek to oppose rural people's access to resources and control of development. On the one hand, community members would want to participate and become empowered so as to have absolute control over resources meant for development within their communities on the other hand, development organisations also feel their inability to control the resources used for interventions will mean a loss of power. This means losing control of intervention management, an aspect which Sahley and Pratt (2003) believe some organisations are not ready to accept, because they believe that would take away their power while empowering communities to enable them to manage their own development (Nyamugasira, 2002).

Desai (2002a:120) has pointed out that NGOs are 'prone to ossification, particularly if they are dominated and controlled by charismatic leaders who are unresponsive to new ideas and view innovation as a threat to their authority'. Arguably, such organisations will succeed if they empower the people to become agents of their own development, which could result from radical changes to the power structures and institutional arrangements that have to be effected from top to bottom (Thomas, 2000b). Development that benefits the poor will not occur unless they are given the powers to control and manage resources through the practice of participation and influence development plans to make a physical and socio-economic impact (Burkey, 1993; Kotze and Kellerman, 1997). However, Pedler et al (2004) argue that, transferring power is one of the necessities of empowerment, but that alone is not enough. Empowerment should come with a real power attached, because 'power is rarely given away and has to be taken' (Gill, 2006:212).

Development organisations are accountable to their funding agencies and the taxpayer, so limiting control of resources to development facilitators seems justified, making them display some reluctance to transfer control and management responsibilities to community members, even though the status quo is facing a lot of issues (Mohan, 2002). In addition, being accountable to donors and making development interventions have significant impact on the lives of the target groups makes development organisations limit the transfer of power to communities (Fowler, 1995; Open University, 2001; Lewis, 2002). Over the years, some organisations have been trying to promote community empowerment through knowledge acquisition, training of rural people to acquire basic skills, building their confidence through capacity-building activities and making them self-reliant (Sahley and Pratt, 2003).

Community members can only become empowered and play an active role in decision-making when they are made to participate actively in every development activity (Desai, 2002). Such empowerment could distinctly affect the lives of the whole community no matter how culturally diverse it may be (Thomas, 2000a). Nyamugasira, (2002) further stated that a commitment to local community empowerment will enable development organisations, particularly NGOs, to organise themselves in a manner that would make them shift development responsibility to community members no matter how inexperienced they may be.

Development organisations and institutions are many and have diverse programmes, yet their objectives converge around the elimination of human suffering and promotion of effective and sustainable livelihoods, so the application of their expertise in development is an effective way of enhancing community empowerment and also helps to promote effective development. Empowerment may seem difficult to achieve but it could be done through capacity building (Malik, 2003). In this regard development institutions and organisations will have to be supportive or facilitative rather than directive or being in full control of the management of resources (Mohan, 2002; Sahley and Pratt, 2003). There are various ways through which individuals, organisations and even communities could be empowered. However, the choice it will depend on the organisation, the programme objectives and the target group.

2.8.2 Participation and Levels of Empowerment

The level at which individuals would be empowered depends on the development objectives, the role that individuals are expected to play and whether the people needed to perform a particular task lack the necessary expertise to enable them play their expected role within the organization or community. Somerville has observed that empowerment can take place among individuals, at district organizational levels and even at the household level (Somerville, 1998 cited in Lyons et al, 2001). For instance individuals could be empowered economically, politically or socially, but it would depend on when and in which organization they work or the communities in which they live.

- *Individual Empowerment:* Individuals could be empowered through the activities they perform within an organization (James, 2001). It equips the individual with the skills needed to undertake the daily routines within their communities or organisations which hitherto they could not do (Thomas, 2000). It gives them the sense of capability to perform creditably in the society, community or organization in which they live.

- *Community empowerment:* The involvement of the community through participatory activities, self-mobilization, or engagement in government or NGO activities could bring about community empowerment (Pretty, 1995; Agarwal, 2001). This form of empowerment could be achieved through community-driven activity or institutionally-driven activity. A community may participate in self-

74

initiated activities or activities externally controlled by NGOs or government institutions. These may require capacity-building to help enable them acquire basic skills to enable them to perform certain duties. As they do so they become empowered through the activities they participate in.

- *Organisational Empowerment:* Organisational empowerment is a way of making individuals that work within an organisation very proactive in their activities (Hilderbrand, 2002; Hemmati, 2002) as they work in synergy to meet the organisational goals. Empowerment of such individuals will not only make them proactive, but also gives them a voice and a sense of belonging that enables them to contribute to their society (James, 2001). A holistic empowerment of individuals within the organisation makes them perform effectively and collectively to improve the activities of the organisation. It gives people a way of expressing their group needs in a way that cannot be ignored (Dugan, 2003). Organisational empowerment, serves as a source of belonging for individuals and not only makes them proactive, but also gives them a voice to enable them contribute to their society. Communities where citizens are balancing existing power relations have a history of grassroots organisations or other social movement through which they become empowered and make useful contribution to their communities (Gaventa and Valderrama, 1999).

There are several ways in which organisations, institutions, departments, groups or individuals could be empowered. An organisation's agenda, its vision and mission, the aspirations of the individuals within it, the political climate, the economic situation, the geographical location and the needs of the community or individuals all have a role to play in people's empowerment. For instance, access to information, a right to basic necessities such as education, good medical care and housing, inclusion or ability to participate in

75

activities that affect ones life and ability to hold leaders accountable for their actions could all form the basis of empowerment (Holland and Brook, 2002; World Bank, 2002). The multidimensional nature of issues relating to poverty and deprivation and the efforts to meet certain basic social needs clearly shows which aspect of empowerment will be needed to make individuals proactive and able to make a meaningful contribution to their community. The fulfilment of certain basic needs calls for empowerment that could be observed in various categories. They include:

- *Access to information:* Informed citizens who have access to information can take advantage of any opportunity to improve their way of life, exercise their basic rights, and improve their level of knowledge either through education or information sharing (Holland and Brook, 2002; World Bank, 2002). TV and radio programmes, telecommunications and the Internet all expose people to information from within their communities, organisations, nations and even from around the world. These information transfer media should be available to every citizen in every community. For individuals to become empowered and act responsibly and confidently, they have to be well-informed about issues around them and should be able to take advantage of and manipulate things (Fulop and Linstead, 2004:200). Access to information allows individuals to know their basic rights.

- *The right to basic societal needs:* People should have the right to education, good health facilities, affordable housing and be able to make use of resources available to them in their environment (Holland and Brook, 2002). These basic necessities should be available to every citizen and every nation must be able to provide them to her citizens. Holland and Brook (2002) and the World Bank (2002) have argued that access to education is also a way to improve the knowledge power of

76

individuals that would also equip them with ideas to enable them make good choices, understand and assess government policies, make better judgments respond positively to public decision-making and formulate better policies. Acquisition of knowledge is a way of gaining power that according to Foucault makes individuals maintain what they know - an important aspect in development policy and practice (Eyben, 2004). Educated citizens have a better understanding of the communities they live in and can make meaningful contributions towards the formulation of policies that affect their lives (Dugan, 2003). Educated citizens are well-equipped with the knowledge of their community which gives them the confidence to perform their normal activities. Well-educated citizens have adequate knowledge and skills needed to influence decisions and are able to control resources in their communities (Somerville, 1998 cited in Lyons et al, 2001).

- *Participatory and legal rights:* The opportunity to participate in public decision-making for policy formulation and implementation brings about a commitment to change (World Bank, 2002). The right to life, protection of the laws of ones nation and the protection of particular citizens by the law or the judiciary should be necessities of life and every citizen should be empowered to demand those rights. Being able to participate, every citizen should have the right to court systems and legal rights to challenge issues that affect them, and also to protect their existence in society (Woolcock, 2002). These basic rights should form part of the fundamental rights every citizen is supposed to enjoy. Individuals should be empowered to understand that they have the right to basic freedoms, which should not be infringed upon by others. Individuals should have the right to demand accountability from their leaders without fear.

77

The type of empowerment is dependent on individual, community or organisational aspirations, and depends on what is expected to be achieved during the development process. However, the power relations that still persist in participatory practice makes organisations' preparedness to empower rural people somewhat questionable and leaves the rural people in a state of uncertainty.

2.8.3 Empowering Rural People through Capacity Building

Effective rural development would be difficult to achieve unless capacity building is organised for stakeholders and beneficiaries who are in direct control of management. Development that is aimed at efficiency, success and bottom-up support should have a capacity building component (Kotze and Kellerman, 1997). Participation that is aimed at achieving effective community improvement will not happen automatically but requires external support (Hilderbrand, 2002). To build capacity in individuals and make them efficient and effective is a way of helping them to achieve good development goals and help them identify problems they experience irrespective of the community they live in. Hemmati (2002:234) argued that 'if participants lack knowledge or the process lacks balance, then capacity building measures should be considered'.

Capacity building is one way by which individuals, organisations and communities could be empowered to enable them to manage development activities effectively and efficiently. Hemmati (2002) observes that there could be areas where some stakeholders or beneficiaries may lack adequate knowledge to enable them to participate fully in decision-making, to manage resources or even to influence policy or make changes that may lead to revision of development programmes so as to enhance effective and sustainable livelihood activities. However, the acquisition of skills and knowledge would not only help people to perform creditably but, they also form the basis of day-to-day management skills needed in community improvement. Lack of capacity building could lead to ineffective performance and poor results.

Panday (2002) looked at capacity building in two different ways. The first perspective looks at the nature of management, where states, government departments and organisations may need reforms or some form of institutional development to improve their level of operations. In the broader sense, this will include human resource development, good governance and advocacy of decentralising policies to improve the services of government. The second perspective looks at nation building that involves its citizens, from the grassroots to the national level. It calls for participation to make them proactive in their day-to-day community activities and to equip them to manage resources and be able to take responsibility for their actions.

James (2001) examines the two perspectives in definitions provided by the International NGO Training and Research Centre (INTRAC) and which are based on the context and areas where capacity is most needed. That capacity building must be an ongoing process of helping people, organisations or societies to improve and adapt to changes around them. The performance and improvements must be taken in the 'light of the mission, objectives, context, resources and sustainability' while 'organisational capacity building is a conscious intervention to improve an organisation's effectiveness and sustainability in relation to its mission and context' (James, 2001:3). According to Panday (2002), the UNDP looks at capacity building as a process and a form of problem solving. That is capacity building should help individuals, organisations or communities to increase their ability to identify problems, solve problems and to achieve objectives while at the same time broadening their understanding of development issues in a sustainable manner.

Capacity building enhances local peoples' 'ability to perform a particular function or tasks effectively, efficiently' and helps bring about effective rural development management and sustainable livelihoods (Hilderbrand; 2002:328). Paradoxically, building capacity in a rural community does not mean encouraging them to participate in rural development interventions. Rather community members could be involved in Participatory Learning Action (PLA) that would enable them to acquire the necessary skills to perform effectively and competently within their communities (Chambers, 1997). Studies done by Eade (1997) and James (2001) showed that capacity building cannot be viewed in isolation but should encompass the social, economic and political environment which may integrate the activities of development organisations community-based organisations (CBOs), the private sector, households and individuals.

Interestingly, the concept of capacity building has been an issue in the development debate for quite some time. However, the manner in which it is applied, raises a number of questions within organisations and among development facilitators. For instance, questions like why, who and when capacity building becomes necessary still remain unanswered. Eade (1997) and Clark (2002), who have challenged the application of capacity building asked the following questions who diagnoses capacity needs? Who should build capacity? Are organisations that claim to build capacity capable, well equipped and have the necessary expertise to do so? Are the people ready for capacity building? Is capacity building relevant within that prevailing circumstance? Thomas and Allen (2000) and Malik (2003) have also argued that, if members of an organisation are not the beneficiary of the development then who decides who needs capacity and who should build it? At the micro-level 'whose interest is the capacity-building programme serving (James, 2001). Is it to make local NGOs better recipients of aid better implementers of aid or better implementers of northern NGOs development programmes?' Or is the capacity building meant to make them better NGOs? In other words, why that particular capacity building?

Figure 3.2 An extract from Hildyard et al case study in Southern India

> In a study undertaken in Southern India Hildyard et al (2001) noted that development organisations still use a blueprint approach and follow organisational objectives when they build capacity. In some cases a non-participatory approach is even adopted to build capacity. In Southern India, the Catholic Institute for International Relations organised capacity building which aimed at equipping women with the necessary cattle rearing skills to become effective cattle farmers because they observed that cattle milk was in high demand so encouraging women to enter into cattle rearing was a good way of helping them improve their level of income and help alleviate their poverty. However Clair noted that having given the women two-week training in cattle rearing none of the women bought a single cow let alone used the skill they acquired for cattle rearing. The women maintained that the NGOs did not consult them; they were never asked if they would like to go into cattle farming. When asked they maintained that they would have preferred to use the money for something else and not cattle rearing.

Source: Hildyard et al, 2001 cited in St Clair, 1995

In the case study, above Hildyard et al (2001) called it imposed participation. Arguably this is what I term an inappropriate way of capacity building. The capacity building was not well planned or there was no proper participatory process to identify the real capacity the women needed. There was no joint decision-making to ascertain the community's priority needs or other livelihood approaches in which the women could also invest instead of the cattle rearing which turned out to be a waste of time and resources. The views of the women were not sought before the training was initiated. This continues to raise questions as to who should build capacity. Malik's (2003) argument shows that organisations may build capacity because it may form part of their development plan or part of the agenda of the funding agencies. Therefore at what time and at what stage is capacity building necessary or are those communities really ready for capacity building. These are some of the questions that still need to be answered by organisations. Until such basic questions are addressed, the controversy surrounding capacity building will remain unresolved.

Major development interventions collapse within a short period because the 'necessary leadership or staffing to make things happen' does not exist (James, 2001:5). It is therefore argued that, if NGOs are to be effective in fostering capacity building, they will need to liaise with other development organisations, share ideas and expertise and start building capacity within their organisations. If participation is to be effective, then capacity has to be built for community members, stakeholders and even for members of development organisations, so that they can contribute effectively in the management of development activities. Capacity building would build the confidence of the people and make them effective and efficient as they go about their daily activities. Burkey (1999) concludes that the acquisition of knowledge through capacity building increases one's consciousness, help one to make better decision and enhances ones understanding, leading better performance and creditably improvements in one's way of life.

2.8.4 Partnership: A Tool to Enhance Community Participation

The concept of partnership is used by some experts to mean a relationship of shared goals and ideology that may link individuals or organisations (Ling, 2000; Mawdsley, 2002). According to Harriss (2000), Ling (2000), Penrose (2000) and Kotse and Kellerman (2001) a relationship exists between individuals, organisations, departments, agencies nations, donors and recipients, NNGOs and SNGOs, public and private sector organisations which could all be termed as partnerships. In the United Kingdom and some European countries, partnership is widely used to embrace activities between the public and private sector (Harriss, 2000). Partnership is now widely used in many parts of the world to explain coordinated activities between development organisations and beneficiaries. Like participation, partnership also means different things to different people (Kotse and Kellerman, 2001). To Bashyam (2002:516-517), partnership means 'involving poor people, and those who work with them, in the analysis of poverty, its different manifestations and its causes, and hence its reduction and, hopefully, elimination'. It does not necessary mean just the analysis of poverty, but also the joint efforts of individuals or organisations to tackle it.

The concept of partnership has recently been growing in popularity and recognition among NGOs, governments and donors (Panday, 2002). Fowler (2002) observes that in the past two decades development organisations have realised that no one party can achieve development growth and eradicate poverty. That means to effectively tackle poverty, communities and organisation have to work in synergy, in order to achieve their common goal. Rondinelli, 2002; Fowler, 2002 and Anwar, 2003 argue that organisations and agencies which extend development interventions to include all beneficiaries and stakeholders, increase the efficiency of service delivery systems and widen ownership. In addition to the development benefits organisations may derive from partnership, it also brings organisations and stakeholders together. It promotes mutual respect, collaboration in problem solving and encourages stakeholders initiatives (Gill, 2006).

Like participation, partnership also means something different to different people, and the interpretation of the approach and its usage seems to vary from organisation to organisation. Lorenz (1989) looks at partnership in two different dimensions: firstly that it entails long-term commitment, shared interest and work towards a common goal. However, no matter the issues affecting them, partnership makes them have a common interest that will be of benefit to all partners, irrespective of the position of the members and power they hold. The quality of stakeholder participation is strengthened by information sharing, but Lorenz argues it could also lead to exploitation by more powerful groups, who could capitalise on the relationship to further their own agendas. In partnership, powerful

83

individuals may either 'undermine or challenge' the overall agenda of the weaker or recipient groups. It is, however, argued that cultural backgrounds, ideological beliefs, power relations and philosophical differences could also affect the effectiveness of the partnership and might sometimes make it difficult to work (Mawdsley et al, 2002; Zelenev, 2005). Anwar (2003) and Malik (2003) observe that although every organisation or community has its respective role in the development process, none can work without the support of the other.

In Figure 2.3 there is an illustration of how NGOs and other development institutions in association with community members could use these concepts of participation, empowerment, capacity building and empowerment to ensure effective rural development management. The Figure 2.3 below demonstrates how NGOs and other development institutions could work in partnership with rural community members to sustain effective development activities.

Fig 2.3 Effective Rural Development Management through Participation

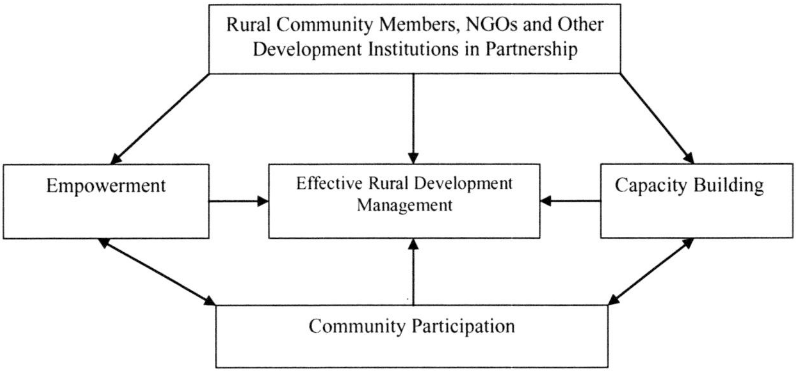

Source: Author

84

As illustrated in the Figure above, effective rural development will be achieved through partnership with development institutions, community members and NGOs. Such partnership will enhance rural people empowerment and their participatory efforts. Capacity building and empowerment help to complement effective community participation which becomes a vital ingredient to effective rural development management. Working in partnership, and in participatory way, gives community members the opportunity to learn and practice their skills. Gill (2006:12) argues that, mutual respect is not gained by victimising or punishing 'those responsible for mistakes', but rather by acknowledging that, individuals have something to offer through decision-making, partnership and contribution towards solving problems within the community.

As indicated in the Figure above, community participation, capacity building and empowerment, all contribute towards effective rural development management. Effective partnership, therefore remain central and gives the people at the grassroots a sense of belonging and an opportunity to build their capacity and make them active partners in the management process. Where areas of capacity building are identified, individuals that lack the needed capacity building will be given the training necessary to make them acquire the skills that will make them effective and active participants in the management process. Partnership and participation will help to empower the local people and make them very proactive.

It would be concluded that, participation can bring about empowerment, but individuals that lack the capacity to participate will need capacity building. However, community members will not be empowered, if facilitators are not themselves empowered. Development facilitators should identify the need to build capacity within their organisation, so as to build the capacity for the rural people, to enable them become

85

proactive and contribute to their society. Ensuring effective capacity building and good partnership will not only empower rural people, but it will enhance their capacity to contribute towards effective rural development management.

2.9 Summary

The concept of participation has been the central focus of most development activities for over four decades. However, previous and recent development discourses still have some gaps in its application. Some critics have indicated that some of the weaknesses and biases that still hinder effective participation include gender issues, power relations and lack of organisational preparedness to accept and integrate local knowledge in participatory practice with the fear of lose of power and control. Participation has been practised for many decades, the missing link in participatory practice is still not addressed. In many developing countries, more especially in sub-Sahara African countries, social norms, belief systems and some cultural practices seriously hamper individuals lack of preparedness to participate in development decision-making.

While development organisations are aiming at encouraging the less powerful and build their capacity to make them very proactive in participatory practice, social norms and cultural practices are also hindering some rural people effective participatory practices. It has been observed that, little is featured in recent development literature as to how these negative practices in many developing countries could be addressed or integrated in development literature to shape recent development policy and practice. The involvement of people at the grassroots level has not improved development in many communities.

Participation in development policy formulation and practice aim to counter the conflict of power and power relations which some critics argue are weakening community support and relegating a lot of potential and active individuals out to of the boundaries of active decision-making, because the key problems effecting participation are not addressed.

Chapter Three

Development, Community Participation and Local Governance in Ghana

3.1 Introduction

In chapter two the concept of participation was critically reviewed to ascertain how it is being applied by development organizations in development practice. The chapter also examined the significance of neo-liberal development theory, and its relevance for development practice in the developing world, and the difficulties countries are experiencing as a result of the adoption of the theory. The chapter also looked at the relationship between participation, power relations, empowerment and capacity building. In this chapter the concept of participation will be examined further to evaluate how it has influenced and continues to influence grassroots level development decision making. It will examine Ghana's development plans, pre- and post independence, how the concept of participation is applied in grassroots decision-making and how notions of participation influences the system of decentralised local governance in Ghana[7] in her decentralized system of administration which was introduced in the late 1980s. Finally, the chapter will look at the system of governance at the local level and the nature of grassroots participation.

---

[7] Ghana is located in the West Coast of Africa (see appendix 7). It shares a border to the west with Cote d' Ivoire, to the north and northwest with Burkina Faso, to the east with Togo and to the south with the Gulf of Guinea. Ghana lies just above latitude 3^0 north of the equator and just 7^0 below the tropic of Cancer (Latitude 23^0). It is dissected by longitude 0^0. Geographically Ghana occupies about 239,460sq km. The vegetation of Ghana is mostly savannah, which accounts for about 2/3 of the vegetation of the country, and which is mainly located in the north. The tropical rain forest which covers part of the middle belt and the south west of the country also forms about a third of the territory, while the remaining third is covered by mangroves and swamps. Ghana is divided into ten regions and sub-divided into 134 districts, which include the metropolis (that is the regional blocks). The capital Accra is situated in the Great Accra region on the eastern coast.

3.2 Development: Pre-Independence Approach

3.2.1 The Colonial Government Development Strategy

The development strategy adopted by the Gold Coast (now Ghana) was based on that of earlier colonial administrations (mostly Dutch and the Portuguese) that governed Ghana, the territory before the British colonial rule. However, after the Second World War, the development policy changed, because, earlier development plans did not integrate rural community development and colonial effort was concentrated in big cities and key administrative areas of the country. On September 19th 1949, the Gold Coast Government issued a Memorandum on Community Development and Local Government (DCD, 2006). The aim of the memorandum was to speed the economic and social development of the country by harnessing the community's own energies through government policy documents and community social capital. This approach became operational in 1949 in the form of mobile teams, composed of a few literate members drawn from various organisations based in the Trans-Volta[8] (now Volta Region), Ashanti[9] and Fante[10] areas (see the Ghana District, 2008).

This community development experimentation paved the way for the beginning of the government's Social Services Provisioning, which relied on a few educated people who were prepared to help their less fortunate countrymen. The main aim was to assist the rural

---

[8] Trans-Volta used to be part of Togo and part of the German colony of Togoland. The southern most part, was first colonized by the Danes and was later on transferred to the British, to be administered as part of the Gold Coast, now Ghana. After the defeat of the Germans in World War I, the German colony of Togoland was partitioned. One area portion was placed under Britain rule and became known as the British Togo. The other, under French, became French Togo, now the Republic of Togo. The British Togoland, was first called Trans-Volta Togo and later the Volta Region after independence.

[9] Ashanti is one of the powerful tribes in ancient Ghana and now denotes a region of Ghana where most of the people speaking the Ashanti language.
[10] Fanti is another language spoken in Ghana. The speakers of Fanti live along the coast of the central part of the country. The Fanti-land is the area of Ghana where education was first introduced.

and disadvantaged urban poor communities to improve their socio-economic well being by developing initiatives through active community participatory activity.

3.2.2 Development Approach and Community Involvement

The development approach adopted in the past and the nature of community involvement were similar to what the rural community members called the '*nnoboa*'[11] system (Bob-Millar, 2005). This was a self initiated development activity whereby people in various villages made financial contributions to assist one another to start their own businesses or income generated activity that would help alleviate financial hardships. The approach established a kind of *revolving fund* that every member of the group could tap into, in order to start a new income-generating activity. It was developed through community mobilization, conscientisation and popular participation, where decisions were taken collectively to improve lives and communities (MESW, 2006). This approach opened up avenues for social and economic development, and moved from the old colonial administrations' focus on trade and mining exploration.

During the eleventh century, the arrival of the colonial missionaries to the West Coast of Africa brought the introduction of NGOs' activities into the sub-region; which boosted the nature of development. It would be argued that the growing numbers of NGOs is a recent phenomena, but Ghana had a long history of indigenous or grassroots voluntary organizations that could be dated back into the pre-colonial days, (Mawdsley et al, 2002). The European colonialists that visited the West African coast were missionaries and their mode of operation was like that of NGOs, because their activities were outside the public

---

[11] Nnoboa is a form credit union mostly organised in rural parts of Ghana. Participants contribute money which individuals use to start business or funerals or to support an individual that may be in financial difficulties such as have a house burnt, property stolen, etc. where the individual may not have immediate funds to support him or herself. It is similar to credit union but the only difference is that as for nnoboa the contribution is made when someone needs financial support to continue life.

sector. Mawdsley et al argued that, though some embarked upon the establishment of development projects, their main focus was on the spreading of Christianity, rather than socio-economic development which was supposed to be their underpinning goals (Mawdsley et al, 2002) without any government influence or control. Yet some critics argued that their motives were political or driven by trade ambitions, rather than the social development of the people. The schools they established were used to educate some of the locals to speak and interpret the colonial language, in order to enhance their trading potential and help with administration work. However, the political independence, in the fifties brought shifted the development paradigm from the colonial administration's approach. The new approach aimed to promote rapid social and economic change rather than infrastructure improvement. But according to some critics, this was detrimentally concentrated in key administrative areas which left many rural communities behind.

3.3 Development: Post-Independence Strategy

3.3.1 Development Models: Post-Independence Strategy

The post-independence development strategy adopted sought to develop Ghana as a modern, semi-industrialized, unitary social state like Europe and the United States of America (USA) (The Adacci Atlas, 2005:1) though the earlier plans were to develop the deprived communities which had not benefited from previous colonial administrations. Rural development never formed part of the main development focus, because the emphasis was placed on industrialization (Colman, 2002). According to Colman the industrialisation approach were also adopted by a number of other countries including India, Cuba, North Korea, and Guinea although the industrialization development approach never benefited rural people. The development approach followed the modernization theory[12] development paradigm, but Ghana's agenda went further to include establishment of state-owned farms and cooperatives which were manned by sympathizers of the post independent government. Mabogunje (1989) noted that this strategy was later adopted by a number of countries in the developing world in the 1960s, in order to curb the collapse of rural infrastructure and promote rapid economic and social development in the rural areas (Bates, 1995); although gain, most rural communities never benefited. Bates argued that the main development focus was social and economic infrastructure improvement, in order to enhance the industrial growth being pursued at the time.

Bates (1995) and Wanmali and Islam's (2002) observations show that, the development strategy adopted focused primarily on industrialization, but paid little attention to agriculture, which was supposed to form the basis of economic and social development in the newly independent country. This reflects Dzorgbo's argument about developing countries post independent development strategies. He observed that many developing countries adopted the western industrialization approach but could not sustain industries due to lack of skilled personnel (Dzorgbo, 2001). Bates argues that efforts to boost the economy, through creation of industries (most of which were state-owned) also failed because the resources allocated for this were thinly distributed (Bates, 1995). Unlike the industrialization programme adopted in Europe which solved unemployment problems there, the strategy adopted in Ghana could not curb the high unemployment rate. Therefore, in an attempt to become *an agent of development*, Batley observes that Ghana actually

---

[12] Modernisation theory was a development paradigm that has continued to have a significant impact on development policy and practice and which has changed the theoretical perspectives of development in general. Hettne, (2002) has argued that modernisation theory was aimed at poor nations which intended to imitate the development efforts and programmes of their richer counterparts, with the aim of helping to bridge the gap between rich and poor nations in terms of development.

became *an agent of underdevelopment* and her effort to progress thwarted her development process (Batley, 2002). This strategy was an imitation of the development that occurred in Europe during the industrial revolution (Bates, 1993; Hettne, 2002), but Ghana's approach never brought technological or economic improvement.

Around independence various development plans were drawn up. A 10-year development plan between 1950-1960 and an 11-year plan between 1951 and 1962, both were compressed to form a five year accelerated development programme, which would be implemented between 1959-64 (Dzorgbo, 2001). The strategy was to achieve the social, political and economic objectives of the country. The plan chosen was made up of wide variety of ideas and views from the public, however it did not give clear insight of how those policy instruments had been chosen (Bates, 1995). The approach followed the then socialist development strategies, which were adopted by the Soviet Union, some Eastern European countries, and China.

Between 1972 and 1976 the Acheampong administration of the National Redemption Council (NRC) introduced what was called '*Operation feed yourself*' (Ghana, 2005). The aim of this programme was to increase food production through communal farming, which was initiated and supported by central government. The agenda aimed to engage the public, mostly at the grassroots level in food production and self-reliant activities. It was a self-mobilization development plan rather than being an outsider-driven (Pretty, 1995) development strategy. The main focus was on provision of labour, which led Agarwal (2001) and Parkes and Panelli (2001) to describe the initiative as *material incentive participation* rather than an *interactive form of participation*. The main focus was just to mobilize rural community members to cultivate land for the production of crops and the provision of labour was the only incentive the rural people could offer. The programme

93

made a significant contribution to community improvement, but the efforts of Ghanaians waned due to the world oil price hike in the mid-1970s, which affected the transportation industry (Ghana, 2005). Unfortunately, the economies of many countries around the world were affected. The development plans adopted never made provision for the peasant farmers to improve and sustain their livelihood activities. However, 'within the context of development plans, a fashionable strategy of dealing with the problem of poverty' (Mabogunje, 1989:89) importation of substitution industrialization from the west never helped to improve Ghana's economic situation and, therefore, aggravated poverty. The industrialisation approach adopted, alienated rural dwellers and resulted in rural to urban migration (particularly of the youth) in search of white-colour and non-existant jobs. This aggravated the already huge unemployment problem in the urban centres, because the education system did not prepare young people for urban employment and encouraged them to dislike the rural way of life.

The elements of the different development strategies are illustrated in Table 3.1 below, and could be summarized as follows: from 1957 to 1966 Ghana practised socialism; from 1966 to 1969 it was capitalism; from 1969 to 1972 was capitalism; from 1972 to 1979 quasi-socialism; and from 1983 to the 1990s capitalism (Dzorgbo, 2001). Ghana's

Table 3.1 Regimes and Competing Models of Development in Ghana (1957-2000)

Name and type of regime	Date	Leader	Main elements of development strategy/policy
Convention People's Party (CPP) liberal democracy later authoritarian, anti-West and pro-East	1957-66 9years	Dr Kwame Nkrumah	Structural transformation and economic nationalism; state-led industrialisation and large-scale capital intensive agricultural schemes, distrust for peasant agriculture, state regulation and control of the economy, social redistribution and egalitarian system, anti-local capitalism
National Liberation Council (NLC) military dictatorship, pro-West and anti-East	1966-1969 3years	General A Ankrah	Gradualism and free-market economy: state sector activities restricted mainly to infrastructure and public utilities, a balance between agriculture and industry, stress on growth and efficiency, promotion of private foreign and domestic investment
Progress Party (PP) Liberal democracy, pro-West	1969-1972 2.5years	Prof K. A. Busia	Gradualism and free-market economy: economic growth and efficiency, the promotion of private foreign and domestic investment but with emphasis on the development of indigenous entrepreneurial class
National Redemption Council (NRC) and later Supreme Military Council (SMC), military dictatorship, pro-East and anti-West	1972-1978 6years	Col Acheampong	Re-etatization of society: economic nationalisation and non-policy regime, social re-distributive policies
Supreme Military Council II (SMC II), military dictatorship, pro-West	1978-1979 1year	Gen Akuffo	Free-market economy
Armed Forces Revolutionary Council (AFRC) military dictatorship, pro-East	June 1979 112 days	Fl.Lt Rawlings	No development strategy, moral revolution anti-corruption crusade, anti-commerce and re-distributive policies
People's National Party (PNP) liberal democratic, pro-West and East	1979-1981 2years	Dr Hilla Limann	Gradualism and free market economy: promotion of private foreign and domestic investment
Provisional National Defence Council (PNDC), military dictatorship, pro-East and anti-West	1981-1983 2years	Fl.Lt Rawlings	Dependency – inspired actions: class struggle, anti-business policies, confiscation of means of production and property as a prelude to socialism
PNDC, military dictatorship and civilianized as National Democratic Congress (NDC)	1983-2000	Fl.Lt Rawlings	Economic liberalism: free-market economy via structural adjustment programme
New Partrotic Party (NPP) Democratic governance	2000- 2008 8years	John Agyekum Kuffour	Economic liberalisation and free trade; development strategy to achieve millennium development goal, through poverty alleviation strategies and women empowerment

Source: Adapted from Dzorgbo, (2001)

unstable economy became worse due to the instability of government – the result of a series

of military interventions between 1966 and 1981. To curb the failures in development

strategy adopted, alternative approaches were designed which adopted a top-down

development approach, in order to encourage greater community participation. The

approach was not even participatory because major decisions were from top-down instead

of bottom-up approach that could enhance the level of community participation.

3.3.2 Nature of Development: The Contemporary Strategy

The development strategy adopted after independence was different from the plan initiated during the colonial era because community members were not actively involved as partners in the implementation of all agendas. The concept of participation never formed part of the main focus though there was community member engagement in some of the decision-making, their involvement was partial or passive. The nature of citizen involvement could therefore be classified as *consultative* (Pretty, 1995; Agarwal, 2001 and Parkes and Panelli, 2001) because although views were solicited from rural people they were not allowed to actually influence any policy. The strategy was to improve rural life through food production, so agriculture extension officers became the main facilitators who gave the rural people the needed capacity building to make them proactive and participate. This type of participation was described by Pretty (1995); Agarwal (2001) and Parkes and Panelli (2001) as material incentive participation.

Before and immediately after independence the development initiatives were controlled by the Ministry of Agriculture (MoA) and the Extension Officers (EO). The emphasis was on the development of rural industries and crop production. In addition, the Western style of industrial development approach (Bates, 1995: Mawdsley et al, 2002) adopted also placed a lot of emphasis on crop production, in order to feed the newly established industries. The strategy pivoted on agricultural development that is crop production rather than human and social development, especially of people in the rural and less developed areas. So the creation of the Ministry of Rural Development (MRD) became necessary to bridge the gap between the developing urban communities and the underdeveloped rural areas. The agenda focus was rural community development, but it also emphasised the national agenda of development. However Johnston and others have argue that without improvements to the infrastructure, adequate health facilities, safe drinking water, good education and improved telecommunications (the prerequisites for rural development), improvement of agriculture alone (Johnston and Kilby, 1995; Wanmali and Islam, 2002) will not achieve significant improvement in the lives of the rural poor.

In the early 1980s, the government embarked on an economic '*clean-up*', and subsequently adopted the IMF Structural Adjustment Programme (SAP), in order to improve the fragile economic situation (Dzorgbo, 2001). The aim was to revive the economy, increase investment and promote development. The economic development strategy was in line with the neo-liberal development approach (Thomas, 2000a) which was to encourage, the economic growth of poorer nations through economic liberalization and the involvement of the private sector in the government's development efforts. The SAP, which was locally known as Ghana's Economic Recovery Programme (ERP) was officially adopted in 1983. Ghana was among the few African 'countries that, according to Mawdsley et al, (2002), implemented the SAP initiative. Yet the country continued to rely on loans from western countries for investments, and development projects, while the economy remained fragile. This reflects McGrew (2000), Batley (2002) and Pearce's (2004) argument that, those developing countries that pursue the SAP as a result of a neo-liberal development agenda, never develop economically and continue to languish in poverty. The ERP paved the way for the inclusion of CSOs/NGOs to assist the government (Desai, 2002) in its development initiatives, as advocated by the neo-liberal development agenda. This shift of the development paradigm also encouraged the government to involve the private sector in the achievement of her development objectives, for example, the building of schools, roads, market stalls, etc.

The introduction of the district assembly concept (DAC) in the late 1980s served to involve the people from the grassroots in political and development decision-making. The concept featured prominently the Ministry of Rural Development (MRD) (which later became Ministry of Local Government, Rural Development and Environment, (MLGRDE) development agenda. At the district level, development was to be spearheaded by the Assembly, through its elected members and Unit Committee Members (UCM) (Ofei-Aboagye, 2000). This also formed the basis of Ghana's decentralization programme which was instituted nationwide in the late 1980s. The decentralized system of governance (to be discussed later in this chapter) encouraged public participation in development decision-making and policy formulation, the subject of the MLGRDE development agenda. However, participation was passive (Pretty, 1995; Cornwall, 1995 and Parkes and Panelli, 2001) because major decisions were still taken by the district chief executives[13], the officials of the MLGRDE in the capital and by the coordinating director and planning officer at the district assembly (DA) and at village level the UCMs influence most decisions. The local people are not directly involved decision-making if one is not part of the unit committee, so their participation is just material incentive type.

The MLGRDE mainly focused its agenda on formulation of local government policies; monitoring the effectiveness of the local system of governance and effective implementation of the decentralization concept; advising government on local government issues, and the promotion and administration of local government training institutions The MLGRDR acts in an advisory capacity to the district assemblies and helps to improve by-laws (Afei-Aboadye, 2000; Ghana, 2005) and, in collaboration with the DAs, support the

---

[13] The District Chief Executive in Ghana is like the mayor of a big city. He or she is the administrative officer or governor of the district. They are government appointees and are supposed to be resident in the same district as where they serve.

activities of NGOs operations through cost sharing and capacity building – in order to promote social development in the district.

The DRD has branches in all the 138 districts and the majority of its staff works in the districts. Their main duty is to promote interactive relationships with the community members. The objectives are to achieve a quality social life and effective economic growth, to enhance grassroots political community participation, and to improve the lives of vulnerable and disadvantaged groups – in line with the government vision 2020 agenda (Osei-Aboagye, 2000). In summary, the establishment of the DRD aims to encourage the socio-economic well being of both rural and deprived urban communities. The department pursued the following objectives in the country's rural development programme.

- To assist in the eradication of illiteracy and unemployment among the adult population

- To facilitate the dissemination of development related information to the people at the grassroots' level

- To feedback to government the views and opinions of the people about national policies and development programmes - thereby creating a two-way communication channel between government and its people

- To provide technical services supporting the construction of essential socio-economic infrastructure in *needy* communities, and encourage the use of self-help methods

- To transfer employable skills to the youth through training in mass education institutions like the Rural Development College, the Women's Training Institutes and the Technical Institutes

- To extend support services to the communities, through animation, mass mobilization and grass-roots organisation and to sister development institutions.

- To expose women to opportunities for enhancing their socio-economic status

- To provide guidance and counselling services, and help to resolve conflicts within the communities and other local organisations

- To undertake socio-economic surveys of needy communities, in other to enable them to assess their situation and initiate economic projects

- To ensure an enhanced community participation in local development efforts and national reconstruction processes (see appendix A)

The DCD had six (6) development priorities namely; Adult/Community Education and Animation, Functional Adult Literacy, Home Science Education, Self-help Construction Projects, Youth Skills Transfer and Extension Services. Also the MLGRDE developed programmes through the DCD, aimed at supporting rural women's income generating activities (MLGRDE, 2006; see also appendix B for details of the DCD programme).

The DCD is one of the decentralized departments under the MLGRDE. The department aimed to support rural and urban poor people especially women through income generating activities, such as food processing, garment design, (batik making, also called tie and dye), in order to increase level of household income, improve nutrition and enable them meeting of their basic needs. The department liaises with micro credit financial institutions to support the rural women in income generating activities (MLGRDE, 2006). The DCD also undertakes reproductive health and HIV/AIDS education through the District Response Initiative (for details of their activities see appendix B). And the department works in association for example, the District Assemblies Poverty Alleviation Fund (DAPAF), the Rural Banks, and the Social Investment Fund (SIF), AARDDO Credit, etc. However some

100

critics argue that because such credit institutions are located in the capital few women in urban settings can access this facility. This is regrettable since most of the women who need financial assistance to start business live in the villages. Additionally, the money allocated is highly inadequate, so even if the scheme was extended to the villages, a lot of applications might still not be able to access funds.

After gaining control in the election of December, 2000, the New Patriotic Party (NPP) accepted the Highly Indebted Poor Country (HIPC) arrangements of the WB and IMF. This helped Ghana to benefit from debt cancellation initiated by these two financial institutions (Mawdsley et al, 2002). This arrangement formed part of the efforts to revive the economy and help improve the lives of poor people mostly in the rural areas in the country through self-help projects and other income generating activities.

3.3.3 Development Organizations and Development Activities

This lack of adequate funding, which prevented the governments from being able to extend development to the rural areas opened doors for the formation of NGOs during the post independence era. These NGOs were able to assist some of the communities that did not benefit from the government's share development plan. Before 1930 only three organizations were officially registered as NGOs (Bob-Millar, 2005) but the number has continued to increase since. then The Ministry of Employment and Social Welfare (MESW) figures show that at June 2003 there were 2942 officially registered NGOs/CSOs in the country. And by 2005, the number was estimated at over 3,000 (MESW, 2006; Adu, 2005). The actual figure of NGOs operating in the country is not known because many of these organisations operate without registration. It is argued that the increasing number was due to the introduction of the Economic Recovery Programme (ERP) in 1983 (Mawdsley et al, 2002). The initiation of the EPR by government to improve the economy and tackle

101

growing poverty justified the involvement of NGOs in assisting government's development efforts and this also served as a basis for the growing number of NGOs in the country.

In spite of the effort being made by the Department of Social Welfare (DSW) to register all NGOs in the country, lengthy bureaucracy in the registration process at the Registrar-General's Department has contributed to the failure of local and indigenous NGOs to register (MESW, 2006). The registration procedure and the amount of money involved, means some NGOs (especially the indigenous ones) simply don't register (Bob-Millar, 2005). This has limited the availability of data and relevant information on the NGOs that operate in Ghana. Gary also observed that because of the bureaucracy involved, a greater number of the indigenous NGOs do not register and that a government attempts to persuade them are resisted (Gary, 1996 cited in Mawdsley et al, 2002). Of the number who is registered, about 60% concentrate their activities in Accra, while the rural people who desperately need support still continue to languish in their misery.

The agenda of some NGOs remain unclear. The government has been relies on NGOS to assist socio-economic development and address the development imbalance between rural and urban areas (Adu, 2005). But critics argue that although communities have benefited from the assistance of NGOs, some NGOs have lost the focus of their development objectives (Adu, 2005; Bob-Millar, 2005) and others do not have a defined clear focus and agenda. And many NGO malpractices are cited. Non-cooperation with central government, exploitation of rural people in the name of poverty alleviation, and false claims of tax exception, are some of the malpractices which have been associated with the NGOs. In Kazakhstan, Luong and Weinthal, (1999: 1270) observed that formation of local NGOs became political, and instead of focusing their activities on the social and economic development of the needy and the poor they rallied their support for and existence for political parties. Most of them focus on profit generation and accumulation of funds to sustain the employment goals of their members and the sustenance of the organisation itself rather than community improvement.

The MESW identified the main community development work the NGOs had assisted with as being relief, rehabilitation of disabled people, civic education, economic empowerment of women through income generation activities, vocational training, youth services, care of the aged and the vulnerable, and advocacy (MESW, 2006). NGOs could be categorized into four main groups, not based on their activities, but on their performance and the area they operate.

i) Indigenous i.e. community organisations without external affiliation.

ii) National organisations without external affiliation (sometimes called national indigenous).

iii) National affiliates of international organisations with indigenous leadership.

iv) International organisations operating locally.

In spite of the variety of activities and programmes, Luong and Weinthal (1999) and Mawdsley et al (2002) argue that, availability of funding from donor institution has led to the evolution of new and indigenous NGOs, which do not have specific development agenda, existing rather as a means of employment for their members and the sustainability of the organization. The paradigm shift in the development thinking also increased awareness of the need to improve their communities and the level of participation of people at the grassroots level in development decision-making and sustainable development policy formulation. This prompted the introduction of a decentralized system of governance which brought in the district assembly concept and local governance through community participation which will be discussed later.

3.4 Local Governance and Community Participation

3.4.1 Local Governance in a Decentralized System

Good local governance and effective community participation is the way of enhancing community development in participation and increasing the level of public decision-making, with the aim of the 'achievement and promotion of human development' (Jenkins, 2002:485). Although local governance is very relevant to grassroots active participation in development decision-making, understanding and application of the concept make it very complex and difficult for institutions to implement. The meaning, interpretation and application of this concept of governance is complex, but in a decentralized administrative system, governance can be divided into two main dimensions (Dwivedi, 2002; Pugh, 2002 and Johnston and Gudergan, 2007), in order to make its meaning more explicit. The first dimension is to decongest state power and spread it among many individuals so that they can address the unilateralism and traditional roles of the government (Dwivedi, 2002; Johnston and Gudergan, 2007). The second dimension is to increase the involvement of those at the grassroots, so eliminating the dominance of the few individuals and interest groups involved in decision-making, and enhancing the support and commitment of those at the grassroots (Pugh, 2002).

The Structure of Local Government (1994) showed that until the PNDC changed administrative structures through the introduction of the DAC, there were few opportunities for people at the grassroots to actively participate in development decision-making and in some areas there was no such opportunity at all. The development of the Ghana's vision 2020 policy document strengthened the work of the establishment of the district assembly system (Ofei-Aboagye, 2000) and creation of the Ministry of Local Government and Rural Development (MLGRD), in order to develop a 'vibrant and well resourced decentralized

104

system of local government for the people of Ghana to ensure good government and balanced rural based development' (MLGRD, 2005:1). This created a participatory opportunity through the DAC where local people could also contribute in ideas-sharing regarding the development of their communities. A decentralization system of governance improves democratization, enhances decision-making at the grassroots level, and promotes efficiency (UNESCO, 2004b cited in Dunne et al, 2008). However, it could be argued that creation of a decentralized system of governance not only created the opportunity for local people to participate in governance but that it was also a way of creating essential rural development structures that provided supplementary employment for those who were destined to spent the rest of their lives in those communities (Johnston and Kilby, 1995).

The purpose of establishment of the decentralised system of governance was to shift development decision-making away from central government to the DAs, through the transfer of power away from the national administration (Afro Barometer, 2008; One World Action, 2008). The establishment and development of a vibrant and well-resourced decentralized system of local government in Ghana also aimed at ensuring good governance and a balanced rural based development (Ministry of Local Government and Rural Development, 2005). However, decentralisation never helped the rural communities to achieve the stated objectives. Works undertaken by Dunne et al, (2008) showed that even a decentralized system of governance produces less than the desirable results. Ofei-Aboagye, (2000) argues that the Local Government Act also stipulates that effective accountability, transparency, popular participation (both in political and development) decision-making were among the reasons behind the establishment of the local government structures; yet there is lack of transparency in the DA system of accountability, and decisions are taken by only a few individuals.

Governance at the local level provides a form of *prevailing patterns* by which public power is exercised in a given social context' (Jenkin, 2002:485). At the institutional level this power is exercised by the facilitators for example development workers of NGOs as they engage community members in the participatory process. At the district and village levels power is exercised by a few individuals who are mostly retired teachers, civil servants, chiefs and elders. The majority of the community members are excluded from this participatory process. However for communities to be able to exercise this degree of power effectively and in an all inclusive manners, Pugh identified some areas that needs to be considered. He said that all community members (not only a few influential ones) should be given greater opportunity to input into decision-making and to build their 'capacity to consider and propose new and alternative strategies' towards the development of their communities (Pugh, 2002:290). This supports Johnston and Gudergan's (2007) argument that the involvement of the community members does not only enhance their commitment in participation and decision making, but also it raises horizons of integrity and social capital.

Local governance has many development and political merits, but Dwivedi argues that it also has its disadvantages that weaken it as well – for example it excludes many people at the grassroots whose lives are affected by political decisions (Dwivedi, 2002). At grassroots level, the elite also turn to hijack power and control of resources to their advantage. Some of the weaknesses of the local governance were highlighted by Andersson and van Laerhoven. They argued that some local government officials are not ready to share their 'political power and control over financial resources with local folks' (Andersson and van Laerhoven, 2007: 1087). This according to Pugh constrains the activities of a decentralized system of governance and grassroots participation and decision-making. Pugh further explained that the neglecting the ideas of interest groups when formulating development policy, is unlikely to enhance the capacity of local institutions and governance (Pugh, 2002).

The establishment of the local government structure in Ghana became operational when Act 252 was enshrined in the 1992 constitution. This makes it mandatory for the DAs to plan and become responsible for their own communities development (Structure of Local Government, 1994) in a participatory process. Assembly members in conjunction with unit committee members (UCMs), were responsible for socio-economic development in the communities within the district (Congress Country Studies Library, 2005), thus facilitating the development of the socio economic life of community members through popular participation (MLGRD, 2005).

Act 252 makes it mandatory for grassroots level participation in decision-making regardless of the level of education of the citizens - provided they are over eighteen and customarily resident in the district (Structure of Local Government, 1994). Until the introduction of the decentralized system, the nature of governance was centralized and there was little or no opportunity for the people at the grassroots level to participate in development decision-making even at the local level. The government's decentralization programme aimed to address the weaknesses in the governance system and shift development responsibility from central government (Afrobarometer, 2008). For over three decades of the decentralized system of governance major decisions were still taken by authorities in the capital. This means there is the need to revitalize the system of democratization, open avenues for grassroots participation in both political and development decision-making (One World Action, 2008). At the district level, only the district chief executive and a few officials took major development decisions, and at the village level the assembly member and some unit committee members mostly made decisions on behalf of all community members.

Governance at the lower level was aimed at transferring power from the central government through the various DAs down to the local people on the unit committee, but at the grassroots level power and decision-making was limited to a few UCMs and the assembly members. The decentralized system of governance had objectives which underpinned its establishment, as indicated by Ofei-Aboagye, (2000).

- To promote equitable and responsive participatory development strategy

- To bring governance and development decision-making closer to people at the grassroots level

- To serve as a basis for training local people in political and development activities

However, nearly three decades after the introduction of the DAC, major decisions are still taken by the District Chief Executive (DCE), the Planning Officer (PO), the District Coordinating Director (DCD) and the Presiding Officer[14]. The assembly members are not included in decision-making. The assembly meeting is a consultative rather than interactive form of participation (Pretty, 1995; Agarwal, 2001) where there is little opportunity to influence policy. Decentralization was designed to increase levels of participation of different interest groups and to enhance the capacity of the assembly (Amin and Thrift, 1995 cited in Pugh 2002) but it excludes those whose voices are not heard in the decision-making process. For example women and the youth still have no voice in decision-making, unless one is an assemblyman or a member of the unit committee. Major decisions are still taken by the Assembly, thus lowering the level of participation rural peoples. This low level of participation as indicated by Johnston and Gudergan (2007), not only jeopardize good

---

[14] The Presiding Officer is an appointed speaker in the DA. His/her duties are similar to that of Speaker of Parliament in the national assembly. In most cases the Presiding Officer is a government appointee and might be an elected member of the Assembly

local governance but also weakens its effectiveness. It also reduces community support in local governance accountability, because the process requires consultation with community and other stakeholders in order to increase confidence and trust in the participatory process.

3.4.2 Local Governance and Community Participation

The introduction of the decentralized system of governance through the establishment of district assemblies and unit committee membership at the village level was aimed at enhancing the level of local participation and transferring of governance to the grassroots (Abacci Atlas, 2005). The transfer of power to the people at grassroots aimed to involve local people in the design and implementation of development programmes and projects, in order to improve socio-economic life in the villages (Dixon, 1990; World Bank cited in Jain, 1997). Additionally, it aimed to promote local economic and social development through public-private partnership based on the neo-liberal development paradigm (Ofei-Aboagye, 2000). The extension of benefit of development to reach people who will be seeking to improve their own lives and economic well-being through organizationally driven or self-help development activities in synergy, follow the neo-liberal development agenda. It is argued that people in rural communities in the developing world are 'continually devising new and innovation strategies for expressing their agency in development arenas' (Hickney and Mohan, 2004:3), either through participatory practice in development or a system of local governance involves those at the grass-root.

The relevance of the local system of governance makes it necessary to increase community involvement in decision-making and encourages people to become more proactive in the nation's development and political process, which turn promotes rapid development

(Smith, 2002). Ofei-Aboagye, (2000) argues that a comprehensive approach to extension of power to the districts through the DAC began in 1988. Nevertheless, some critics argue that the institutionalization of local governance was not intended to replace the existing structures of administration (CIVICUS, 2007) but rather to complement, reinforce and improve it, while bridging the gap between local people and central government. However in the absence of CSOs in the participatory process - to monitor the inefficiencies in participatory decision-making - officials are unlikely to place the public good before their private or political goals (Verwey, 2005). It is therefore, argued that local governance is traditionally focused on input (Scharpf, 1997) rather than output of work. Participation of local people is core to development, so emphasis must be placed on how participation should be practised instead of how *effective* or *efficient* the system governance is supposed to be.

Although the conceptual focus was on participation at the local level, the application of the approach was different. Arguably, participation has failed to engage with issues like power or the conflict of power relations (Hickney and Mohan, 2004). Participation through communal labour was designed to enable people to assist one another or to undertake community driven development projects. Putnam and others refer to this form of participation as a *social capital* or as '*horizontal capital*' or '*localized social capital*' (Putnam et al, 1993 cited in McAslan, 2002:140). But this did not become well established in the local governance. The strong social capital at the village level helps in strengthening this form of grassroots governance initiated through the DAC, which have participatory practice in its component. This supports the argument of Cooke and Kathori (2007:5) that the recognition of local people's ideas and acceptance of their involvement as an 'alternative to the outsider-led development' agenda became appropriate for development organisations and institutions.

Rural community members welcome the principles of participation in their own way. They express participation in a local saying, as *'tell me I will forget, show me I might remember and involve me I will learn'*. The concept participation 'emerged as a recognised approach to development some 3-4 decades ago its practice remained as virtual enclaves among isolated, sometimes romantic adherents, until recently' (Gariba, 2005:1). Even though the use of the concept differed among development organizations, the various development objectives which always reflected community development aspirations, weakened the momentum and application of the concept. It is however, argued that, although the people at the grassroots appreciate the benefits of participation, at the local government level participation is very weak (Afrobarometer, 2008). This is because the majority of people cannot utilize the opportunity offered by the reforms. Participation has gained recognition especially in projects design and implementation. But it had little recognition in Ghana's development agenda in the first two decades after independence. This was because of the government's efforts to improve infrastructure, in order to boost industry - rather than the economic social development (Bates, 1995) of the majority of rural dwellers.

Public participation was introduced when the government decentralization system became fully operational though some critics argue that this was a *gimmick* and that it was a way to sustain the PNDC government at the grassroots level so that it could remain permanent in office because it had some political motives (Dzorgbo, 2001). The weaknesses identified in the public system of participation encouraged the Extension Service Department to develop three approaches to address the system problems (Gariba, 2005). The first was to allow the local people to *de-learn* the old systems and learn new process in participatory workshops.

The second was to equip communities with the skills to identify their priority needs and design ways of meeting them. And the third was to engage community members in participatory activities that could help them address poverty reduction needs.

Community participation has been accepted in development policy and practice, but its application still remain constrained because 'donors require shorter, abbreviated and rushed training and community facilitation sessions in order to fit development project time-frames and budgets' (Gariba, 2005:5). Observation made by Woroniuk and Schalkwyk (1998) indicate that participatory practice needs time and requires continuous support, so development organisations must dedicate enough time for the engagement of rural people in participatory practice. This helps to achieve objectives and to win community support and trust. Woroniuk and Schalkwyk argument is especially relevant in areas where development facilitators rarely visit and interventions need constant and continuous monitoring and evaluation.

In a study to evaluate the effectiveness of the Poverty Reduction Strategy Papers (PRSP) and the Ghana Poverty Reduction Strategy (GPRS) a SWOT analysis was adopted. The aim was to involve people from the grassroots and CSOs in planning Ghana's poverty reduction strategies, however 'the level and quality of participation, as gathered from the field and the Ghana Association of Private Voluntary Organisation in Development (GAPVOD) commissioned report was very shallow' (Abrokwa, 2005:4). The report showed that the rural poor, especially farmers who form the majority of the country and rural population were not given the opportunity to present their concerns, so findings did not reflect the views of the poor whose problems the PRSP and the GPRS were trying to address. Rather the findings expressed only government priorities and initiatives.

This is the same as the findings of institutions like the World Bank (WB), which emphasizes the need for members of rural communities to be allowed to participate in development policy formulation and practice that 'major decisions continue to be taken by outside experts' and that in most cases external agencies decide the perimeters of participation (Datta, 2003:55). To improve the life of rural people in a sustainable way, they have to be engaged in active participation and proactive decision policy formulation and implementation. This helps to improve living standards on a 'self-sustaining basis through transforming the socio-spatial structures of their productive activities' (Mabogunje, 1989:94). Unfortunately, participation is still limited to only a few individuals and agencies involved in development. However for participation to work individuals and institutions must relinquish their power, which Pretty (2003) has observed is relatively difficult for a number of organisations, including the WB.

3.5 Summary

Rural community development in Ghana can trace its roots back to the colonial days, but the approach has not always been the same and strategy has changed over the years. This was due to military governments which did not have sustainable plans or which failed to follow well-established development strategies, and which adopted un-sustainable economic policies and ill-planned development strategy. Development which was supposed to improve the lives of rural dwellers, focused on industrialization. The approach which was adopted in many developing countries like Ghana never helped rural dwellers. In Ghana, this necessitated the introduction of a decentralization system of governance in the late 1980s, which focused on the participation of the people at in the grassroots level in development and political decision-making. However, the level of participation was partial

113

or passive and decision-making still remains in the hands of just a few influential community members and leaders.

The works of One World Action (2008) in some Asian countries shows that decentralized governance is sometimes undermined by a few elites who normally benefit from the status quo. Strong social capital at the village level is supposed to enhance participation at the grassroots level, but because decisions are still taken by just a few influential people such as Assembly Members and unit community members, widespread community participation remains weak of only partial and this does not help to improve the lives of the rural poor. It can therefore be concluded that although the government introduced decentralization policy three decades ago, the level of grassroots participation has little changed development in the villages has not improved.

Chapter Four
Research Methodology and Design

4.1 Introduction

In chapter one the research methodology was briefly explained, in order to offer insight into the strategy adopted for gathering the data for the investigation. This chapter explains in more detail the research methodology and the philosophical underpinnings adopted for the study. It examines the motivation behind the selection of the research topic, the rational behind the adopted research method, the main research questions and the objectives of the study. The design took into consideration the key philosophical perspectives adopted and how they matched the data collection technique. This chapter will also explain the sources of data and the approach used in gathering the data. And it explores the researcher's fieldwork experience and some of the ethical issues that were considered when gathering the data. Finally, the chapter looks at some the limitations of the chosen methodology.

4.2 The Research Motivation

The motive behind this study was the realization that although the concept of participation has become part of development practice in the last three decades there are major constraints that make the application of the concept difficult. Ever increasing concerns among organizations, researchers, stakeholders and development practitioners, focus on issues like where and when participation is appropriate, how it is best orchestrated, and who should be involved. A decentralised system of governance was adopted in Ghana in the late 1980s. It focused on the grassroots level in order to encourage proactive popular acceptance of political and development participation. But it has failed because it has not addressed the barriers to community participation in rural development. Supporters of grassroots participation, argue that it encourages the involvement of community members in development interventions in their communities, which they never had any influence over before. Participation encourages people to be proactive and to work towards the achievement of sustainable development objectives (Francis, 2002, Desai, 2002; Kotze and Kellerman, 2003 and Cooke and Kothari (2007).

Community participation has been embraced by funding agencies and CSOs because it is argued, it is only through participation that rural community members can become involved in the development intervention in their communities (Cooke and Kothari, 2007). This observation reflects Mosse's view of participation, which he argues is a way of transferring control of resources and power to local people (Mosse, 2007). But critics argue that participation is a threat to the overall control of resources and the management of intervention by development facilitators (Roche in Open University, 2001).

Local people can contribute significantly through offering their knowledge during the participation process and development decision-making. It also helps to streamline government decentralised system of governance and the assembly's development plans. Grassroots participation also demonstrates an appreciation of the value of the knowledge to development policy and practice. But fear of loss of power, which Roche explains, threatens the DA concept of decentralized governance – which sought to pave the way for the involvement of people at grassroots level in participatory planning and development decision-making in their communities (Roche in Open University, 2001). This is because those in governance 'still face other pressures to get things done and other measures of efficiency than those provided by measures of participation' (Mosse, 2007:24). The fear of lose of control of power, resources and management responsibilities, have all become some of the barriers hindering effective participation of people at the grassroots.

116

In Nzema East District (NED) NGOs that undertake development rely on external project officers for the management of intervention. Notwithstanding active community participation could empower community members and assist them to be more proactive in their development efforts. But active participation seem difficult to practice. Cooke and Kothari, (2007:8) question whether participatory methods have driven out other approaches, which have advantage over participation. They also question whether 'group dynamics' can 'lead to participatory decisions that reinforce' the interests of the already powerful. Are the constraints in the effective application of participatory practice still issues that need to be investigated? Can effective community participation help improve the lives of rural people and make them proactive and able to make a meaningful contribution to the task of improving their communities (Cleaver, 2001; LaFord, 1995). It is because of these uncertainties that an empirical study is required to analyse the paradoxes and barriers that hinder effective rural development. This is the motivation for this investigation.

4.3 The Philosophical Standpoint: Interpretivists and Constructivists Perspectives

To understand the way rural people participate in development activities and the difficulties development organisations experience when they involve people at the grassroots in development activities, made the use of interpretivist and constructivist philosophical perspectives very relevant for this investigation. However, Gray (2004) argues that the research epistemological and ontological standpoint also dictates and influences the philosophical underpinnings of the research methodology used. The adoption of the interpretivist[15] and constructivist[16] philosophical perspectives helped to ascertain the

---

[15] Fay, (2004:113) argues that the interpretivists view social phenomenon as a form of social construct which reveals the 'comprehending human behaviour, products and relationships consists solely in reconstructing the self understandings of those engaged in creating or performing them'.

paradoxes and barriers that affect participatory practice in community development in NED. This supports Fay's argument that social science research remains 'plagued into two related dichotomies; that between understanding and explaining' (Fay, 2004:133).

Community participation has not only been weakened by biases in the nature of its application or the power relations involved (Chambers, 1983; 1997), but also by various barriers and paradoxes, which this study aimed to investigate. It is therefore argued that an understanding of the nature of community participation and the complexities involved calls for the information gathered to be interpreted and well constructed as suggested, for example, by May (2001), Fay (2004) and Gray (2004), in order to make community members participatory practice and their engagement with development organizations more comprehensible. The data that is already in the public domain needed to be re-constructed (Blaikie, 1993 and Sayer, 2004), because as Flick (2004) argues this is a way of invoking the evolution of new knowledge. Constructing the data findings and reconstructing[17] the existing data helped to discover the guiding principle of community participation while identifying the barriers and paradoxes involved in the application of the approach (Sayer, 2000; Flick, 2004; Gray, 2004).

Gray (2004:24), argues that 'in terms of epistemology, interpretivism is closely linked to constructionism'. Therefore the intertwining nature of the two philosophical perspectives make them a unique option for understanding, interpreting and constructing how community members participate in development activities in NED, whether the intervention is community driven or initiated by a development organization. This confirms Gray's (2004) further pointed out that the philosophical standpoint of the social

---

[16] Flick, (2004) believes that social constructivists are concerned with how knowledge is developed, what type of knowledge become appropriate and how it can be evaluated as useful knowledge.

[17] Sayer, (2000), Flick, (2004) and Gray, (2004) agreed that existing data could be explained in a different way to suit new phenomena. They call this reconstructing a social event to suit another situation or event. This can clarify understanding and from the basis of a new body of knowledge.

epistemologist's acquisition of knowledge through interpretation, construction and re-construction of some social realities, remains justified. As a social scientist, it remains appropriate to seek the meaning of the community development activities through qualitative means and to interpret their causes, and when they occur (see Potter, 1996; Fay, 2004; Whyte et al, 2004).

To understand the way community members participate in development activities in NED and why they do what they do required the adoption of an interactive approach, which made the use of one-to-one encounters and focus group interviews being the most appropriate methodology for the study. The aim was to understand the agents (the researched) so that the researcher could acquire the requisite knowledge needed to complete the study (Hart, 1998; Fay, 2004). It is however argued that community development activities are just voluntary contribution which one has to offer to his/her community. Some people may not know why they have to participate and in some communities participation is understood to be a form of *social obligation* that is an honour for members of a community or inhabitants of the area to become involved in.

As indicated in the earlier part of this section, the adoption of interviews (for the community members, development facilitators and the district assembly development officials) was based on the researcher's philosophical epistemological perspective which gave respondents the opportunity to explain the way they participate in development work initiated by local people themselves or by any external development organisation. These perspectives necessitated the use of focus group discussion and one-to-one informal interviews because this helped to give a better understanding of the people and their social life, and more especially their day-to-day development practice (Robson, 1999; Silverman, 2000 and Gray, 2004).

119

4.4 Research Methodology: Research Design, Strategy and Data Collection Technique

4.4.1 Research Design and Strategy

This research adopted the inductive research approach to investigate the paradoxes and barriers which made participatory practice more complex and which undermined the achievements of development objectives in rural areas. To understand the way community members participate in development activities, why they participate and how they participate; an interactive approach was needed which made use of one-to-one informal interviews and focus group discussions. This aided an understanding of the agents (the researched) and enabled the researcher to acquire the requisite knowledge needed (Hart, 1998; Fay, 2004). This perspective necessitated the use of interviews, which, according to Robson (1999), Silverman (2000) and Gray (2004) would allow the researcher to understand the way people interacted with their environment and carried out activities in their communities.

The research aimed to explore ways in which people at the grassroots level are involved in development activities that employ the participatory principle and the nature of inconsistencies and complexities in the application of the concept. The study never tested any hypothesis, however as an exploratory study it did investigate, how the district assembly (DA) and the Italian NGO – Co-operation for Development of Emerging Countries (CDEC) applied the participation concept in order to empower rural people and encourage them to be proactive in local development activities.

The study did not follow the feminists' approaches which view development interventions to be gender biased and which, as a result has encouraged feminist researchers to look into ways of integrating women's views into decision-making on development policy formulation and implementation. Rather the research was centred on overall community inclusion in participatory practice and the proactive empowerment of rural people in development activities within their communities. This enabled an investigation of the paradoxes and barriers that are associated with development practice. It is argued that community development activities are achieved through the *voluntary contribution* one has to offer one's community. In some communities participation is understood as a form of social obligation that should be seen as an honour for members of a community and inhabitant of an area.

4.4.2 Research Method and Data Collection Technique

The nature of the research, the research questions and the skills and resources available dictated the research tools, which were used to obtain the data for this research (Morse, 1994; Laws et al, 2001; Robson, 2003; Blaikie; 2003). The adoption of a one-to-one informal interviews and the use of a focus group discussions approach, helped to generate new ideas and understanding that produced evidence that might challenge not only the researcher's belief but also those of wider society (May, 2001) particularly in the area where the research was carried out. The questions were designed in a semi-structured form so there could be room for probing into unclear responses. This also gave respondents the opportunity to clearly express their feelings about the phenomenon under investigation.

Qualitative data for a study of this nature could be gathered by using interviews, participant observation or non-participant observation. However, the use of semi-structured interviews was the best option since the community members were. Most of the participants were interviewed using focus group discussion, because they live in the same villages, they have an equal level of experience and socio-economic life-style, and they share the same sentiment in terms of issues in development within their communities, so their contribution towards responses in focus group interviewing was considered appropriate. It enabled them to put ideas together and provided good responses for the interview questions. There were many people in the villages to be approached and so one-to-one interviews would have been so time consuming that the study would have become longitudinal – and this was not the intention. Besides, filling in a questionnaire would have been a daunting task for most of the respondents even if the local language had been used, since most of the village people were illiterate. To triangulate the interview data, some secondary data were gathered from the DA and research documents from the district office and the MESW.

The focus group interviews were conducted for community members in three different villages. The district coordinating director, the planning officer and the district chief executive were those interviewed formally at the DA. The two officers of the NGO (Co-operation for the Development of Emerging Countries – (CDEC) were also interviewed. The local officer and his Italian counterpart of the NGO were interviewed individually. In addition eight village members were interviewed formally in the four villages in order to triangulate the focus group interview data which were gathered from the villages. The subsequent sections will detail how the data collection tools were implemented.

4.4.3 Access to Research Area and Sources of Data

To avoid the researcher being continually 'seen as extensions of their political sponsors within the setting despite denials to the contrary' (Punch, 1994:86) the parties involved were informed about the nature of the research what was being investigated and why their involvement was important. With some knowledge of the people involved the economic activities in the area and levels of education, I made some preliminary visits to the participating villages and interacted with the interviewees and briefed them about the nature of the research what would be done and what would be expected of them. This was in line with Punch's argument that 'the determination of some watchdogs to protect their institutions may ironically be almost inversely related to the willingness of members to accept research' (Punch, 1994:86).

Before the first visit, letters had already been sent to the District Chief Executive (DCE) and the District Coordinating Director (DCD) to ask permission to conduct the research in the district - this was positively responded to. During one of the visits arrangements were made to get rooms for the interviews with the DCE, DCD and the planning officers. Assembly members in the participating villages were informed about the study. The DCE wrote supporting the introductory letter, which had been provided by the university. The letter from the assembly requested the assembly members to mobilize the people for the focus group interviews and the one-to-one interviews, although none of the participants were coerced to participate. They were asked for their consent, and willingness to participate was agreed upon during a visit.

The study data was obtained from two main sources, primary and secondary.

(i)   The primary data was obtained from rural community members in selected villages where development activities are very active. The data was gathered from four villages; namely Ankobra, Asenda, Asemko and Nkroful. In the district every village has a Unit Committee. The membership oversees development within the village. In all there were six (6) focus groups interviews conducted. Six (6) members in each group. And eight people were informally interviewed, two from each village. The District Chief Executive, Coordinating Director and the Planning Officer were interviewed and two development workers of the NGO were also interview. Additionally, two senior employees from the regional office of the Ministry

123

of Employment and Social Welfare and the national director of the Department of Rural Development were also interviewed.

(ii)   The secondary data was obtained from documents from the district assembly, the MESW and Department of Rural Development. In addition, information about the NGO and the nature of activities it conducted in the district was obtained from the regional office.

Experts in the field of development, who had knowledge of development activities within the district and experts in the field of development in general were also consulted (Morse, 1994). This approach reflects what Morse calls *intensity sampling procedure*. Research institutions that had previously undertaken research activities in the district were also contacted for information about the nature of development activities, security and safety concerns relating to the area.

4.4.4 Selection of NGO, Villages and Individuals for the Interviews

Identification and location of individuals for data collection (Morse, 1994) formed the basics of the data gathering procedures adopted. The Italian NGO involved in the study was the Co-operation for the Development of Emerging Countries – (CDEC). The district is one of the most deprived in the country, in terms of development, but despite introduction of the government decentralization programme about two decades ago the area has not attracted many NGOs. There is especially a dearth of international NGOs in the districts in the northern part of the country, and development has been very slow. Five NGOs were contacted for the study but only the CDEC officials accepted to participate. Although other NGO were active in the villages, their offices could not easily be located and so contact was difficult. Often NGO offices are located in the capital, Accra, and only occasionally do officials visit the area. And there was another problem, grassroots NGOs often did not

124

register, did not have offices and so did not want to be identified because they did not want to pay registration fees. Granting permission for a researcher to conduct interview meant their illegal activities would be exposed so this permission was difficult to obtain.

The selection of respondents from the NGO was based on the role they play in the NGO (Morse, 1994) and how they involve the people at the grassroots' level in their activities. Their prior knowledge of the organisation's activities in the district and whether they were willing to talk to the researcher was also taken into account. The key respondents of the NGO were the local project coordinator and the manager of the organization, who is an Italian colleague. They are the people in charge of the day-to-day management of the NGO, so they were the key knowledge informants for this research.

Selection of the villages for the study was based on two factors: (a) the nature of development activities in the village and (b) whether there had been recent development work in the village. The involvement of district assembly (DA) and whether the activity was community-driven or initiated by an external development organisation was also taken into account. Selection was not based on the number of development activities that were taking place in the village, but was rather done randomly, since most of the villages had self initiated development activities going on. Some of the villages had more on-going development activities than others and some of the villages were more proactive in their development activities than others. However the selection was done based on the community readiness to participate in the study.

The villages where the respondents were ready to talk to the researcher were prioritised over those that were reluctant to do so. Most of the development interventions in the villages focused on infrastructure, e.g. market stalls, bore holes and pit latrine construction and micro credit schemes. The infrastructure development activities were instituted by the government through the District Assembly Common Fund (DACF) and the micro credit schemes were initiated by CDEC and local banks. Although the assembly in conjunction with the Rural Banks within the district had earlier implemented credit schemes in some of the villages, the NGO seemed more active than the assembly and more women especially had benefited from the NGO initiated scheme than from projects initiated by the assembly.

The respondents were selected based on their performance in activities within the respective villages, but those who expressed willingness to participate were prioritised. This approach was adopted to avoid the situation which Laws et al, (2002) and Hopf (2004) described, where an *opportunistic researcher* gather information from respondents who might not be ready to participate in a study, but who could be coerced to participate. All the villages had development committees that managed their development activities. The Unit Committee (UCs), as they are nationally called, have been in existence since the assembly concept became fully operational in the late 1980s. Most of the respondents (whether those who agreed to participate in a one-to-one formal interview or in a focus group) were members of the UC, but they were randomly selected to avoid any influence or biases in interview responses.

4.4.5 Visits to the District and Villages

Before the start of the data collection informal visits were made to the district office when I was briefed by officials about the villages that had agreed to participate in the study. The DCE informed the assembly members living in the participating villages about the research and of what would be expected of the members that were willing to take part. During the visits issues such as the safety of the research assistants, the researcher and the respondents were discussed. Interview venues and scheduling was also discussed during these visits. At

126

the district office the officials (the Coordinating Director, the Planning Officer and District Chief Officer) agreed that the interviews could be conducted in the conference room, during office hours. A briefing period gave me the opportunity to explain to the district officials the objectives of the study and how it could benefit the district if successfully completed. The ethical guidelines were also discussed. The District Coordinating Director who became very interested in the research, requested a copy of the thesis when the study was completed. The coordinating director and the planning officer agreed to be interviewed the following week since they had tight schedules during the week the initial visit was made.

The visits to the villages were made during weekends. The initial plan was to assess the possibility of organizing the interviews during the weekends – preferably Saturdays and Sundays - because most people do not work during the weekends. It became clear that because three of the villages - Ankobra, Asenda and Asemko were situated along the coast and it is illegal to go to sea on Tuesday the participants in those villages agreed to be interviewed on Tuesdays instead of Saturdays and Sunday. On Sundays most of them go to church and on Saturdays they attend funerals. At Nkroful the fourth village participants agreed to be interviewed only on Saturdays. However, knowing the exhausting nature of participants farming work, and because some of the participants were mothers and married women, the times agreed seemed convenient for all participants. In spite of the circumstances, the data was gathered with some ethical considerations to avoid insufficient data gathering. Efforts were made no to compromise data quality by limiting study timeframes.

4.5 The Interview Schedule: District Assembly, NGO and the Villages

The interviews scheduled for the key informants in the selected villages, officials of the NGO and the district assembly began a week after the initial visits. The one-to-one informal interviews, conducted in the DA, were done in the first week of the fieldwork - that was during the third week of April 2006. During the initial visit the officials in the DA initially agreed to be interviewed in the conference room, but on the interview day, they insisted that the interviews to be conducted in their offices. Initially it was a bitter pill to swallow, knowing the nature of government officials and the number of telephone calls that may come to the office during the interview process, since it was to be conducted during office hours. However during the process interviewees never received calls nor did they make any. That seemed to indicate their cooperation. The District Coordinating Director (CD) and Planning Officer (PO) agreed to be interviewed during the first few days, but the planning officer refused to have his interview taped. Without breaching ethical rules, the research assistant was able to take notes while I conducted the interview. To assist the planning officer ensured the research assistant had enough time to make good notes. All the interviews lasted nearly 45 minutes.

Like the interview conducted for the district assembly officers, the facilitators of the NGO were also interviewed in their office. The local coordinator and his expatriate manager were interviewed the same day. Although the two officers work in the same office they were interviewed at different times. Separate interviews were necessary because the expatriate officer was in the office most of the time, while the local officer was always in the field monitoring the organization's project. The interview with the expatriate officer lasted an hour, and that of the local officer lasted an hour and fifteen minutes. The local coordinator spoke at length and gave detailed information about the operation of the NGO and its activities in the district and the villages. This demonstrated his familiarity with the area, and with the local socio-economic situation and the nature of development interventions.

The focus group interviews were conducted mainly with the rural community members, some of whom were members of the UC. The interviewees in each village were divided into three groups of six women, six men and six youths - that meant each group was made up of six members (see figure 4.1 below – for details of the interviews scheduled see Appendix G). The youth group was made up of three males and three females. This gave three focus group interviews conducted in each village, a total of six (6) focus group interviews for the two villages. Different people were interviewed separately in an attempt to avoid any form of *power relations* that could influence the smooth flow of the discussions – because, for example most women feel intimidated in the presence of men. In the presence of their husbands or older relatives they may feel uncomfortable about talking freely and in detail. The separation of the youth from the men was also necessary to avoid any form of intimidation on the part of the men and to ensure the men did not feel disrespected by any freely expressed and open comments the youth made. All the interviews lasted between forty-five minutes to one hour.

Fig 4.1: Interview Schedule Diagram

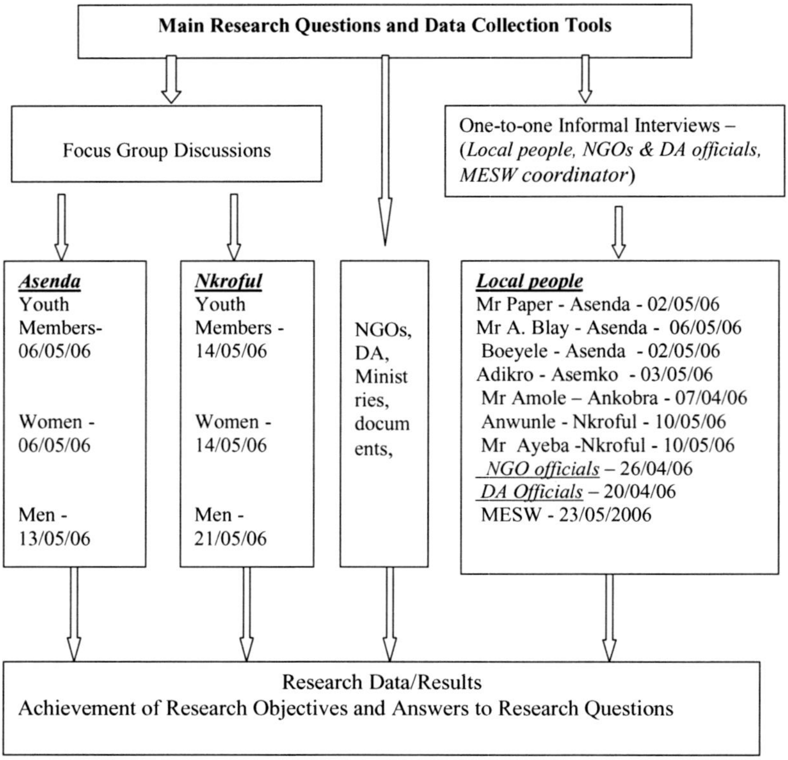

Main Research Questions and Data Collection Tools

Focus Group Discussions

One-to-one Informal Interviews –
(*Local people, NGOs & DA officials,
MESW coordinator*)

Asenda
Youth Members- 06/05/06

Women - 06/05/06

Men - 13/05/06

Nkroful
Youth Members - 14/05/06

Women - 14/05/06

Men - 21/05/06

NGOs, DA, Ministries, documents,

Local people
Mr Paper - Asenda - 02/05/06
Mr A. Blay - Asenda - 06/05/06
Boeyele - Asenda - 02/05/06
Adikro - Asemko - 03/05/06
Mr Amole – Ankobra - 07/04/06
Anwunle - Nkroful - 10/05/06
Mr Ayeba -Nkroful - 10/05/06
 NGO officials – 26/04/06
 DA Officials – 20/04/06
MESW - 23/05/2006

Research Data/Results
Achievement of Research Objectives and Answers to Research Questions

Source: Author

Before the interview, the questions were piloted among some of the community members who did not take part in the study. The responses provided were good. Few amendments were made to the questions. However, this helped to simplify some of the questions that were asked and how they could be put to obtain the optimum responses. Non-verbal responses also made it necessary to adjust the strategy to be used for the conduct of the interviews. This helped anticipate comments from interviewees (Robson, 2002), about the interview schedule and the process. Piloting the interview questions gave me the opportunity to practice how to facilitate when conducting interviews (Laws et al, 2003) especially in a rural setting using the local language.

The one-to-one interviews were conducted in areas where the interviewees themselves had suggested they would like to be interviewed. The respondents who participated in the one-to-one interviews all agreed to be interviewed in their homes. All the one-to-one interviews were conducted in the afternoons so that the women who might be busy cooking evening meals for their families could have the chance to participate. The interviewees who participated in the focus group discussions were interviewed in the local Junior High School, because the school was on holiday and there were a lot of empty rooms where the discussions could be conducted without interruptions. All the respondents who took part in both the focus group discussions and the one-to-one formal interviews were illiterate so the interviews were conducted in Nzema (the official language spoken by the people in the district), so that participants would be comfortable in expressing themselves freely and in detail. This reflects the view of Laws et al (2003) hat the best way of encouraging respondents to speak openly and freely, is by *coming to their level* in terms of expression or social relations.

The friendly and relaxed atmosphere in which the interviews were conducted helped to diffuse any tension that would have discouraged the interviewees mostly the women and the youth, from talking freely and openly. To diffuse any tension, an open question was asked which made the interviewees feel relaxed and comfortable during the discussion. I maintained my neutrality, and never asked leading questions or supported certain types of responses, but encouraged every respondent to participate in the discussion. The recording of the interview made it possible for responses that were provided undertone or very fast to taped for better analysis. During the interview the respondents reached a compromise on some of the issues but different opinions were expressed and every response was recorded. After the interview, a summary of the discussion was communicated back to all respondents for comments and further clarification before the record was finalised.

4.6 My Real Fieldwork Experience

The fieldwork took approximately four months, although there were some days when I did not visit the research area. The data collection started during the second week of April, through to the end of July 2006. The respondents were mostly illiterate and their livelihood activities were farming or fishing, so they had free weekends, when they attended funerals (mostly Saturdays) or church services. The weekends are the only free days that most of the people have some rest and have time to attend to any other non-essential duties so it was suitable for the conduct of the interviews. Apart from the focus group interviews, all the other interviews were conducted during the week days, when convenient for the interviewees.

The days of the interviews were agreed upon by all respondents but it became very difficult to get some of the interviewees at the time of scheduled interviews especially the focus group interviewees. During some of the focus group discussions, some of the respondents could not be found either they had to attend funerals or visit a sick relative at the hospital or attend to some family issues. On one occasion when one of the focus group interviews was about to start in Nkroful, a lady came to tell the other respondents that a pregnant woman was in labour and needed help. There was no nearby hospital nearly so the interview had to be cancelled and rescheduled for another day. This and other minor problems made the data collection drag for the four month period. In one of the villages, a one-to-one interview which was scheduled to start at eight o'clock in the morning could not start - the man told me one of their '*ahead*[18]' had arrived so he was going to buy fish. It was a resting day for people in the village and nobody was supposed to go fishing but the man needed fish for his wife who was a fishmonger – so the interview had to be called off. It was necessary to re-scheduled the interview, but no date was agreed.

In order to accommodate respondent willingness to participate the day proposed by the respondent was accepted by the researcher, but in spite of all these difficulties the interviews were successfully conducted by the end of the fourth month. Initial data analysis started when the data collection was underway, but intensive analysis only began after all the data had been gathered. The initial analysis made it possible for some of the questions that the interviews could not address to be re-written – so that all research objectives were achieved.

4.7 Data Analysis and Presentation of Results

Traditionally it is acceptable to analyse data after it has been gathered, but some researchers argue that the analysis should start as soon as data gathering is underway (Strauss and Corbin, 1990; Silverman, 2000; Robson, 2002). I began writing the transcript the night the first interview was conducted. The transcript makes 'features of the recording more transparent and accessible and also enables the researcher to see the vocal and non-vocal activities that unfold on the tape' (Clayman and Gill, 2004:593).

The method of the analysis chosen was based on the research tradition adopted for the study. Formal one-to-one interviews and focus group interviews are forms of conversation through which information can be gathered from informants (Robson, 2000; Laws et al, 2003). However, the approach was based on the researchers' epistemological stance (Fay,

---

[18] Ahead is the name given to small fishing companies that undertake off-shore fishing along the coast of Ghana and other West African countries. Fisherman use outboard motors to power their boats and travel from one coastal village or town to the next. It is a form of migratory fishing activity.

2004) and the methodological objectives of the study (Blaikie, 2003; Gray, 2004). The data was analysed using the conversational analytic approach (Gray, 2004; Christenson, 2004), because it made the focus explicit and the data more comprehensible (Gray, 2004). Because the study is also hermeneutic in nature (Lee and Fielding, 2004) it gave me the opportunity to apply the social constructionist approach to interpret the responses, that were gathered during the investigation.

The transcript was conceptualised by breaking the responses into paragraphs sentences and phrases, in order to make the meaning explicit and comprehensible and to highlight the phenomena that unfolded in the interviews (Strauss and Corbin, 2004, Clayman and Gill, 2004). The transcribed data was coded using the open coding approach which Strauss and Corbin (1998:62) explained that it offers a more appropriate way of 'naming and categorizing phenomena through close examination of the data'. The coding was done by *cutting and pasting* and collating similar responses under different headings (Bryman and Burgess, 1994). The coded data was put into the NU*DIST computer software package for final analysis, before the results was presented in the report.

The final report was compiled after completion of the data analysis, taking into consideration the key concepts - like participation, power relations, empowerment and gender relations. The objectives of the study, and the paradoxes and barriers identified during the investigation and how they affect development and participatory practice in communities in the district were also noted. The results was presented in three chapters, which focused the DA's engagement with the rural community members, the application of the concept of participation by CDEC and the snarl-ups and dilemmas facing the rural people in participatory practice. The presentation was aggregated in a manner that avoided any identification of the gender, age or name of respondents (Morse, 1994). This meant a guarantee of participants' anonymity and confidentiality was assured (Morse, 1994; Laws et al, 2003), and contributed to the maintenance of a high standard of ethical principles during the investigation.

4.8 Ethical Considerations

Ethical issues are embedded in most research processes (Laws et al, 2002), more particular development studies, which is anthropological in nature. Ethical issues simply explain the codes of practice and acceptable moral behaviour one needs to consider when undertaking research (May, 2001; Hopf, 2004). Researchers inevitably encounter ethical problems (Hopf, 2004) because research activities usually involve different stakeholders, with different backgrounds, aspirations and ideologies. The participants involved in the research were made aware of the benefits of the research and, especially, of the individual benefits which might be derived either directly or indirectly. Their role in the research was also explained and they were made aware of what was expected of them if agreed to participate (Silverman, 2000; Laws et al, 2002; Hopf, 2004). The voluntary nature of their participation was emphasised. Research is a form of epistemological study which philosophical perspectives may either follow a subjectivity or objectivity paradigm. While some ethical problems could be related to power relations between or within organisations, others may be associated with cultural, politics or ethnicity. The following ethical issues were taken into considerations in planning the study, undertaking the fieldwork and during the presentation of the results.

In research 'it is considered unethical to collect information without the knowledge of participants, their informed willingness and expressed consent' (Kumar, 1996:192). The consent of all participants was sought and enough time was given to them to decide if were willing to participate in the study. Additionally, enough time was given to respondents to enable them to comprehend the objectives of the research which enabled them to make informed decisions about whether they wanted to participate (Silverman, 2000: Laws et al, 2002: Hopf, 2004). It was made clear to participants that they could decline to be part of the research, and that their involvement was entirely voluntary (Hopf, 2004). And the importance of research for the district and country was explained to the participants (Laws et al, 2002).

Research participants have their own priorities, which may or may not be similar to that of the research. Efforts were made to avoid any intrusion into the participant's private lives. This was done for example, by avoiding questions that could intrude into the participants' private lives, and which might not have any bearings on the research anyway. Anything that could cause harm to the participants, for example causing them to be stressed, depressed or anxious (Kumar, 1996: Robson, 1999) as a result of their participation in the data collection was avoided. Anything that it was considered could damage rapport between the researcher and the participants, either in a form of bad language or ill treatment, and which could endanger trust also reduce participant willingness to continue, was avoided (Hopf, 2004). Efforts were also made to avoid triggering displeasure during the data collection that could make the participants not welcome the researcher back, if it became necessary for further data to be gathered (Laws et al, 2002).

During the research some of the respondents wanted to know if the research was part of a government programme to provide the village with a proper toilet or assist them to build good market stalls or if the research would bring a development project to the community. Some of the respondents felt they had been used for several research projects and that many people (especially journalists) always visited the area to interview people. So they wanted to find out if they were not going to waste their time and go through the interview

136

process for nothing - as had happened in the past. The purpose of the visit was explained and what was expected of them was clarified. They were given the choice to withdraw at anytime. Although their withdrawal would delay the data collection, it was important to establish the option in order to abide by the ethical rules.

The success of the research depended on how secure the researcher would be during and after the data collection. In anthropological research, researchers sometimes become very subjective due to their personal beliefs, values and norms. However, subjectivity differs from bias (Kumar, 1996). With this as one of the guiding principles efforts were made to avoid any bias that could influence the data which was gathered. All information that was gathered was reported back to the respondents for their comments and approval, before the data was finally compiled. This was to guarantee their support of information that entered the public domain (Robson, 1999). The findings were reported objectively to avoid unethical interpretation of the data, (Kumar, 1996) which might not reflect the interest of the participants.

4.9 My Position as a Researcher and the Research Participants

Another interesting experience was my position as a researcher and the research subjects. As local from the research area - although my home village was not part of the selected villages for the research positioning myself as a researcher and interviewing individuals from the same district was a challenge to me. However, at the start of the data collection, it was considered very important to observe what Gray (2004) describes as striking a balance between *insider* and *outsider* status, because as member of the district, my position would have influenced the respondents behaviours and the responses they provided for the study. Therefore, a better understanding of my position as researcher and a local community

137

member at the same time enabled me to position myself to avoid any form of influences or biases on the part of the respondents which could affect the validity or reliability of the data.

Although being a member of the local area would have made the data gathering difficult, however it helped to increase my understanding of the people better, and also helped in the selection of the right people that could provide information for the study. NED is one of the areas in Ghana where witchcraft and black magic is seriously practised. The district is often classified as a dangerous area (in terms of witchcraft activities and the use of magical powers) so a lot of researchers will not like to visit to undertake a research study, let alone contacting individuals in the area for interviews. My position as a researcher contributed to deepen my knowledge about the use of magical powers to influence decision-making and participatory practice. This helped to enrich the data gathering and enhanced the degree of validity and reliable of the results.

4.10 Validity and Reliability of the Data

4.10.1 Validity – Internal, External and Content

The research was validated internally, externally and in content (Cohen et al, 2007) to enhance the effectiveness of the data which was gathered. Equal numbers of respondents were selected from the two villages to participate in the focus group discussions. This was done to ensure better generalization of the information that was gathered (Gray, 2004). The respondents were put into smaller groups of six, with youth members being in separate groups from the women and men. The women and men also remained in separate groups. Although the number of questions was the same, the responses provided in each discussion

138

were different, because the respondents had different views on some issues and when comfortable within their groups they could freely express themselves about issues that affected them in their active participation. This would have been difficult if all of them had been together during the discussions.

Rural life in most Ghanaian communities is similar both economically and socially. As a result the selection of respondents took into consideration, their background and socio-economic activities. Gray (2004) considers this approach helps to ensure and strengthen the external validation of data. The separation of the men from the women and the youth from both the men and the women also enhanced the external validity. All the participants shared similar a socio-economic lifestyle and almost all the respondents had the same livelihood (that is they were either farmers or fishermen), but the separation eliminated power relations and gender biases, that might have affected some of the discussions. Besides, it also helped to reduce the tendency of some of the respondents not to feel comfortable enough to talk or freely express their opinions in the presence of their husbands, elders or fathers and mothers.

The questions posed during the investigation explicitly addressed the issues that confronted the NGO, the DA and the local people when they were engaged in participatory practice. The link between the question and the method chosen determined the 'types of results obtained and ultimately the usefulness of the results, or the pragmatic application of the study findings' (Morse, 1994:223). The use of the local language, Nzema also ensured better understanding of the issues at stake and helped participants to provide appropriate responses. The rural community members' active and effective involvement in development interventions was ensured by comparing the findings and finding ways in which the results could be used to address the problems the organisations encounter when they engage community members in participatory activities (Gray, 2004).

4.10.2 Reliability – Stable and Intra-judge

The reliability of the study was based on its stability and intra-judgement. The study was *stabilised* by conducting the interviews during the weekends, and in the late afternoons when most of the participants either had nothing to do or were not very busy with their home activities. Some of the key informants agreed to be interviewed in the evening, as this was more convenient to them. Some of them were occupied most of the day because they were farmers, fishermen and fishmongers. Some women preferred day time interviews because in the evenings they were busy cooking for their families. Some of the interviews were conducted at the weekends as this was preferable, because on Saturdays, most of the villagers only had funerals to attend and these funerals were usually in the mornings so participants had the afternoons free.

To avoid intra-judge unreliability, the study was done in a continuous and consistent manner to avoid what Gray (2004:94) describes as 'bias on the part of respondents' that might have arisen as respondents could provide responses they might assume could be acceptable to the researcher. Additionally, efforts were made to avoid recall of respondents for further data, which might be biased. An audio tape recorder 'with technical quality of recordings' (Perakyla, 2004:326) was used to tape most of the interviews conducted during the study. The recorded messages were played back to the respondents for clarification and approval. In spite of the efforts made to make the study reliable and valid, there were some few limitations affected the methodology used for the study.

4.11 Limitations of the Research Methodology

The respondents were made aware of the objectives of the study and their consent sought. They were also told they could opt out if necessary. Some of the respondents could not be interviewed within the agreed time frame and that affected some of the smooth flow of the interview schedule. At the district office there was not enough literature about the activities of the NGOs operating in the district and the record, which did exist was patchy. The use of two or more NGOs could have provided a more diverse response and better reflected the nature of other organisations operating in the district. And non participant observation could have provided different responses since the elements of subjectivity could have affected the responses provided.

4.12 Summary

The research methodology chosen was based on the philosophical perspectives that underpinned the study. In an exploratory study to investigate the participatory activities of rural community members in the management of development interventions it was considered appropriate to use the social constructionist and interpretivist perspectives to examine the issues under investigation. The use of focus group interviews for the community members was not only appropriate but rather *most* suitable since they had similar experience in the same socio-economic environment. The informal interview, organised for the development officers for the NGOs and the district officials, was deemed appropriate for the study. Ethical considerations were taken seriously in the course of the study and factors such as the nature of the research design, the research area and the type of respondents, were taken into consideration when attempting to make the results more reliable and valid. Despite this there were some limitations that affected the methodology used for the study. However, the study remains valid and is reliable enough to take place.

Chapter Five

Nzema East District – Profile of Research Area

5.1 Introduction

In chapter four the research methodology and design was examined. It explained the motivation of the study, the main research questions and objectives of the study. The chapter also looked at ethical issues considered when gathering the data for the study. This chapter looks at the research profile and the villages that were involved in the study. The chapter critically looked at the socioeconomic activities in the district; the nature of development over the years, the district assembly concept (DAC), the district assembly common fund (DACF) and how the fund has affected development in the district. The final section of this chapter, will looks at the participating villages and how socio-economic activities have affected development pattern.

5.2 The Nzema East District

5.2.1 The Geographical Location of Nzema East District.

Nzema East district is located on the south coast of the Western Region of Ghana. It is bordered to the west by Jomoro district, to the east by Wassa West and Ahanta West Districts, to the north by Wassa Amenfi District and to the south by Gulf of Guinea, (a section of the Atlantic Ocean). The district administrative capital is Axim, which is located along the coas, about three kilometres West of Cape Three Points and eighty one kilometres west of the regional capital -Takoradi. The language spoken in the area is Nzema. The district has a population of about 142,959 - this is made up of 71,673 males and 71,198

143

females, (Ministry of Local Government, 2006). The district has approximately seventy eight towns and villages. The settlement is basically nucleated type with about a third of the towns and villages situated along the coast. The remaining towns and villages are about five or more kilometres away from the coast.

The vegetation of the district is tropical rainforest with some mangrove swamps along the coast (near the estuaries). The coastal belt stretches across the southern part of the district and as a result has made the land very infertile for farming. The only crop that thrives well along the coast is coconut. Because the soil is very salty, coconut is the only crop that thrives well along the coast, yet only a few people in the villages have coconut plantation. In some of the villages, the coconuts have been attacked by coconut bacteria, which have destroyed a lot of plantation in the area. The district lies in the equatorial region of the country so, it registers the heaviest rainfall. Expects believe, it is due to the Cape Three Points which influences the yearly and heavy rainfall in the district and makes it records the heaviest rainfall in the country. However, the continuous rainfall does not enhance agriculture, activities, because the land is not fertile for cultivation of crops.

The destruction of coconut plantations along the coast has affected agriculture and economic activities in most villages along the coast. This has also affected the population pattern in the district. The socio-economic activities in villages along the coast are very slow due to lack of jobs. People who in the past, used to rely on coconut oil processing as their main source of livelihood and income, have moved out of many villages in search of other jobs, because there is no enough copra to sustain the oil processing business, as a result of the destruction of coconut crops. People in the villages are mostly fishermen and their families or fishmongers who buy fish from the fishermen and sell in the hinterlands.

144

There are other people who do buy-and-sell, but because the economic activity is very slow, unlike the interior, poverty is still high in the villages.

5.2.2 Socio-economic Activities in Nzema East District

Like most rural areas in Ghana, the rural people in NED 'settlements represent not only an aggregation of farming population' but rather fishermen and fishmongers whose activities are based on communal labour (Mabogunje, (1989:109). Villages within the district are all nucleated, like most districts in the western region and other parts of the country. The type of settlement is a reflection of the history of Ghana and even West Africa during the pre and colonial days, where most people who lived in nucleated settlements could help one another in times of wars and external invasion or aggression. They live together so that they could help one another during farming season through communal labour and other community development work. Mabogunje (1989) argues that, the nucleated type of settlement is a form of security, and has economic reasons and benefits. As they live together neighbours could assist one another in need, and could use that to make financial contribution to neighbours who may want to start their own micro enterprise activities. As they live together, they can also assist their old and sick relatives in times of need. This synergic way of life has strengthen the social capital in the villages and also strengthened the level of support for one another.

Most of the people in NED are peasant farmers, fishermen or fishmongers but this depend on the location of the inhabitants. Those living along the coast are mostly fishermen and fishmongers, while those who live far away from the coast are mainly farmers. The fertility of the land increases as one moves further away from the coast. Some of the fishermen are migrants, from the Volta and Central regions oF the country are mainly – Fantes and Ewes. The fishermen move from coast to coast to do their fishing business at areas where they

145

could find market for their catch and the condition of the sea is good, so they do not have permanent homes in the area. The fishermen sell their catch to the local women, most of whom are wives of the fishermen. The women sell their fish in the hinterlands and in some cases in the big towns and cities mostly at Aiyinasi, Takoradi, Agona Nkwanta, Tarkwa, Obuasi or Kumasi. Besides, fishing, some of the people use traditional methods, to process coconut oil, which they sell to other traders, who buy and sell them in the regional capital Takoradi, and other major cities where they could find market. In some cases the oil is sold at areas where the traders could make huge profits.

In addition to fishing and farming, other commercial activities go on in the village and town in the district. Some of these people are mostly hairdressers, dressmakers, petty traders (whose activities are just buy-and-sell) and teachers. Due to the huge unemployment in the district, in every village there are many school leavers who may be idling with the hope of getting jobs which they do not know when they may get one. Unlike the coastal area, activities in the interior are very active. In the hinterlands, because of continuous rainfall in the district, farming is year-round. The absence of the sea and lack of rivers, leave the people with no option than to go into farming. Unlike other parts of the country where the irregular rainfall pattern makes farming unsustainable. The farmers cultivate crops like cassava (the most common crop in the region), cocoyam, maize, etc and other vegetables. Cassava, which is the main resource for the processing of gari, is cultivated throughout the year and contributes to the busy gari business.

There are medium sized stores where almost everything sold in the regional capital or even the capital can be found. Apart from internet *cafes* that are limited to the regional capital, access to telecommunication has increased significantly throughout the district. The growing economic activities in the interior, has also contributed to the growing population

146

in the villages and towns. The 2000 census revealed that out of a total population of about 144,959 people in the district just about a quarter live along the coast, with the remaining living in the hinterlands (Ministry of Local Government, 2006). The rapid population growth justifies the active economic activities in the villages in the interior. The fast growing economic activities, has forced a lot of people along the coast to migrate to the interior to do business. Like districts in the Northern and Upper Regions of the country, NED 'lack of non-agricultural investment and underdevelopment of markets result in few opportunities for economically meaningful off-farm employment or income generation' (Whitehead, 2004:1), this makes the cost of living very high compared to other parts of the region.

School enrolment is very low, due to what Georgiou and Tourva, (2007) describe as lack of parental support which affect improvement of academic performance and school enrolment. In all, there are Three Senior High Schools (SHS), One Technical Institute, One Secondary and Technical School, Forty Eight, Junior High Schools (JHS), One Women's Vocational Training Institute, One Community Nurses Training College and one hundred and ten (110) primary schools in the district (Ministry of Local Government, 2006). Besides, there are six (6) privately owned Preparatory Schools in the district. Almost every village or town has a nursery school, though some of the big towns and villages have more than one. It depends on the size of the population, availability of teachers and funds to pay the teacher's salary. Because some of the teachers are not trained, they are paid by the community's own contributions and support from the Assembly. However, with this number of schools, enrolment is very low at the Primary and Junior High Schools. Studies conducted by Akyeampong, (2007) shows that, school enrolment continue to dwindle as the children

147

progress into the Senior High School and at Further and Higher Education levels. This has reflected in the huge unemployment in NED.

Lack of Teachers Training College (TTC) in the district has also contributed to the shortage of teachers in the schools. A private TTC which was established in the early 2000, to train teachers to feed the local schools, could not be sustained, because of lack funding to pay the teachers salary and government's inability to integrate into the public training college system has made the college to collapse. The college was established by the Saturday Adventist Church, with negotiations being made by the DA to have it absorbed by the government to become one of the public TTC in the country, so that supply of teachers and payment of their salary could be done by the government. The purpose of the establishment of the TTC was to help to curb the teacher shortage in the district (Cobbinah, 2001). Most of teachers are Pupil Teachers[19]. The district has a Community Nurses' Training College, which was established in 2002, to train nurses to feed the local hospitals and other health centres in the district. It has helped to increase the number of health professionals in the health centres.

5.2.3 The Nature of Development in the District

In order to promote development in the rural areas, the National Commission for Democracy (NCD) proposed the establishment of a District Assembly Concept (DAC), which aim was to accelerate development in the districts and improve governance at the grassroots, to make the local people very proactive in political and development decision

---

[19] Pupil Teachers are instructors in mostly basic schools who are employed to teach in schools in areas where there are no trained teachers. Such instructors used to be Middle School Leaving Certificate (MSLC) holders, but some of such instructors hold GCE 'O' and 'A' qualifications.

making. However, towards the late 1980s when the DAC became fully operational, the nature of development took a different turn (Ghana, 2006). The DAC became mandatory and formed part of the country's constitution under the 1994 National Development Planning Commission Act 480 and the Local Government Act 642, section 46; which states that, rural development planning should be at the community level, and people involved in decision-making must be local people. The work of Ofei-Aboagye (2000) showed that the DAC formed the basis of the government vision 2020 development plan which was published in 1992 by the Rawlings administration. The same Article 462 also makes it mandatory for members in the DA to carry out their own development planning and programmes. Act 241 empowers them to take full responsibilities of development within the communities.

Before the PNDC government came into office in December, 1981 most villages in Ghana had what used to be called Town Development Committees (TDCs). The work of TDC was mobilisation of rural people for community initiated development activities, e.g. re-constructing dilapidated schools structures, building of markets stalls for communities that never had market to buy and sell their goods, and building of toilets. Members of the development committees were retired teachers and school leavers who could not find jobs or could not further their education (and idling in the villages) peasant farmers and fishermen. The work of the committee was entirely voluntary, so people in full time employment like teachers, nurses and other salary workers, never took part in most community work. Saddle (1978:115) observation shows that, the approach was different from the initial development strategy, which focused on 'dissemination of the urban-based approach to progress, an impression which is reinforced in the minds of rural dwellers by the diffusion' of urban form of services. The initial development approach was in line with the colonial government development strategy, which was primarily based on space-economic, and the emphasis was placed on exportation of raw materials to earn foreign exchange.

During the PNDC era, the TDC was done away and replaced it with Committee for the Defence of the Revolution (CDR). However, according to critics like Gariba, (2005) and others the establishment of the CDR was a strategy to help the government gain support at the local and remained permanent in office. The CDR therefore took over the activities of the TDC, but went further. It became evident that, although members of the CDR were not supposed to be partisan and were not supposed to use their position to demand any assistants from government functionaries, rather their work was on the contrarily. They used to help the government to arrest critics of the revolution and mobilise electorates for the government during election. The CDR was controlled by the PNDC, even though it was supposed to be free from government influence. It is argued that the establishment of the CDR was to mobilise people at the grassroots and also spread the ideology of the ruling government which denounced multi-party democracy (Gariba, 2005). The involvement of the people at the grassroots level in development decision making was to cover-up the government intentions of denouncing multi-party democracy.

5.2.4 The District Assembly and Development in the District

Development in NED has been very slow compared to other districts in the Western Region. The district is predominantly rural, with little or no manufacturing industries unlike the Wassa West and Bibiani-Anhwiaso-Bekwai districts which have a lot of mining companies and a few industries. The only coconut oil processing company which was based in Essiama, collapse during the mid 1990s. Development activities in almost every district in Ghana are under the auspices of the district assembly. The introduction of the government decentralisation concept was to promote public participation in development decision-making, but at the district level development decision-making are still in the hands of the District Chief Executive, the District Coordinating Director and the Planning Officer. Occasionally a few of the assembly members are invited to participate in district level decision-making process. All the rural communities have representatives (assembly members), but their main duties are concentrated on political issues rather than development (The Local Government System in Ghana, 2006). The assembly members were to be responsible for deliberations, evaluation, coordination and implementation of programmes that are appropriate under the district's economic development plan.

Lack of community participation in development practice brought about the introduction of the CDR, but the absence of constitutional legitimacy of the military government necessitated the introduction of principles of grassroots participation through the DA. Later, Unit Committee Membership was introduced to replace the CDR which formed the basis of the DAC and has been the corner stone of popular and grassroots level democracy in Ghana today. Development has since been under the various district assemblies. Funding of the assemblies (as established in the 1992 constitution) constituted five percent of national revenue and was always approved by parliament (Ofei-Aboagye, 2000; Afrobarometer, 2008). That money is called the district assembly common fund (DACF) and became the main source of money every district uses to embark on development projects and programmes in their communities.

5.3 The District Assembly Common Fund (DACF) and the Highly Indebted Poor Countries Fund (HIPCF)

The introduction of the DAC led to the creation of the DACF and the HIPCF and later the President Poverty Reduction Initiative Fund (PPRIF), which were all aimed at helping the rural people to start their own income generating activities. The introduction of the DACF was under section 252 of the 1992 constitution. However, subject to the provision in the constitution, at least five percent of the budget fund was to be given to the districts through the DACF, as earlier explained, was based on parliamentary approved formulae. However disbursement of the funds at the district level is not based on any criteria or procedure. How much every community is supposed to get, which area should be given priority and what development programme must be followed first, are all deliberated upon by the District Chief Executive, Planning Officer, the Coordinating Director in the assembly and the Presiding member of the Assembly.

The introduction of the DACF was aimed at boosting the level of development in deprived communities in the country, more especially those that hitherto were not benefiting from the central government's development initiatives. Act 445 of the 1992 constitution, also states that, the DACF was to help various assemblies' to initiate self-help and community or locally driven development projects. This could be in a form of micro-credit schemes for local people to start their own micro-business ventures. Quoting from the WB sector policy paper, Jain (1997:24) noted that Ghana's approach fell inline with the WB rural development strategy, that aim at helping in the creation of 'new employment, improve health and education' for the people in rural communities. Ghana like most countries in the developing world, has majority of her population living in rural areas, so the introduction of the DACF was a welcoming idea for most people in the country, especially those in rural

152

communities that over the years have not benefited from government support. The purposes of the establishment of the Fund among other things were to;

- Ensure equitable distribution of resources for development in every part of the country in a sustainable manner.

- Improve and provide affordable housing in poorer communities and improve upon the health delivery system in every part of the country.

- Establish a democratic process, through the district assemblies and promote a sustainable self-help development programme, while strengthening the decentralisation programme.

- Improve and expand access to education, through provisioning of educational infrastructure, logistics and provisioning of quality education to every school going child.

On paper the policy look very good, but in reality most communities seem not to have changed much since the introduction of the policy about three decades ago. Proper and affordable housing is still a problem for many people in all villages. Mostly rural people still live in dilapidated houses, while many live in thatch-houses, because they cannot afford to build concrete houses. Although the policy is to support local people in creation of jobs, yet the unemployment is still high, while rural to urban migration remain on-going. The strategy was value based (Thomas, 1996; Robinson et al, 2000) and was to be engulfed in a complex activity within the changing and prevailing rural circumstances (Esman, 1991). Creation of employment was very difficult so the main focus of the DACF was to provide credit facilities to the people to establish small and medium scale enterprises, but just a few individuals were benefiting. Although government placed a white paper on it, the implementation of the credit facility was not initiated, until the early 2000 when the millennium development initiative was also implemented.

Unlike the DACF which was introduced in the 1990s and was enshrined in the constitution, the HIPC fund was introduced in the early 2000, when Ghana satisfied the requirements of the World Bank and IMF poverty reduction strategy initiatives, which some highly indebted poor countries, including Ghana had some of their debt cancelled. It brought some financial relief to countries that adopted the new development initiative, although most people seem not to be benefiting from the programme. In Ghana, the HIPC fund became another source of revenue to support the nation's development projects.

5.4 NGOs Activities in the Nzema East District

Although NED is one of the most deprived districts in the country, it does not attract attention of many NGOs although government support for the district has been very small. According to the MESW (2006) report yet the introduction of the DACF and the recently initiated HIPCF are contributing towards the development of many districts in the country, development in NED is slow. Unemployment remains very high in most villages. Unlike other districts in the region where there are many mining companies, NED has no mining company and there are no industries. .

During the early 1980s the 31s DWM became one of the NGOs that was operating in district, with a few self-help programmes scattered in some of the villages. By August 2005, the number of NGOs that have registered in the western region were just 37 (Ministry of Social Welfare, 2006). Out of this number, just five were operating alongside a few international development NGOs in the district. Currently there are 24 NGOs operating in the district, 5 are international NGOs, which could trace their roots to Europe, apart from the United States Agency for International Development (AUSAID) which sometimes supports community initiative projects in the district. In the district, the NGOs have concentrated their efforts on vocational training (mostly dress-making), gari processing, renovation of schools, building of toilets, bore-holes, market stalls, among others. Some of the NGOs work in collaboration with the DA, by providing financial and material support towards infrastructure improvement.

5.5 Profile of the Selected Villages.

In all, four villages were selected for the investigation. The villages were not randomly selected (as already discussed in the previous chapter), but the selection was based on development activities in the villages and the community members readiness to participate in the study. All the four villages selected have similar socioeconomic activities because apart from Nkroful, which is about four kilometres away from the coast, all the three villages are situated along the coast. Their main economic activity is fishing and the women are mostly fishmongers. All the villages have at least some on-going community-initiated development project. Some of them have projects that were initiated by the district assembly and some local NGOs, e.g. ADRA.

5.5.1 Ankobra Village

Ankobra is a fishing community along the eastern coast of NED. The village links the communities in the interior part of the district and the coast. However, Ankobra is situated along the estuary of the river Ankobra, which the village had its name. Ankobra is at a strategic location for commercial activities. It serves as an entry point into the district for those in the northern part, whilst traders from the coast also use the area as their point of entry to the north to do their business. The main source of livelihood for the men is fishing, while the women are fishmongers. The location of the village at the estuary makes it a strategic position for other fishermen to dock and sell their catch to the local women.

155

Unlike other fishing communities, in the district, fishing in the village is almost year round. Some fishermen bring fish from the river, while those who go to sea also bring fish from the sea, thus making the fishing activity continuous throughout the year. In other words, because, the sea becomes rough most of the time, it makes fishing activity very difficult. The river serves as an alternative source of fishing for the fishermen, when the sea is rough. Because the fishing activity is very busy in the area it makes community meeting relatively difficult. Especially during active fishing season, the men are always at sea, while the women are also engaged in the processing of fish to get them ready for market. Like other communities in the district, there are dress makers, hair dressers and other petty traders, but the main activity in the village is fishing.

5.5.2 Asenda Village

Asenda is just about three kilometres from Ankobra. It is also a fishing community so most of the women are fishmongers, but a reasonable number of the people do trading. A small number rely on the processing of coconut oil as their main source of livelihood or income generating activity. There are some traders who sell their wares in kiosks,[20] while others sell their wares on tabletops[21] like the most villages in the district. The village is one of the communities that has attracted NGOs in the past, especially from the Adventist Development Relief Agency (ADRA) Department for International Development (DFID) and United States Agency for International Development (USAID). A newly established training college in the village was initiated by ADRA, the main support of development projects in the area. However lack of financial support never helped in the sustenance of the

---

[20] Kiosks are shops with two big window-like doors which is open upwards. Items sold in such shops include local drinks, provisions and toiletries they are the most popular shops in most villages in Ghana.

[21] Tabletops are tables which are used to display items like sweets, biscuits, etc. the items are usually displayed in the day and collected at night. The owners take their items home and displayed them in the day for sell.

college and has necessitated a takeover by the government, though the takeover had not been successfully during the time of the study. Most development activities come from the ADRA, because there is a Saturday Adventist church in the village and the leaders use their influence to solicit for development assistance from ADRA. Besides, the NGOs assisted projects, the village has initiated a number of development projects from locally generated funds and assistance from the DA. Unlike the other villages in the district, the people in Asenda are more united and their communal spirit is very high. Their Unit committee is one of the most active in the district. This has reflected in a number of projects that were taking place in the village.

5.5.3 Aseemko Village

Asemko is a small fishing community situated between Ankobra and Asenda. The people are mainly fishermen and fishmongers. Just a handful of the women are dress makers and traders. Although a few of the people are farmers, the farming activity is not very active because the land is not very fertile and does not support cultivation of crops apart from coconut and sugar cane plants. Because the soil is not suitable for farming, the only activity is coconut oil processing, because the raw materials (copra) is available. In the last 10years the coconut trees have been attracted by a disease and had destroyed most of the coconut trees in the area. This has also reduced the supply of copra for the coconut oil processing company in the district. Commercial activities in the village are slow compared to other surrounding villages. The women rely on fishing activities which is also seasonal and in most of the time the sea is rough so the fishermen do not go to sea. During such periods the

157

people in the village work on their farms, but the farming activities are just subsistence[22] type with the cultivation of cassava just to feed their households. Those who are not farmers buy their food-stuffs for their families from nearby villages.

Unlike Asenda the Unit Committee in Asemko is very inactive. In the past ten years, the village has not had a chief so the leadership is in the hands of an adikro[23]. Because the village has no chief mobilisation of the people for development activities is very slow and has reflected in the lack of development activities in the village. Occasionally, the assembly member in the area organises the people for development activity, but those development activities are initiated by the assembly. The assemblyman who is supposed to liaise with the DA and help in the initiation of development activities does not live in the area. Mobilisation of the people for certain communal activities are organised by the adikro with assistance of the elders in the village. Like other villages in the district, the young men just ideal in the village without jobs. Some of them depend on remittances from family members or relatives that live in the mining areas or in other parts of the country or abroad for their livelihoods.

5.5.4 Nkroful Village

Unlike the other villages, Nkroful is the only village in the interior. The village is about five kilometres from the coast. The main livelihood activities is farming, buying and selling. In the last ten years, some illegal goal mining activities called galamsey[24] was initiated by the

---

[22] Subsistence farming is a type of farming where the farmer cultivates just a little amount of food for his/her family. The crops are basically food crops and not cash crops and there is nothing for sale. Such farms are owned by households.

[23] Adikro is someone who represents a chief of an area. Usually such people act as a chief in areas where due to either chieftaincy disputes or lack financial resources to install a chief or the rightful candidate has been found and as a result such people are made to act.

[24] Galamsey is a form of gold mining done in most villages in Ghana where there are mining companies or some mining activity had taken place before. It is done by the local with the use of local materials for the

youth in the village. The galamsey business affects mobilization of the people (especially the youth members) for development activities. The village is the birth place of the first president of Ghana, Osagyefo Dr Kwame Nkrumah; as a result, the area attracts a lot of tourists from many parts of the world, but the people have not taken advantage of it to develop the village. The government assistance to the area has also been very limited. The only Senior High School in the village is among the newly listed deprived High Schools in the country which the government has earmarked to up-grade into model High Schools. There are dress makers, traders, and some employees of Nkroful Agricultural Secondary School and other civil servants. The used to be a coconut process company (the Essiema Oil Mills Company) which was situated about one kilometre away from the village. The company used to manufacture coconut oil and soap. Between the 1960s and the late 1970s, it was the major employer of the people in Nkroful, but production dwindled in the early 1980s during the government structural adjustment programme which was embraced by Ghana. It finally collapsed in the middle of the 1990s.

5.6 Summary

Nzema East District is one of the most deprived districts in Ghana but has still not attracted enough government support to undertake development projects. Over the years, development activities used to be financed through community internally generated funds, until the introduction of the DACF and HIPCF. The introduction of the DACF and the HIPCF is helping to make a difference, but the benefit has not been adequate enough, looking at the size of the district and the level of deprivation. Commercial activities in the area are relatively slow, because the main source of livelihood is the sea, which is also not reliable because, in most of the time, the sea is always rough, so the people have nothing to

mining activity. It is mostly don by the youth who have either dropped out of school or those who have completed school and do not have any intention of looking for employment.

do for a living. Because the land is not rich, most of the people are subsistence farmers. The unemployment is also high in most of the villages compared to other districts in the region. The locally processed coconut oil business, has also been affected as a result of coconut bacteria, which has attacked most of the coconut plantations in the area. This has increased the rural-urban migration, because most of the people (more especially the school leavers), cannot find job in the district.

Chapter Six

Local Governance, Decision-Making and Community Participation

6.1 Introduction

In Chapter Four the government's decentralized system of governance which paved the way for grassroot participation in political and development decision-making was critically examined. The aim was to address the slow pace of development in Ghana, especially in the rural areas. The main issue raised was to ascertain how the concept of participation was applied by the DAs and NGOs that work with people at the grassroots. This chapter looks at how the decentralized system of governance that was adopted nationwide has influenced the nature of development practice and decision-making in communities of the district. It examines how the concept of participation is applied in development activities, which players are involved and what problems could be envisaged. The chapter will finally examine some of the key problems affecting participatory practice, with particular reference to power relations, youth and some gender issues.

6.2 Local Governance and Rural Community Members in Development

6.2.1 Decision-Making Structures and the Nature of Governance

Grassroots participation in development decision-making became part of the government's decentralization programme in the late 1980s, but the controversy and bureaucracy surrounding application of the concept has raised a lot of concerns. In Nzema East District (NED) many people are not directly involved in governance. Active development and political decision-making is basically concentrated at the district assembly and with assembly members and district officials. However, in the early 1980s when the government introduced the district assembly concept (DAC) many people became actively involved in

161

decision-making through the unit committees. So governance, as many people would put it was brought to the doorstep of the people at the grassroots. The Unit Committee Members (UCMs) who were mostly elected members in the villages were brought into decision-making, alongside the assembly members of the village or electoral area, the chief or *adikro* (where there is no chief) and the elders. Mobilization of the members and resources, implementation of development activities and management of any development process were all under the auspices of the UCMs.

Decision-making which is supposed to be participatory and should involve the people at the grassroots is just a form of consultation with the community members by the UCMs and assemblyman or woman. During the focus group discussions at both Asenda and Nkroful all the participants emphasized that the community members are just consulted on issues of development, but are not involved in active participatory decision-making. Most of the community members are just representatives during decision-making. Decision making at the community level mostly involves the men, women, youths and *adikro* or chief as well as the village assembly member - although final decisions are taken by the UCMs. At the district assembly the final decision is taken by the District Chief Executive, District Planning Officer, the Coordinating Director and the Presiding Member of the assembly. In Figure 6.1 below the decision-making procedure and the nature of the people involved have been illustrated to show how development decision-making takes place within the various villages and towns and in the district assembly.

Fig 6.1 Illustration of decision-making in the district – from the village to the assembly

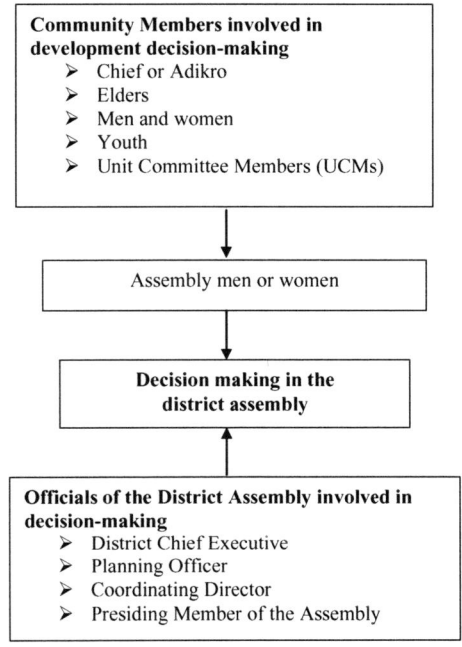

Source: Arthur

The district Coordinating Director and Planning Officer confirmed this during an interview. They explained that, it would be very difficult and a waste of time to directly involve the community members in decision-making. The community members are consulted in during decision-making at the village level by their assembly member, such meetings do not involve officials of the assembly. Meetings with the assembly officials only include the assembly members and do not even involve the UCMs who represent their respective villages and towns.

Before independence the various villages had a well-structured traditional system of administration which was headed by a chief or *adikro*[25] of the town or village who ruled with the support of his elders[26] in the villages. They were all still are the most respected people in the village. They could use their authority and position to mobilise the people, organise them for development activities without any difficulties and use their authority to influence decision-making. Even today, the chiefs and *adikros* still have authority over their subjects, but their duties have been reduced because of the assemblymen and women who work as liaison between the district assemblies (and the government) and their respective communities. Active development decision-making is taken by the UCMs, by mobilizing the people and implementing development activities and programmes. The role of the assembly members is still very significant, even when the intervention is not community-driven and mobilization of local resources would not be necessary for accomplishment of the intervention. This reduces the authority of the chief or *adikro* in the community.

People in rural areas differ in terms of their political, economic and religious beliefs as do their development aspirations. This diversity of interest also hampers the efforts of government to rapidly tackle the problems that need priority attention. The conflict of interest in terms of which community should be given priority, which development programme must be executed first and so on was acknowledged by the women during the focus group discussions in Asenda and Nkroful. They hinted that, in most of their meetings, a lot of people suggest different interventions for the community that need urgent attention. Yet during their deliberations there is always confusion and most of their participatory decision-making ends in a stalemate. One of the interviewees (a woman) furiously said 'the

---

[25] Adikro is a traditional ruler who has less power than a chief though he does the work of a chief. He is often called the acting chief, and this happens only when there has not been an installation of a chief in the area.

[26] Elders of a community are usually the older people and sometimes may also be members who are in the same clan with the chief or *adikro*. In some cases they are advisers to the chief or *adikro* and they help in the day-to-day administration of the village or town.

164

men always come to the meeting drunk. They refuse to accept whatever issue a woman will raise during our meetings'. The attitude of the men seems to be damaging the effectiveness of participation by the village and development in general.

The management of development intervention in the villages is now in the hands of the UCMs instead of the elders as it used to be before the coming of the District Assembly Concept (DAC) in the late 1980s. The control of development by the UCMs has become effective because of a lack of trust of the chiefs and the elders as a result of misappropriation of funds. This therefore makes the involvement of the community members in decision-making absolutely paramount, though active participation involves only the UCMs and the assembly members. This has shifted the development management paradigm from the traditional authorities[27] to government representatives, mostly the UCM, in the various villages and towns. This paradigm shift was the basis of the government decentralization programme that aimed in the late 1980s at involving people at the grassroots in political participation and development decision-making towards the achievement of rural development goals in the late 1980s.

6.2.2 The Assembly Members and Unit Committee Members in Decision-Making

The introduction of public or grassroots political and development decision-making brought about the election of representatives from all villages and towns at the district assembly (DA). The assembly members (AMs) of the various towns and villages represent their communities at the DA in participatory development decision-making. The District Coordinating Director explained in an interview that the assembly members are the representatives of their communities in terms of the assembly's development planning and

---

[27] Traditional authorities are the chief or adikro and the elders who rule the village or town and maintain law and order in the village.

processes. He acknowledged the vital role the AMs play in development decision-making. In his response to ascertain the vital role of the AMs in development he pointed out that,

> Development decision-making is taken by the members of the villages and towns in collaboration with the assembly members in the village. The community members suggest which areas or projects they consider necessary to be given urgent attention. Proposals are sent to the DA by the assembly member in the area. The district officials, mainly the planning officer, the district chief executive and I (the coordinating director) decide finally which proposal must be given priority and should be financed or supported based on the funds available to the assembly.

Development decision-making is supposed to be participatory, but the general response from the interviewees showed that it is a form of consultation with the assembly members and officials of the district, mainly the chief executive, planning officer, coordinating director and the presiding member of the assembly, taking the major decisions. It was noted that assembly's proceedings are supposed to be in the local language, but all deliberations are held in English, thus making it difficult for some of the members to participate actively and effectively in decision-making. Just few individuals who can speak English are privileged to participate in the decision-making process. This is what one interviewee from Asemko believes limits the effectiveness of participation to the literate few and alienates the illiterate majority.

The UCMs, like the assembly members, have also been playing a crucial role in the decision-making process, especially in development issues at the village level. This was made evident during an interview with the District Coordinating Director who explained that some of the UC are doing an excellent job within their communities. However he further hinted that 'in some of the communities some of the UCMs are not very active'. But during the focus group interviews at Asenda and Nkroful all six groups acknowledged the benefits the communities derive from the work of the UCMs. One lady in Nkroful who had also served on the unit committee for nearly ten years, said;

> The UCMs manage all development interventions in this village. The community members come in only when they need labour from the whole members. It could be in a form of carrying sand, water or gravels for development projects. The people trust them and have confidence in the UCMs so there is no problem if they are allowed to manage projects on behalf of the whole community.

Even on committees where the UCMs are considered not to be very active, their work is still appreciated by the community members. In some cases they work with NGOs that come to the village to train and assist those who need livelihood skills to enable them set up their own business or some other income-generating activity. One woman, a UCM in Asenda explained during the focus group interview that,

> We assist some of the NGOs that train the local women in *gari* making and coconut oil processing; especially those who have some skills in these areas. Sometimes we help in disbursement of money to the women who may put their names down for loans to enable them start their businesses. Sometimes we assist them through the local banks to secure loans for their micro-enterprises.

Overall the community members (CM) were satisfied with the work of the UCMs and wished them to continue working for the community. However, there were some sentiments expressed about financial mismanagement within the UCMs which, according to the interviewees, reduces trust and weakens their support in participatory decision-making. Nevertheless, there was a general satisfaction that the UCMs are doing a very good job regardless of the slight financial problems that are sometimes encountered. As one man from Nkroful said, '*ekuro biara Mensah womu',* which literally means in every community there is someone who definitely has some short-comings and whose work may affect the performance of an organisation, no matter what. In all, the members acknowledged that,

167

although the community is not a hundred percent free of corrupt individuals, cases of financial mismanagement are very rare because of the work of the UCMs. They work hand-in-hand with the elders in the communities, so difficult individuals are sanctioned according to the norms of the society, which serve as a deterrent for others.

6.2.3 The Elders and Community Members in Decision-Making

Before Europeans came to the West Coast of Africa, the various communities along the coast had their various systems of leadership in the towns and villages. The leaders were mostly chiefs and elders of the villages. However, because of the significant role the elders play as brokers and peacemakers in the various towns and villages, it become very difficult for any government to neglect them, if they have to win community support in development decision-making or win their support even during elections. This among others, has necessitated the formation of the Ministry of Chieftaincy Affairs by the ruling New Patriotic Party (NPP) government to assist in decision-making at the grassroots. However, some critics argue that, it was a way of honouring the chiefs and the elders so that they would also mobilize their *subjects* (who are mostly the community members) and rally support for the government of the day.

In the villages the elders still influence development decision-making. They use their positions to mobilise the members through *gong-gong*[28] beating for community gathering and development decision-making or for communal work. The establishment of the UCMs has reduced their active involvement in decision-making, although they still have great influence especially in the brokering of peace, conflict resolution and community mobilization for development work. The elders liaise between the government and

---

[28] Gong-gong is a metal can which is beaten in most rural communities in Ghana. It is usually used to summon the community members in the village to the chief's palace or to meet in the house of the elders. Sometimes, when someone dies it is also used to assemble the community members or to make community announcements.

community members and represented the community at the district or regional offices on development issues usually ones that involve land disputes.

One unique development approach that became evident during the investigation is the level of synergy among the community members which was observed to be improving their participatory activities, even though a few problems were identified. The social capital that used to exist in the pre-colonial days, where the rural people used to assist one another during cultivation of crops and other communal work, still exists. The good communal spirit that has contributed towards the development of the various communities is still active, though some of the interviewees expressed some concerns. For instance, because of the level of poverty in the villages, when some members take loans from their colleagues to start a business or engage in a micro-enterprise activity, they default on their payments. This has reduced trust among some of the community members and has made it difficult for others to obtain help locally to engage themselves in livelihood or income generation activities.

In the areas of communal labour or engagement in community-driven or organisational-initiated development activity, the communal spirit is unique. At Asemko one lady explained that 'fines are paid by individuals who fail to participate in community work, whether it is organised by the elders or by the whole community'. So people participate actively in community work. This could be regarded as a coercive form of participation, though the objective is to accomplish the development goal and not to empower the members through their engagement in the work. Everyone is always willing to help and there is unity when implementing development activity. A man from Nkroful explained that 'we work as a family because we know each other. If there is problem and you don't help, when you get problems nobody will come to your aid'. They support one another so there is

169

greater cooperation among the community members. Though sometimes there are problems, but they are easily resolved because of the social norms that people have to abide by.

6.3 Development Decision-Making at the District Level: Divergence Views

Community participation in development decision-making has been a good strategy for development organisations (both local and international), but the approach has been criticized because of the biases and power relations that tend to skew decision-making towards a few influential groups and individuals. These biases were observed both at the village level and the district assembly. Before the start of the study, it was thought that biases could be more prevalent at the district assembly because of its control over financial resources, this was not, however, the case as observed during the investigation.

6.3.1 Decision-Making at the Village Level

Funding agencies like the World Bank have been championing the affairs of rural people over the last three decades and have come to appreciate that participation by rural people in community-level development decision-making is very important, yet in NED communities this does not happen. Lack of employment in the district has reduced and weakened the level of community participation in the villages. The youth do not actively participate in development decision-making, because they view participation as a waste of time. In both Asenda and Nkroful the youth members do not appreciate community participation or even their involvement in decision-making. They stressed during the focus group discussions that,

> We don't participate in most of the development decision-making because of lack of jobs. We will not participate in discussions that will not be of benefit to us. We

would prefer to work and make money rather than involving ourselves in participatory decision-making. How can we waste our time participating in activities that will not generate any income for us?

There was a general acknowledgement from the youth who participated in the focus discussions that the assembly expects every member of the community to participate, but the youth do not appreciate that. The youth members explained that most livelihood activities that are undertaken within the village are activities for women. They sited examples like *gari* processing, *abonkyen*[29] making and selling of fish at the local market, among others, as jobs that are done by women. Some of them (especially the young men) explained that they could participate in the dressmaking training but, because it is not a lucrative venture they would not make enough money for themselves and their families. At Asenda one young man said that they do not like dressmaking at all. At Nkroful they acknowledged that

'Ever since the *galamsey* business started in the village no young man will stay home during the day to participate in decision making. Fines are paid by those who fail to attend decision making gatherings, most young men and women prefer to go to galamsey sites and do their business and pay any fine that the elders would impose rather than attending such meetings'.

When asked why they do not do the galamsey business on other days when there were no meetings, so that they could participate in such decision-making meetings, they pointed out that there are UCMs who take major decisions so that is their responsibility. The UCMs take decisions on-behalf of the community members; even if you are at the meeting, you will not have the opportunity to talk. It was acknowledged that it is of no importance to

[29] Abonkyen is a locally manufactured soap in Ghana. It is made from plantain and cocoa peels that are dried and burnt. The ash is added to coconut oil and sodium hydroxide and boiled to prepare the soap.
Galamsey is a name given to the illegal mining of gold. People who are engaged in such illegal mining activities are referred to as galamsey operators

171

attend such meetings when there is no chance to talk or voice your concerns. One lady in Nkroful explained that, 'after all, if you do not attend you will hear whatever they will discuss, so it is a waste of time. Besides if you are at the meeting you will not have the chance to talk, so it is better to stay away and do your business'.

It became evident that the assembly initiates programmes that they feel could help the rural people who are not engaged in livelihood activities but not what the people themselves want. Decision-making at the community level is more consultation rather than participation, and development decision-making is dictated by the district assembly officials through the assembly members and the UCMs rather than giving the opportunity for local people to discuss issues and make decisions. The youth members reiterated that participatory decision-making is supposed to be the work of the elders and the old men and women in the villages because they have nothing else to do. At Ankobra a fishing community, one interviewee explained that;

> As a fishing village, most men and women will prefer to go to the beach, buy fish and go and sell it at the market, rather than wasting our time on discussions that will not bring direct and immediate benefit to us. We want to do something that will put food on our tables for ourselves and our families. We will participate if the assembly is willing to give us money to do our businesses, but not just to waste your time and participate, for what?

This was clearly justified because, as one woman from Asenda also pointed out during the discussion.

> The officials from the assembly come at a time that people are busy going round their daily activities. Sometimes they come unannounced so most people may not even be aware of what will be happening or would not know why they may be needed. So if meetings are unannounced, how could we participate when we don't know what they want, or do they think we don't do anything in the village? We are also busy people.

172

Decision-making is limited to the elderly, the chief or *adikro* and the elders who might be assisting the chief in his governance. If the village has an assembly member, then he/she with some UCMs may be involved in the decision-making process. The youth members in this case are completely neglected and not involved in the village level decision-making. Views from the youth and the women, as noted above are not taken into consideration in decision-making. It was revealed that the attitude of most of the community members, especially the men, has reduced support of the youth in community participatory activities and decision-making. Details of youth involvement in development activities will be discussed later in this chapter. At this point we will divert our attention to ascertain how development decisions are taken at the assembly.

6.3.2 The District Assembly in Development Decision-Making

The introduction of the DAC in the late 1980s brought significant improvement to the lives of people in a number of rural communities in the NED. This improvement was manifested in areas such as micro-enterprise activities, which made a lot of people become involved in micro economic activities for the first time, in order to improve their lives – especially, women in the villages studied. In addition to the improvement of rural livelihoods there was an improvement in infrastructure like toilets, market stalls and schools. Introduction of the DACF and more recently the HIPCF (channelled through the district assemblies) has helped a lot of people improve their lives in the villages.

It was intended that decision-making would take place, the grassroots level but in the assembly only its members are able to represent community members. Unlike with political participation, which has seen the active participation of people at the grassroots level, the findings show that *effective development* decision-making rests solely on the shoulders of

173

assembly members. This is contrarily to the main objectives of the district assembly, which aimed to involve local people in a holistic manner, in the planning of development activities in their own communities. The assembly advocates for community participation but this seems difficult for the authorities to achieve.

As was explained in the previous sections of this chapter that decision-making related to implementation of development interventions in the district is hierarchical, however the major and final decisions are taken in the district assembly (particularly by the District Chief Executive, the Planning Officer, the Coordinating Director and the Presiding Member of the Assembly), in conjunction with the assembly men and women. Decision-making is based on availability of financial resources and what the assembly prioritises in its development agenda. This is evident from the responses gathered from the planning officer and the coordinating director of the district and some of the interviewees who were members of the unit committees. But during such assembly decision-making influential members push for acceptance of programmes in their areas, and these are often implemented irrespective of assembly development priorities. Figure 7.2 shows some external forces that continue to influence development decision-making and how they affect interventions that are undertaken within the district villages.

Fig 6.2 Development Decision-Making in the Villages

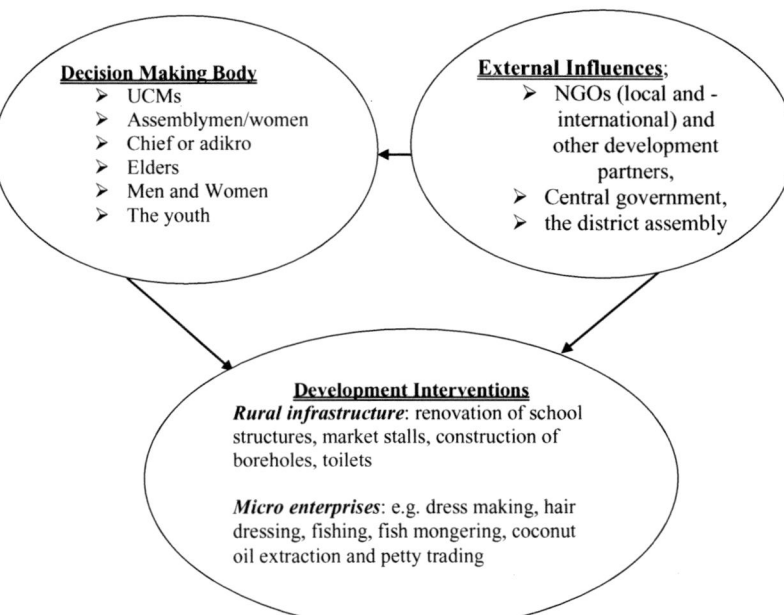

Source: Arthur

This analytically portrays the influence that NGOs, governments, and the district assembly have on decision-making at the village level. The financial power possessed by these bodies gives them the mandate to exercise their influence on decision-making in the villages. The rural people do not have the money and, therefore the power to influence and implement development decision that could bring improvement to their communities. Decisions could be taken at the village level but the assembly or NGO concerned coerce the people in the village to accept whatever project or intervention they consider appropriate for receipt of funding. Mostly programmes proposed by the village people are not funded. The assembly, and even the NGOs, implement projects they have identified in *their* development agendas. But in spite of that the interviewees from the four villages said they were happy with what the assembly and the NGOs do for them. Progress to achieve development activities such renovations of schools structures, building of toilets, etc slow and the villagers' involvement is limited but the local people appreciate the level of improvement which has been achieved and the support they are receiving from these organisations. However, if community participation would achieve effective benefit, then paradoxes in participation have to be addressed in order to win community support and trust in development work.

6.4 Community Decision-Making and Participation Paradox

The participation of local people in community activities has suffered a lot of absurdity. However, while some schools of thought encourage the involvement of the youth, for instance in participatory practice, some community members, mostly the elders and elites argue that the youth are too immature to be involved in active decision-making. The lack of transfer of power from the elders to the youth for example and gender issues are among the paradoxes of participatory practice, especially when the youth and women are concerned and these issues raise concerns which have to be addressed.

6.4.1 The Youth in Decision-Making: Is Power Relations Still an Issue?

One main reason for involving the youth in community participatory is to ensure that they become familiar with future challenges ahead of them when become proactive in community development activities. However, active participation observed during the investigation was limited to a few adults and key influential groups. So do issues of power relations prevent the youth from participating in decision-making? Some schools of thought believe that active community participation that involves the youth help them to harness

176

their potential and this is key to achieving continuity and effective and sustainable development for a community in her development efforts. Surprisingly, despite this awareness it became evident during the study that some elders and key influential groups in rural communities are against the participation of youth in decision-making.

Participation of the youth (mostly young men and women) in development activities in the villages has been hampered by intimidation and treats from the elders. The chiefs, elders and men in the villages intimidate the youth who actively participate and threaten those that are outspoken during the decision-making process. These attitudes not only hamper effective participation but also scare those who may wish to participate in the future. One respondent - a youth member from Asenda - explained during a focus group interview how youth members were intimidated by elders of the village. He said:

> 'A twenty five year old man from this village decided to contest in the district level election to become assembly member of this area. The elders alleged he was too young to stand for election. Some said he was not married, did not have children and did not have a place to sleep (that is he does not own a house) so nobody should vote for him. We want those who are responsible not those who may not have time for us'.

To the elders those who have wives or husbands are considered responsible and qualified to stand for election. The community members consider marriage as a major social responsibility, so if one is not married he or she is classified irresponsible and not fit for office. This form of social exclusion has made the youth (who are mostly not married) to become inactive in participation of community activities, unless there are penalties against those who abscond. This behaviour from the elders is preventing the youth from participating in decision-making that should involve will involve the *whole* community. Instead, all participatory decision-making is carried out by the UCM, the assembly

177

members and the village elders. This was observed to be an issue that did not go down well with the youth in the villages. They explained that,

> 'More often than not most of the youth members do not attend participatory decision-making even if they are invited. Decisions are taken by the elders. We are not considered or invited to participate in active development decision-making. Even if we are present, our views, ideas or suggestions are not taken. Most of the elders consider us to be children with no experience or have nothing to offer'.

During the focus group discussion the youth express mixed feelings about how the men exercised their powers over everybody during the decision-making process. A twenty eight year old man said, 'what is mostly annoying is that some of the meetings are not organised by the community but by some NGOs, but they will not allow you to talk'. The youth members wish to participate but the opportunities are limited for them to be actively involved. They are either prevented from participating or withdraw from participating for fear of being reprimanded or threatened by the elders after the meeting.

This concern was noted among the youth members who are not married, those not in serious relationships and those who do not have children. The elders said, 'you should not be very outspoken, because when it comes to writing, you would not be able to write. So only those who can write must be given the chance to talk'. As the saying goes, *the pen is mightier than the sword*, and only those who can write have the *power* or are given the opportunity to participate in decision-making. As a result, rural people are always excluded from active decision-making, because of their social commitment, their vulnerability, and their lack of entitlements, because of their inability to read and write. The problems confronting the rural poor become compounded due to their inability to write and this is a problem not only affecting the youth but all illiterate men and women in the villages, so far as participatory practice is concerned.

6.4.2 Power and Gender Relations in Participatory Development

Power and gender relations are also factors affecting participatory practice at the grassroots level. The dimension of power, the struggle for power, disempowering the powerful (mostly the men) to empower the powerless (mostly the women) has also become a difficult task for development organisation. Development organisations are making efforts to empower women who had previously been relegated to the bottom of the decision-making hierarchy. Generally men dominate decision-making, and represent women in all levels of governance, whether traditional or political (Massaw, 2000). Arguably, it is also naïve for outsiders to raise the issues associated with gender and power relations when in reality they are in partial support of keeping power to themselves (Woroniuk and Schalkwyk, 1998) and have done little to address gender inequalities.

Gender disparity, like power relations still predominates in the villages in NED despite over three decades of feminist advocacy, which has argued that the issue of gender should be addressed because women have a vital role to play in development policy and practice (Pearson, 2002). The relations of power and how they are exercised over others, especially women, are not only a problem related to development institutions in the district, but one which affects almost every institution there. In the rural communities power relations were observed to be a problem not limited to the district assembly but also throughout the rural communities and villages. During the focus group discussions the women's groups said that men control every bit of the participatory decision-making process. The women said that sometimes it was very difficult to participate if you were a woman. One lady from Nkroful explained during a one-to-one informal interview that,

> 'The men do not respect us; they don't want us to talk. Even when you are raising an issue they turn to mumble and grumble. It makes you feel embarrassed at times.

179

In the end whatever a woman will say is not taken into consideration. Sometimes they may listen to you, but your point will not be taken or implemented'.

And the elders may threaten to beat women who oppose the views of the men. In some cases, if a woman runs her own business in the village, the men and the elders try to dissuade the community from buying from her by classifying her *witch*. And she may be may be excluded from taking part in future community development activities. In some cases the men may even attack the woman at night through *witchcraft* activities, so the women are scared to participate in community decision-making. This kind of intimidation is common in the villages for people of both genders who oppose the elders, but it is worse for the women.

This problem of power being exercised by the men over the women was not an isolated case observed during the study. Rural development has targeted women because they are the most vulnerable and weak, apart from children, and their commitment surpasses that of men. The duties of the women range from subsistence farming to child care, they need to participate actively in development issues to empower them enough, to become better equipped to effectively address the socio-economic problems they face in their communities and also to help improve their livelihoods. Other societal problems make it unattractive for the women to play their role in participatory practice as citizens who have equal rights and responsibilities with men. Lack of respect for women in the villages, coupled with the way they are intimidated by the elders and other men is making participation very difficult for them. One lady from Asenda who has also served on the UC, explained that,

> The men do not respect us at all; they don't, at all. Even if an important point is raised by the women at meetings the men will not take it. The men use their powers to influence decision-making and over-rule issues raised by the women, because they don't respect us.

180

Perhaps this sentiment seems to be a cultural phenomenon because in African society men are considered the head of the family. So, in the presence of men, women's decisions are considered irrelevant. But the views expressed by the women doing the focus group interviews show that they do not appreciate the idea of the men dominating decision-making and the way they 'lord over' them. The power relations debate still remains ongoing in the development discourse, because many agencies that firmly support participation feel reluctant to release power (Mohan, 2002; Francis, 2002). The assumption that, social capital of rural community members is unique, that they have common interests and agendas, and that they live in harmony without any conflict of power, is naïve. This assumption restricts the spread of participatory practice, which also affects the social and political structures in rural communities and rural development institutions (Francis, 2002). These, among other bottlenecks in participatory practice, have prompted rural people to view participation as a development concept that needs to be reshaped to effectively address the problems of participation and participatory practice in enhancing development in rural communities.

6.4.3 Financial Mismanagement and Mistrust among Stakeholders

Financial mismanagement is another issue that was observed to have weakened trust among stakeholders of development in the district. It became evident that the rural people do not trust officials of the assembly to manage intervention in their villages. On the one hand, some of the village people feel that the authorities of the assembly overestimate the cost of development projects so that they could get a share of the money allocated to the project. On the other hand, the officials of the assembly also feel that, if money get into the hands of the local people, it will be misused or embezzled. This has reduced the trust the community members have for the assembly officials and even NGOs that are active in the villages. The

181

rural people also believe that the development workers are corrupt while the facilitators think the same about them. This attitude has persisted because any such corrupt; individuals are likely to go unpunished (Quah, 2002). However, due to the limitations of the data, it was difficult to substantiate the argument posed by the rural people that there is corruption within the assembly, while the assembly officials also could not justify how the rural people are corrupt or embezzle development funds.

Putnam's analysis of a study carried out in Italy indicated that trust is built among communities in which there was active participation that had registered high performance and economic growth (Harriss, 2000). This also explains the variation in performance between the north and south of Italy, and confirms the level of social capital that exists in the north because of the trust that community members had for their leaders. In spite of the strong social capital observed to exist in the villages in this study, there is a lack of trust in assembly members by community members. This supports the Afro barometer's (2008) investigation to ascertain whether Ghanaians trusted their assembly members, but noted that there was little or no such trust. Thus, the majority of assembly members do not want assembly budgets to be made known to community members. It was observed that the assembly members are not honest with their budget and do not want to be transparent to the local people either. Though it was observed that the district assembly is using the DACF to assist in development activities in the villages, there is a lack of trust of the assembly officials, because the village people regard them as corrupt. The Afro barometer (2008) also observed that the local people have negative sentiments and reservations about their representatives, because of corruption.

One important point raised by one of the UCMs in Asenda was the benefits that could be realised from community involvement in the management of finances for development. At

182

both Asenda and Nkroful the interviewees who also work on the UC said that there is transparency in all financial management, so the rural people trust the UCMs more than the officials of the district assembly. At Asenda the interviewees explained that the officials over-estimate the money earmarked for development intervention, but this is not common with the UCMs. They explained that,

> If the money is given to the UCMs, they negotiate for cheaper items for the project. Most of the items that we need could be provided locally which reduces the cost of the projects. For example sand, gravel, water, labour will be provided by community members. This will make the cost of the project relatively cheap. We can do a lot of things with what we get from the assembly.

At Nkroful the story was not different. The UCMs also explained during the focus group discussion that,

> We have local people who can undertake most development projects at a very affordable cost that could help to reduce the cost of the intervention. We could get experts within this area to do the work very well and at a cheaper cost, because we will provide labour and even some resources like sand, gravel or water. Besides, it will increase community satisfaction about how the money was to be spent.

Leaving management in the hands of external officers will reduce trust and weakens community participation and support. At Asenda the *adikro* explained during an interview that 'more often projects done within this village are community-initiated projects, so the whole community knows how much is gathered, how money is disbursed and who should be accountable and to whom'. He maintained that the people involved are trusted for the work they do, because it enhances community participation and helps in the promotion of development activities within the community. Paradoxically the District Coordinating Director (DCD) had some reservations about community members' direct involvement in

183

management, especially financial management. In his reaction to the views expressed by some of the local people he said,

> 'Most of the local people are illiterates and have little or no bookkeeping skills. How could we release moneys that have to be accounted for to such people? After all such people are not accountable to the government. If the money is embezzled we will be accountable. For me, I don't see it ideal to involve community members in financial management'.

In contrast, the interviewees in all four villages feel that if they are given the opportunity to manage financial resources, they would be empowered to effectively manage development on their own and help reduce costs. This will win trust from the people and enhance their level of participation in any development activity. The interviewees expressed their dissatisfaction during the focus group interviews about the way development interventions are managed by officials who do not live in the villages. This has weakened trust for the officials and, therefore the effectiveness of participatory practice. Development facilitators expect grassroots accountability but, in reality, their activities distort the structures of effective accountability.

Development organisations claim they want the rural people to participate in whatever intervention they undertake, to become empowered so that they can take control of their lives, but in reality they resist control by the rural people. Therefore, who must be blamed for lack of participation? The system of accountability that lies on the shoulders of development facilitators makes them skew control (especially financial control) away from the rural people. So long as institutions and organisations have to render accounts to the taxpayer and funding agencies, the transfer of financial control to the poor in order to win trust and enhance community support in participatory practice will continue to look unlikely. Brehm, (2001) concludes that, in theory, accountability to the people at the grassroots is important, but funding agencies tend to hijack the mechanisms of accountability and shift it towards the donors. So how participatory practice could be reshaped to promote effective community support and enhance rural development, has been a concern not only among stakeholders but also leaders in development.

6.5 Improving Rural Livelihood: The Assembly's Approach

It was observed that the assembly has no special strategy in place to improve the lives of people in the rural areas, but their main activity is centred on liaising with the local banks to acquire loans for those who may wish to start their own business. This initiative was confirmed by the District Planning Officer during an interview with him. He explained that, 'the DACF and the recently introduced HIPCF are helping in funding a lot of projects in the district'. When asked about the type of projects the fund had helped to implement, he stated that the assembly has collaborated with the rural banks to help rural people to secure loans to enable them TO establish their own businesses. He further reiterated that,

> 'The rural people do not have money, let alone property, they could use as collateral to enable them take loans from the banks. The assembly decided to take that initiative by liaising with the banks so that they could give loans for those who would like to enter into small scale-business but have no money to start'.

This initiative was a big boost for the rural people to improve their lives. The explanation given by the Planning Officers clearly shows that the assembly is not helping the local people because the government had introduced the DACF and HIPCF which the assembly is supposed to disburse to the local people for their micro-enterprises but that is happening. The HIPCF was introduced by the government as part of her development assistance for people in the villages to enable them start their own businesses. The Assembly in

185

agreement with the local banks assist the people to secure loans to add to money they receive from the HIPCF to initiate the business.

It was observed that a reasonable number of the rural people, mostly women are engaged in activities that could give them income. This was confirmed by the women who were interviewed in all the four villages and who acknowledged that they have benefited from the bank's credit facility. In spite of this help from the assembly, two women from Ankobra stated that they were not aware that it was the assembly's effort that made it possible for them to secure the loans from the banks. The agenda falls in line with the recent President's Poverty Reduction Initiative Strategy (PPRIS) which was introduced in the early 2000. In view of that, community members consider the initiative as part of the PPRIS and not as support from the assembly. The programme targets poor people and is meant to assist them (especially women) to get into income generation activities and to establish small businesses. These should help to alleviate their poverty by improving their living standards and also contribute towards national development. Critics of the government argued that the PPRIS only benefited a few individuals who were supporters and sympathizers of the then government of the day.

In an interview with the District Coordinating Director to find out if they receive assistance from other development organisations, he said that the assembly occasionally gets help from some international NGOs and other development partners that sponsor projects within the district. He mentioned organisations like USAID, ADRA and the WB as some their main sponsors. The poverty reduction initiative programme was aimed at helping poor people especially the women. Mapping out strategies to address poverty or improve local livelihoods requires active community involvement and decision-making, and the reshaping of best participatory practice to address the expectations of rural people and those that desperately need development assistance.

6.6 Reshaping Participation: Expectations of the Rural Poor

Reshaping participatory practice to benefit the rural people has been an issue of concern for development organisations and institutions and an issue in the development debate. The question is how can participatory practice be reshaped? The concept of participation has suffered a lot of set-backs in its application because of bureaucracy and some bottlenecks, but there is little attempt to improve the way the concept is practiced to meet the expectations of rural people. Some critics have argued that it is important to consider other development paradigms (Chambers, 1983; 1997; Clarke, 2002 and Desai, 2002). The development paradigm has shifted towards concepts like a 'bottom-up' approach, 'people-centred', institution centred, as some of the alternative paradigms of development practice. Some NGOs are also generating 'new forms of participation which are not rooted in place, but stretched across space where' communities may virtually exist (Mohan, 2002:53-54), but even then, some of the changes have not been well rooted within organisations and in communities.

The difficulties facing the rural poor are how to make a living and how they can improve and sustain development within their communities. To enjoy at least one decent meal everyday has been a dream of every rural dweller more especially those that live in poverty in NED communities, but this reality seems difficult to achieve. It was observed that development programmes that adopt a participatory approach do not make provision for rural community members to achieve the anticipated benefits. The expectations of the rural poor in participatory development activities are enormous but development organisations follow their own agendas and objectives, ignoring the benefits that the rural people will

187

derive from their participatory work. Table 7.1 shows a summary of some of the benefits

that rural people expect when they actively participate in development interventions. It also

suggests how participatory practice could be reshaped for the rural people to realise the full

benefit of participation. It illustrates what some interviewees consider could be achieved

through active participation in development practice.

Tab.6.1 Characteristics of participation and expected benefits for rural people

Participation Characteristics	Expected Benefits
Decision-making	As community members participate they • Express concern about what they want, why they want it and can identify the sources • Become stakeholders, contribute to it and help towards its implementation • Become responsible for and make contributions towards its improvement.
Monitoring of interventions	When the interventions are executed within the communities • The rural people will have enough time to monitor • Problems can easily be identified and rectified, because they are always available • Those responsible can easily be contacted since everybody is available and within reach • It improves the effectiveness of work if the monitors live within the community
Financial issues	Community members will be able to • Know how much can be spent and take responsibility when it fails • Render proper accounts to the satisfaction of everyone • Check and control misappropriation and embezzlement of funds • Cut down costs because labour will be cheap since community can may provide local resources • Identify the people they can trust and be able to manage their finances effectively
Overall management	The role of the rural people becomes paramount in the overall management because • They are always available if the need arises • Financial misappropriation is minimised if not eliminated • It improves the quality of work and increases community satisfaction and responsibility • They provide support because they will appreciate that the intervention belongs to the community • The strong social capital makes community members better able to manage their own intervention than external project facilitators (who may live outside).

Source: Arthur

The views expressed by the rural people as indicated in the table above, show explicitly some of the benefit of participation, but do the assembly officials in the district consider that? Or will the organizations operating in the rural communities realize that and make the rural people active players. There is 'more to participation than a series of exercises' (Woroniuk and Schalkwyk, 1998:1), but how will development organizations make this a reality for the benefit of the rural poor making them proactive and equipping them to take control of their own development and improve their lives? How long will development organisations continue to manage development when they do not live with the people, do not know their cultural values and do not understand how they do things? How would the rural people have their reality counted, so that they could be put first, as Chambers (1997) put it, so that they could be placed in charge of their own interventions and improve their communities?

6.7 Participation and Effective Development Management

6.7.1 Participation and Empowerment Rural People

To empower individuals in a community means to raise the capabilities of those individuals so that they can be equipped with the knowledge and skills that which hitherto they did not have (Anwar, 2003; Lukes, 2005). People can participate effectively if they have the power to participate and do so on equal terms. Empowerment can happen when power is distributed equally. Rural community members could be empowered if they were given the opportunity to participate. The DAC of participation requires that the people at the grassroots participate actively in development planning and activity in their communities, but decision-making is limited to the UCMs. All the interviewees acknowledged that community participation only happens when a particular intervention requires labour. A lady from Nkroful explained that her role in the UC membership has helped her in many ways. She cited an instance where she was involved in financial management and was once appointed a treasurer of the UC, although she is not educated. She said,

> 'Hitherto such duties were reserved for the literate members of the committee, mostly the men who are school leavers. They are usually made secretaries and treasurers of the committee, and not an illiterate like me. Those of us who did not go to school are not considered for position like this within the committees'.

The respondents explained that there are various ways through which they have benefited from the activities in which they participated, although most of the benefits are limited to a few, mostly individuals. Yet the illiterate ones who agree to take some responsibility are permitted to do so. This, according to the respondents, gives them the opportunity to become empowered and take on better and more challenging responsibilities. The key players of community participation are the UCMs and few educated people who may have time to take part in decision-making meetings. There is a lack of opportunity for people to be involved in active participation, because of the introduction of the UC which became fully operational in the villages. This makes capacity building very important in making the people very proactive in their activities.

6.7.2 Capacity Building and Effective Development Management

Building capacity for rural people is a way of helping them to acquire the necessary skills to enable them to take responsibility for their lives and development in their communities. People are the greatest asset of every organisation; therefore improvement of the performance of the people within it will help enhance organisational performance. It is not possible to improve the activities of the organisation without building the human capacity (Cook, 1995). Building capacity requires the effective diagnosis of capacity needs identification of those who may need capacity building and who should build such capacity are issues that were critically looked at during the study. To what extend is the district assembly or the NGO prepared to build capacity within their organisations so as to help improve the capacity of the rural people in the district?

Capacity building is vital to organisational and community improvement through acquisition of skills by members to make them capable of performing effectively and competently. However critics like Eade (1997), James (2001) and Hilderbrand (2002) have argued that capacity building should entail the social, moral, economic and political orientations and activities of communities, development institutions, community-based organisations (CBOs), the private sector, household or individuals so that they can perform their duties effectively, efficiently and in a sustainable manner. It became evident from the study that there is little capacity building in any of the villages, though development activities were very active and the people were well engaged in the interventions, be they community-driven or organizationally instituted. The District Coordinating Director made it clear that the people in the villages are mostly illiterate so building capacity would be a waste of time. Thus, it was better to make them contribute only labour because the assembly cannot pay to hire workers and, since they do not make financial contributions, the only way they could be involved is contribution of labour. Building capacity according to the Coordinating Director of the Assembly was not on the agenda.

In an interview with the district coordinating director I asked him whether building capacity for the rural people would improve their level of participation in community development activities. He explained that,

> Building capacity could help improve the level of knowledge of the rural people to enable them manage their own interventions effectively, but that has to be done through community education. Such training is supposed to be done by the Department of Civil Education and not the district assembly.

When asked why they are aware of capacity building, but do not take it seriously, he explained that it is not their responsibility as an assembly to build capacity for the rural people, but the responsibility of the Department of Civic Education. The Department of Civic Education is supposed to work with the district assembly in building capacity for the local people, but works independently. The work they do is focused on political participation rather than equipping the people with livelihood skills.

So how do the rural poor harness their potential without capacity building? Raising organisational performance without building capacity does not reduce the performance of the organisation but, rather, wastes capacity and reduces sustainability (Cook, 1995). Effective capacity building will be achieved if the people's aspirations are well understood and integrated into the development process. It became clear from the findings that the rural people appreciate the need to participate in development activities in their communities but the necessary capacity building to enable them to become proactive, harness the resources and improve their communities is not provided by the assembly or the organisation that engage them in their work. So Roche's claims about the need to spend more time with the poor, develop new ways of learning from each other and identify mutual learning as opposed to training based on organisation's or individual's knowledge and another persons ignorance (Roche cited in Open University, 2001) have become very relevant in NED communities. The district assembly and the Department of Civic Education work with the rural poor but not in partnership to help build capacity and empower them so that they can enhance their potential and improve themselves and their communities.

6.7.3 Managing through Partnership: The District Assembly and Rural People in Synergy

Managing through partnership is one of the key strategies from which the district assembly and the people in the rural areas could work in synergy to manage and develop their communities. The rural people appreciate the need for partnership with the assembly and other development partners, but this is far from a reality. They appreciate that partnership is a set of frameworks where different parties and interest groups can negotiate on equal terms (Fowler, 2002), but it became clear that the rural people do not have the opportunity to participate on equal terms with the officials of the assembly and the UCMs who manage development in the villages. Control of financial and material resources by facilitators and the UCMs also skews the power balance away from the rural people and has become an obstacle to partnership (Brehm, 2001). In the NED development activities initiated by the DA are controlled by the assembly mainly in partnership with some of the assembly members, while the UCMs become agents of labour mobilization in the villages. The rural people are considered as a source of labour and not as active participants in development decision-making. The facilitators of the assembly exercise the greatest power because they control resources for the interventions. The involvement of the rural people is as passive participants because their work is mainly provision of labour. Their engagement would be considered as *partial partnership.*

It was acknowledged by the UCMs that, they form partnerships with the assembly because there is no revenue-generating activity in the villages through which they could get money and initiate their own projects. Besides, activities that, need some technical expertise that people in the community may not be in the position to provide will be difficult to implement without assistance from the assembly or the NGOs. The *adikro* in Asemko also

193

explained during an interview the relevance of this 'partial partnership' between the rural communities and the DA. He said,

> Our partnership with the district assembly has been very fruitful in so many ways. For instance we do not have financial problems because physical cash is not given to the community to execute projects. Any project initiated by the assembly does not involve physical cash. We make a financial contribution but it is supplemented by the assembly through the DACF and the HIPCF, which are controlled by the assembly.

He further explained that 'because the community members make financial contributions towards all community-driven project, it makes them feel partners of the project so they contribute towards managing and sustaining it'. The strong social capital within the villages contributes towards the enhancement of their work in partnership with development institutions or organisations. This form of partnership would enable the rural people to harness their potential and, through that, they would work to achieve whatever development objective they may set. Mog (2004:2142) argued that, no matter the amount of time available and the experience of staff supporting a sustainable development programme or project 'it is the local people who are going to do most of the work and make most of the investment required to create change within their community'. If the development institutions and organisations actively involve local people and promote this form of partnership, it would not only help them to build on the already existing strong social capital but also to sustain any interventions executed in the communities. Management of intervention in a partnership manner will not only win community support for the intervention but also enhance its improvement and sustainability.

6.8 Summary

The introduction of the district assembly concept in the late 1980s through the government decentralisation programme increased the level of community participation in development decision-making. However, the major decision-making is done by the assemblymen and women in the respective communities. They take decisions at the district assembly on behalf of their communities, while the unit committee members also take decisions on behalf of community members within the villages. The findings showed that power relations is still an issue that affects participatory decision-making. Both the youth and women face intimidation and threats during decision-making. Outspoken women are called witches and outspoken youth members are considered disrespectful and insolent.

Another problem hampering effective participation, is lack of trust which results from financial mismanagement. It will be concluded that, effective rural development management, would never be achieved through active participation, but if the aforementioned bottlenecks are addressed. Development organisations and institutions can win trust from the community members, but if they become transparent in their work and open themselves for scrutiny, accountability and criticism. When community members lack the capacity, the organisations should help build the capacity to enhance their level of confidence and become active participants. As development organizations advocate for participatory practice in their agenda, they should be prepared to work towards the achievement of participatory priorities rather than pushing to implement their pre-planned agenda.

Chapter Seven

Community Development and Participatory Paradox: the NGO's Approach

7.1 Introduction

In the previous chapter the nature of community level decision-making was investigated to ascertain how it affects participatory practice in NED communities. The issues critically examined were power relations and gender biases in participatory decision-making. I looked at some of the problems associated with the application of the concept; how it was affecting the active participation of the youth and women. NGOs and rural community members seem confused about application of participation and how it could be applied to achieve effective development objectives. The chapter will analyse the assumption that communities and their members are united and live peacefully and that they could co-operate to help improve their communities (Francis, 2002). Finally, this chapter will discuss some of the conflicting views expressed by NGO officials and local people about why, when and how participation should be practised, who benefits from participation, the power relations in participatory practice, and the problems associated with the use of application.

7.2 The Uncertainty of NGOs' Development Activities

One of the major problems identified during the investigation was the uncertain outcome of development activities and the way development organizations work at the grassroots level in NED district. To understand these uncertainties, the investigation focuses on the activities of the Italian NGO (Co-operation for the Development of Emerging Countries) (CDEC).[30] This NGO is involved in activities in NED. An interview with the project

---

[30] CDEC is an Italian language abbreviation which stands for is a no-profit association operating in the field of international co-operation and solidarity. It is recognised as a Non Governmental Organisation (NGO) by the Italian Ministry of Foreign Affairs and the European Union

coordinators of CDEC (both the local and the Italian officer) sought to understand the nature of the work of the NGO. They explained that the activities of the NGOs changed or were drawn up in association with their international counterparts or were re-designed to accommodate expectations of funding bodies and tax payers, in order to ensure support. The NGO has adopted this pragmatic approach over the years because, the CDEC facilitators assume their role is to support the government in geographical areas which state resources cannot reach (Desai, 2002). It has meant they embark on any agenda they see fit, whether local people are asking for help in this area or not. Like other deprived districts and rural communities NED, as a result of its desperate need for development is ready to accept whatever intervention the organizations are ready to finance or execute.

The preparedness of NGOs to work directly at the grassroots level and with the poor has won the hearts and minds of these people in the communities. NGOs that operate in NED have very diverse objectives, just like other districts. Nevertheless most of them focus their activities on HIV/AIDS eradication campaign, capacity building and women empowerment. According to MESW's Coordinating Director, who was interviewed during the study, it became clear that NGOs (mostly local and indigenous ones) obtained funding from international donors in order to sustain themselves. The priority was to ensure the survival of the organisation rather than achieving their main developing objectives, which they had received registration for. He explained that most of the NGOs concentrated their activities on HIV/AIDS prevention because of what he called government *bogus policy* for NGOs. He argued that,

> Until the early 2000, NGOs had to submit just a proposal for funding for their development programmes and activities. The proposals were usually written by development experts, lecturers in universities for a fee and are sent to the respective ministries and appropriate offices for approval.

197

He pointed out that such proposals are always for HIV/AIDS campaign because it became the most favourable development programme that most funding agencies considered because they were related to health. However, whether such NGOs existed or not did not matter, because only proposals were accepted for award of development contract and funds for development projects. It became evident from the interviews that some NGOs not have development agendas and the programmes that did exist did not have any clear focus. The MESW coordinating director explained that;

> Because a lot of grassroots and local NGOs have realised that donor agencies have diverted attention towards HIV/AIDS, and are channelling the resources in those areas, the NGOs have taken advantage of the opportunity. Though most NGOs do not have HIV/AIDS on their development plans, they send proposals for funding to undertake HIV/AIDS eradication campaign.

He explained that some of the indigenous NGOs operated from their homes and did not have offices. Some of the NGOs use funds obtained from donor agencies for different purposes different from that intended. While others use the money to buy cars, build new homes and even to support their families, though he could not provide evidence to substantiate his claims about these activities of NGOs has led to a sharp increase in their number because it is lucrative way of making ends meet or serving as a source of employment for illiterate and semi-illiterate families who cannot find jobs in the elsewhere. The priority has been not to achieve the development goals for the rural areas but to ensure the survival of the NGOs and to raise money to pay for their workers (Townsend et al, 2002).

At the district level there was no data about the activities of NGO operations. Unlike countries like Uganda where over eighty six percent (86%) of NGOs are registered and their activities are well monitored to avoid conflict, abuse of development funds and duplication of their work (Fafchamps et al, 2005) there is no registration in Ghana. The programmes and objectives of the NGOs' operation in NED remain unknown, because they do not have recognised offices and do not register the organisations with the MESW. Limitation information about the activities of NGOs operating in the district was obtained from the MESW. Capacity building, vocational training and religious educational programmes were the main items on the development agenda of these organisations. Only the international development organisations run rural development programmes, which aim to improve rural livelihoods or have programmes that help address poverty and promote income generation activities in the communities of the district.

7.3 Improving Local Livelihoods: The CDEC Approach

Improving local livelihood activities was the approach adopted by CDEC to help the people in NED villages, though it was later understood that this was not part of the initial development plan of the NGO. In NED the main socioeconomic activities in the communities are fishing and farming, while a few individuals are also involved in small-level trading (mostly doing their selling in kiosks and on table-tops), especially in some of the big towns and villages. Beside the petty traders there are dress makers, hair dressers and street venders whose activities are seasonal, and which in some cases, are dependent on sea conditions. The commercially active villages and towns have market days normally organised once a week, when most of the nearby villagers visit to do business. Micro enterprise activities were not prevalent in the various communities, because most people do not have enough money to go into such ventures or cannot provide collateral for the banks to secure loans for micro-enterprise activities.

During the focus group interviews, all the participants explained that although there were a number of development activities in their communities, most of them were *community driven*. Because most rural people rely on the sea for their livelihood and the sea is rough

199

most of the time, many find it difficult to make a living. The respondents maintained that occasionally they solicit assistance from NGOs that visit their village in form credits, to start micro-enterprises and community development projects or improvement of existing projects. They stated the following as being of the projects undertaken in their villages: rehabilitation of market stalls, improvement of toilet facilities and construction of bore-holes and schools. At Ankobra a fisherman explained in an interviewed that the Adventist Development Relief Agency (ADRA) an NGO in the area, had assisted them to construct stalls for their new market place. Before they were constructed, the traders either sold their wares in the scorching sun in the open market or in temporary sheds in front of their houses. These conditions had deterred women from starting a business because there was no proper place for them to work. And this had affected economic activity in the village because people did not know where they could buy what they needed. The interviewees explained that the construction of the market stalls had made buying and selling easier and a lot of women were now in business. It was observed that although the village was small as was the population and business activities were limited people now had enough income to support their families.

The projects are sometimes co-financed by a combination of international NGOs money and contributions from local people. Occasionally the district assembly provides support in the form of materials or personnel. Although poverty is crippling development in the district some individuals have made the effort to enter into micro-enterprise activities, funded by credit schemes from private money lenders and shylocks – mostly ruthless men who demand high interest, but offer loans without collaterals. The study noted that besides the efforts being made by the government, CDEC is also making efforts to help the poor – but this has not been adequate because of the demands for collateral by the banks. This was similar to the observations that were made during the focus group discussions, when some people pointed out that when they needed money to support their fishing business it was difficult to offer enough collateral to enable them to obtain loans from the banks. In response, CDEC changed its development agenda to incorporate micro-credit schemes, and so assist local people who needed financial assistance to enter into micro enterprise activities.

7.4 Community Participation and Micro-Credit Schemes

The idea of using the principles of participatory decision-making in the micro-credit scheme was introduced by CDEC to incorporate ideas from local people in income generation activities, the project coordinator called this *micro-enterprise*[31] activity. Although the CDEC used the term participatory decision-making, it was observed to be a consultative type of participation, because the investigations showed that people expressed their opinion but never influenced the actual policies governing the scheme. The involvement of local people in micro enterprise activities initiated by CDEC was aimed to incorporate their ideas, in order to comprehensively tackle poverty within the various villages in the district. Nevertheless, Shaw does not support the CDEC initiative of combating poverty with the consultative participatory approach because 'rural micro enterprises serve a protective function, but offer limited prospects for poverty exit' (Shaw, 2004:1262). The poor who might be the target of this venture may not necessary benefit from such assistance, because in most cases, the few influential people become the main beneficiaries.

---

[31] Hall and Midgley, (2004) defined micro enterprise as a small business which was usually owned and operated by low-income people with assistance either from the private, public or the voluntary sector. They are undertaken by people who are making efforts to increase their level of income through these kind of activities.

201

Micro enterprise activities constitute a significant part of the rural economy (Dulansey and Austin, 1989) especially in areas where rural development programmes do not feature predominantly in the development agenda. It could be argued that subsistence farming which has been one of the main livelihoods activities for people in the district, 'alone cannot be the means to address poverty in the rural areas' because as they put it, it has many limitations and constraints (Hall and Midgley, 2004:97). Besides, lack of access to and availability of arable land for farming, low and variable agricultural output, drought, and lack of the necessary capital to go into farming have also reduced interest in this activity as a source of livelihood (Kabbaj, 2003). The flexibility of payments of micro-credits and the convenient by which organisations operate the scheme, make a lot of lot of people to appreciate and participate in micro-credit schemes.

The people involved in micro enterprise activities were mostly hair dressers, dress makers, fishermen, fish-mongers and small traders. The aim was to assist them in ideas-sharing and equip them to expand their businesses, while at the same time building capacity for those who were yet to engage with micro enterprise activities. When asked why the CDEC had adopted this approach the project coordinator explained that,

> 'The main objective of our work is to organise the local people, train them about how to work in associations. We believe that through the associations they can work together share ideas and find ways by which they could improve their activities. By doing so they could enhance the social capital already existing in their communities to address some of the problems they face'.

The local coordinator explained that micro-credit schemes were not part of the CDEC original plan. They were included because during meetings with the local women expressed their anger about their predicament. They said, that they wanted to go into micro-enterprise activities, but that they did not have the initial capital to do so. The local banks were not ready to help because they needed collateral which most of them could not provide -

although some said they had had assistance from the assembly. A woman from Ankobra during an interview explained that it was through the assembly that she managed to secure funds to start a business, selling fish in the village.

'The assembly helped me to secure funding to start this fish-selling business. If it had not been the assembly, it was going to be very difficult for me to secre a bank loan to start my own business. The bank officials will not even look at your face, let alone given you a loan. Being illiterate, they sometimes assume we would not invest the money well enough to make profit to enable us to pay back the loan. Without collateral and support from the assembly it is difficult to secure a loan to start a business'.

The difficulty in securing a loan was observed to be the major problem facing rural people who wanted to start a micro-enterprise venture and make a living. This reflects Turvey and Kong's observation about the poor people predicaments, in relations to tackling poverty and emerging from misery. It was observed that in the 'absence of micro-credit the poor are excluded from credit markets except through family, friends and moneylenders' (Turvey and Kong (2008:14). The rural poor might be willing to enter into micro-enterprise activities or go into business but because of the absence of collateral they are relegated out of economic empowerment activities and are made to stay in chronic poverty. CDEC's help for local women to improve their livelihood was justified, but it became evident that most of the micro-credit meetings were attended *only* by women, though it became evident that some men also needed assistance.

7.5 Setting-up Micro-Credit Scheme for Local Women

Micro credit schemes play a crucial role in the informal economy, by enabling small micro-enterprise owners to enhance their business volumes, while it create opportunity for those not in business to create opportunity for those not in business to establish their own micro-enterprise to improve their livelihood (Mogale, 2007). The decline of employment

203

opportunities in communities in NED, and the high rate of rural-urban migration, in search of jobs, has contributed to the increase in number of micro credit schemes in the district. While some experts argue that, micro credit schemes have helped many communities to have some livelihood activities, other critics argue that, 'several decades of modernisation strategies with trickle-down assumption have done little to alleviate mass poverty' in most rural communities (Hall and Midgley, 2004:89).

The high level of poverty which has resulted from the lack of access to arable land for the people in Asenda, Asemko and Ankobra because of the salty nature of the soil has stopped them from farming. The people attempt to escape poverty has resulted in the engagement of subsistence farming practices and the overreliance on unscrupulous money lenders, who offer loans at astronomical interest. The high interest paid, also contributes to people indebtedness, their inability to escape poverty and failure to expand businesses. Hall and Midgley argue that, there is a need for 'a more interventionist approach to generate employment and incomes, while targeting benefits at needy groups without waiting for those problems to be resolved automatically' (Hall and Midgley, 2004:94).

The small enterprise activities being initiated in the rural communities in the district range from street vending, to selling on table-tops and in mini-kiosks. Additionally, a few individuals, especially women, organise themselves to process *gari* and locally produced coconut oil. Others make a living from being hair dressers and dress makers. In Asemko, for instance, because there is no proper market the women sell their wares on table-tops in front of their homes on the side of the streets. The reason for this is simple, if they put up proper structures, like kiosks, this would attract payment of tax to the district assembly, which the traders always try to avoid (that is an interesting point – when you considering that payment of tax for this kind of activity is very much part of a developing economy).

This reflects Hall and Midgley (2004) argument about individual responsibility, risk-taking and personal commitment which are some of the attributes of the rural poor need to escape, survive poverty or make a living.

The social and financial responsibilities make the credit scheme to target women in particular for the micro credit scheme. As Pearson (2000) observed that, targeting women is more rational because they are reliable when borrowing and do not default on their repayments. And targeting women is vital, because it helps to increase their income and status in the community, which could benefit their families more especially the children, because it became evident that many women were single mothers and had no external help to support their families. Setting up micro credit schemes in NED was the second priority for CDEC. The initial programme was to involve the local people in development intervention. The expatriate coordinator explained during the interview that, the aim of the organisations original programme was to assist local communities to finance the refurbishment of dilapidated market structures, school buildings, construction of toilets and capacity building activities. However, our initial meetings with the local women forced CDEC to change its original plan. According to the local coordinator, in their meeting in Asasetre a village where the programme was initiated, the women expressed their appreciation of the infrastructure improvement in their village, but they emphasized that they would prefer micro credit support. Because it will enable them to start their own micro-enterprises to become economically independent - through income generation activities which could help improve their general standard of living.

The local project coordinator explained that the initial plan was not to set up a micro credit scheme, because the main development programme had only just begun. However, during several consultative meetings, with the initial plan was changed. He further explained that,

> 'We began to seek views from the women, by allowing them to explain their problems and tell us the type of assistance they wanted CDEC to offer. We did so, to enable us understand what they actually wanted and how the organisation could help. During the deliberations, we were able to modify our programme to suit what the local people wanted and how they could achieve them'.

The consultation was conducted in conjunction with the local assembly members within the various villages. The coordinator further explained that, after several consultation meetings the people maintained that they needed money to enable them to start their own businesses, so they could pay to send their children to school and support their families. This necessitated a shift of agenda from improvement of dilapidated structures like toilets, market stalls and bore holes, to micro credit schemes that could help local people start a micro-enterprise. Therefore the consultative participatory approach compelled CDEC to shift its original plan and to adopt the micro credit scheme. The local coordinator further explained that,

> 'Involving the local people will help raise their concerns so that their views could be integrated into the micro credit policies. We help in training the members of the executives who are all local people in the micro enterprise. We also observed that if there is adequate capacity building the people will be equipped with the skills to enable them manage their own affairs'.

The capacity building approach gave local people the opportunity to identify their own capacity needs, suggest ways it could be built and helped them to identify who could help in building the capacity.

It became evident from the findings that, some rural people and their communities had become more of a source of information and knowledge for community improvement rather than places where projects could be implemented. This became clear during one of the focus discussions at Nkroful where one of the ladies angrily said; 'you people always come here to ask us questions and request a lot of information from us but you don't do anything for us in this community. We don't have toilet. We *do it*[32] in the bush'. Another woman explained that 'sometimes we hear the government is helping some people, but some of us do not get the information. Just few people are given the information. Before we hear of it, all that they say is there is no money, so next time'. The information is not well publicised, so some people who desperately need micro-credit to start their businesses are ignored. Some organisations have still not realised that micro-enterprise was the 'last hope for economic survival' for a lot of people in a number of the rural communities, because the anticipated assistance from their governments has usually not been forthcoming (Mogale, 2007:350). Their poverty has been further hampered by the exploitation by the scrupulous money lenders who take huge interest from loan they take, so repayment of the load become another burden on them.

7.6 Improving Local Livelihood: Benefits of the Micro-Credit Scheme

The improvement of local people's livelihood is one of the major reasons behind CDEC's introduction of the micro-credit scheme. It was felt the scheme could help local people start micro-enterprises and increase their level of income. Besides, it helps to catalyse rural economic activities and help enhance poor people's assets accumulation. In NED a greater number of the people in the rural areas rely on non-farm enterprises for their daily earnings, in order to generate income for themselves and their families. Fishing and fish mongering are the main livelihood activities for the men and women, in addition to farming, because most of the people live along the coast. And many of them still rely on micro-credit schemes to generate income for their families.

Micro enterprises 'contribute to poverty reduction because they generate social capital in a form of networks that promote economic engagement' (Hall and Midgley, 2004:76). They

---

[32] Do it in the bush means to attend nature's call in the bush instead of using proper toilets as a place of convenience

also provide income for the poor in unfavourable and harsh economic conditions (Dulansey and Austin, 1989). They further explained that, unlike bigger enterprises, that may require training, technical know-how and some expertise, micro enterprise activities can be carried out anywhere. This makes it easier for women in the communities to start their business, despite their busy schedules. The introduction of micro-credit scheme in the district has brought some significant improvement in the lives of the people in the district. The schemes have empowered them and facilitated their economic activities while at the same time they have enhanced their contribution to their families (Pearson, 2000). The study noted several areas where the scheme has helped to improve the lives of the people; either in their homes or within their communities.

7.6.1 Improvement of the Level of Income

The fundamental objective of the micro-credit scheme was to help local people to engage in some livelihood activity through a micro enterprise so that they could increase their level of income and meet their basic needs. Some of the people who were observed to be benefiting from the scheme have registered an increase in their level of income. There was no data to ascertain the levels of people's income before, during and after they had taken credit from the NGO, but during the focus group discussions some of the respondents acknowledged the benefit gained as a result of the scheme. For instance in a one-to-one interview in Ankobra one fisherman explained that;

> We used to have problems in securing loans from the local banks, to buy materials for our fishing business. The officers of CDEC know that we do not have collateral to take any money, but they agreed to help us. They trust us. They know that we will not run away with their money, so they gave us money to buy materials for our fishing company.

Another fisherman also explained that;

208

The help the NGO's offer is always timely. It came at a time that the sea had been rough and was getting better for active fishing activity, so we needed money to buy new fishing net for our fishing company. There was no money and the banks were not prepared to help because they needed collateral which we do not have. It was CDEC that helped us. To be honest the scheme has helped a lot of us, especially those of us in the fishing business.

During the all the focus group discussions in Asenda a similar sentiment were raised about some of the benefits of the have received from the micro-credit scheme. It became evident that the scheme had helped a lot of people to start many micro enterprises in Asenda and other nearby villages along the coast. Nevertheless those who hitherto had their own businesses already used the opportunity to get a loan to expand them. Though they don't get all the money they asked for it was but at least enough to enable them to expand their businesses. In a one-to-one interview in Ankobra a lady explained her difficulties in securing loan from one of the local banks, in order to enable her start her own business. She said,

'I visited many banks, on several occasions for a loan to buy sewing machines for my new apprentice, but I could not get any help, so I gave up. My apprentices would not be able to afford it and their parents also didn't have the money. But, because I wanted to help them, I sought help from the NGO and they assisted me. I have not even finished paying back the loan, but the officers know that I will pay, so they do not harass me'.

There was general consensus among the respondents that the micro credit scheme has helped a lot of people in the engagement of livelihood activities or has helped to raise their level of income. This was not an isolated case during the focus group discussions. All the interviewees admitted that the scheme has helped a lot of people in the communities.

7.6.2 Home-Family Improvement

In rural communities, home-family improvement depend on two things the level of income the household may have (which may include asserts possessed) and the type of income generating activities the individual may be engaged in. Besides, the engagement of income generating activities, in order to increase the levels of income of the people in NED,

209

another area that the micro-credit scheme aimed to help was home improvement. It was observed that some of the participants had benefited, and continued to benefit, from the credit scheme through income generation activities but, that most of them lacked the knowledge of how they could use the extra income to improve their homes. Local building materials are very cheap in the area. Many families with four or more children live in single room accommodation: some live in compound houses with their extended families, while others live in rented accommodation. Living in rented accommodation is not unusual, but in the rural areas because materials are easily obtained from the bush, men who stay in rented houses are considered lazy. Every woman getting married would expect her husband to move out of the family home and live in his own house, even if that house is a thatched and built with local materials.

In Asenda, all the participants of the three focus group discussions acknowledged that through the micro-credit scheme people were able to secure money to start businesses, the proceeds of which they used to improve their homes. When asked why they never solicited help from the local banks, the interviewees explained that the banks never assisted individuals who needed money for home improvement. They explained that the banks assist those who intend to go into micro enterprise activities, but even then collateral would be needed - which most of people cannot provide. They said that not all people benefited from the micro credit scheme, however those who CDEC had helped pointed out that the scheme was beneficial to them in many ways. The women in particular said, that they have been able to establish micro-enterprises through the micro-credit scheme, which enabled them to assist their husbands in maintaining their homes and families.

7.6.3 Improvement of School Attendance

Improvement of education is one of the major problems facing NED but at the village level parental contributions towards educational management is not only based on provision of school uniforms and books, but their enabling children to regularly attend school. Improvement of school attendance remains a significant issue today because, 'in a situation where economic and social forces are undergoing major changes, human capital particularly education becomes increasingly important for all socio-economic groups' (Ayres and Simon, 2003:216). Nzema East District (NED) is among the districts where large numbers of children cannot afford further or higher education – beyond primary and Junior High School. This is because the district has no Teacher Training College (TTC), so most of the schools do not have an adequate number of teachers to sustain further education.

The issue of teacher shortage was another area that was identified as having contributed to the failure of children regularly attend school and their inability to further their education, after completion of the Basic Education. A detailed investigation into why there is shortage of teachers is beyond the scope of this research, but a lack of social amenities in the district could also contribute to this problem - although there is no data to justify that. The introduction of the micro credit scheme was observed as having brought a significant improvement in the lives of a lot of women in the villages. It was seen that some of the parents who said they could not afford the school fees were able to after receiving micro-credit cash. In one of the focus group discussions in Asenda one lady said,

'Hitherto, we could not afford to pay for the school fees for our children, because we did have money. As of now things are different. Even if you decide to go and borrow money to pay your child's school fees, you can easily get help, because

211

they know that you are doing your business, so you will be able to pay back whatever money you may take as loan from the credit scheme'.

It became evident that before CDEC introduced the micro credit scheme a lot of parents, especially single mothers, could not afford to send their children to school, let alone give them money to buy food to eat at school everyday. At the time of the study, the government introduced school feeding programme, where every school going child at the Basic Level schools were suppose to enjoy at least a free lunch everyday whilst in school. It was observed that none of the villages that participated in the study had been included in the school feeding programme so children in those villages still demanded money for lunch from their parents when going to school. Children who could not get money from their parents either missed lessons or did not go to school.

During and towards the end of the study, the government introduced what the Ministry of Education (MoE) calls a capitation grant[33], which abolished the payment of school fees. However, Ayres and Simon (2003:225) who published an account of their work in *Education, Poverty and Sustainable Livelihoods* argue that, 'there is little evidence that marginal improvement to family income alone will solve the poverty problem and it is unlikely to have any significant effect on school attendance'. They explained that it is parental motivation and support that explain educational attainment, but not economic improvement. However the responses from the interviewees do *not* support the Ayres and Simon's claims, because the parents felt the income they got from their micro credit went a long way towards helping them to support their children's education. In addition to school attendance the scheme has also helped to improve the livelihood of people in the villages,

---

[33] Capitation grant was introduced in the early 2000 by the Kufour administration as part of the government millennium development goals, in order to reduce poverty, and increase school enrolment (especially at the basic level). Under the scheme basic school pupils do not have to pay school fees and are expected to have at least one meal at school a day. Bt although the system has been operational for some time most schools have not benefited from the feeding programme.

especially in areas where economic activity is slow and the land does not support food production.

7.6.4 Capacity Building and Empowerment to Improve Livelihood

When individuals lack the basic skills they need to enable them to embark upon the job they want capacity building becomes a necessity. It does not only equip individuals with the skills that enable them to start a business or trade but also rather it empowers them to live an economically independent life. Building capacity to empower the local people was one of the main objectives of CDEC, in order especially, to help local women acquire livelihood skills, through micro enterprise activities. But Murrison argues that the assumption that giving micro-credit to women will automatically empower them is naïve, because there is no direct correlation between the better financial position of women and empowerment (Murrison in Helmore and Singh, 2001). Her observation is that, micro-credit taken by women gives them extra burden, both financially and economically - because they have to work harder to repay their loans, in addition to supporting their families. Running a micro enterprise also gives them an extra burden as most of them continue to have huge responsibilities at home, for example helping sick and old family members and caring for the young. These extra burdens work rather to disempower women. NED has no fertile lands for agriculture, so most people rely on non-farming activities to make a living. Development organisations that work in communities in the district concentrate their activities on non-farm activities. Because, 'boosting the rural non-farm economic activities does not enhance their economic activities to improve their livelihood skills, but also it is a strategy to help them out of poverty (Hall and Midgley, 2004).The project coordinator of CDEC explained during an interview that, the NGO organises

213

capacity building through organisation of associations with the women's working groups. He explained that,

> 'We encourage the women who joined the micro enterprise to form association. They were allowed to elect their own executives, treasurers, secretaries, etc. We encouraged them to do so, so that they could be well equipped to put ideas together and send their grievances to the Assembly for redress'.

The women involve the district assembly in their meetings when they present their problems and they use the opportunity to ask the assembly to secure loans from local banks - because most do not them could not have their own collateral to obtain loans to start businesses. The NGO money is not enough, on its own to fund a business.

The findings showed that there were several ways in which the NGO has encouraged rural people to acquire livelihood skills. As they because empowered they challenges the problem they face in tackling poverty, become sufficient and independent, and useful contributions to their communities. Empowerment encourages rural people to construct 'group identity, improving economies of scale, strengthening collective bargaining power, acquiring new skills and upgrading the knowledge basis progressively to build economic and social power to overcome vulnerability' (Mozumder and Halim, 2006:153). Capacity building and empowerment, to enable rural people make a living through income generating activities, was initiated by CDEC. Now the question is how can they sustain these activities? In other words, what roles can development organisations play in to making the interventions they initiate sustainable? Who should do what and how can it be done? To answer these questions effectively an investigation is needed into whose interest participation primarily is what form of participation is required and what are the paradoxes in participatory practice?

7.7 Whose Interest is Participation? Some Participatory Paradoxes

To determine an answer to the question in whose interest participation is, requires a critical investigation as to *why, how* and *when* community members *have* to participate in development activities that take place in their communities. Stakeholders and CDEC officials in this research had conflicting views. For the last two decades application of the participatory approach to achieving development objectives has been on the agenda of a number of development organisations. Mosse argues that more participation does not necessarily lead to sustainable development (Mosse, 2007) but why should people participate and in whose interest is participation if it does not really lead to improvement? During the course of this investigation it became necessary to ascertain why the NGO consulted on micro-credit and in whose interest was participation in this regard? The local project coordinator said,

> 'Participation is in the interest of the European Union (EU), the sole funding body of this organisation. They appreciate, if the local people are involved in a participatory manner, so that they could be part of the programme and its execution. However, it is beneficial also for the local people, because it makes them become part of the intervention, rather than looking at the project as something that belongs to the NGO or a foreign organisation'.

The local project coordinator explained that, 'effective participation of the rural poor is a good thing because it ensures support and ownership of the intervention'. Recognition of the value of participation by the rural community members, not only creates awareness of the rural poor as being owners of any intervention, but also that they are the sole beneficiaries of it – as they support its sustenance. This explanation seemed plausible but how many rural people appreciate that participation will be of benefit to them? The paradox of the participatory process and the NGO's inability to inform community members of its full benefits has weakened the support of the rural poor for the participation project. It

215

became evident from the study that local people do not believe they will receive any immediate benefit from participating in community activities apart from getting the chance to make themselves available to NGOs which might provide funds for their businesses. Some of the interviewees explained that, development officers do not explain why they have to participate in the decision-making. One woman at Nkroful explained in a one-to-one interview that,

> 'I don't see this form of meeting with the NGOs as participatory, because when they meet with us, don't say anything. They tell us about the money they want to give to us. They just ask how we will be paying back the money. They explained to us the mode of repayment, where and which days we have to make payments'.

Another lady said,

> 'Sometimes we tell them the business we do and what we want to use the money for, but they tell us the money is not for house keeping but for business. If you tell them you don't have any business plan in mind, all they will tell you, is why don't you go into dress-making. But if you don't like to go into dress-making business then what are you supposed to do'.

Micro enterprises became part of the development strategy of CDEC but the NGO was unable to identify any new business ventures, besides dress-making. One question asked during the investigation was would women without business ideas be willing to go into dress making? The micro credit scheme was observed to be good by the NGO, but there were no new micro enterprise plans in place. Women who did not have their own business plans could not join the scheme because the NGO did not have plans to offer them. Even if they were interested in dress-making, no one was available to train them. It became evident that NGO had no plans to organise apprenticeships for women who wanted to go into dress-making, but who lacked the necessary skills. Another questions included was dress-making a lucrative business that would enable people to make money? Where will the dresses be

216

sold? Addressing these questions was not part of the NGO agenda. These are just some of the difficulties NGOs face but cannot foresee when they engage with local people in micro enterprise activities.

The officials of the NGO do not understand the local way of life and how business is done. The term participation is used but its practical application seems to deviate from how the community members understand it. Paradoxically development facilitators remain accountable to their bosses and funding agencies, so they have to enforce participation even if the people are not ready to do so. How can the development facilitators justify they are doing if the people are not participating? The effectiveness in their work depends on the number of people who participate. Evidence of successful participation, so far as the NGOs are concerned, is related to the number of people involved in a particular activity and the number of villages visited. It does not depend on the degree of participation for the measure of its effectiveness (Chambers, 1997). And whose job is to report if there is participation or not? Development workers need to sustain their jobs, while beneficiaries also need continuous support from the NGOs, so the ineffectiveness of participation is not well documented by development organisations, while the beneficiaries of the development also do not see lack of participation as a set to their inactiveness in participatory activities.

Low level of participation means intervention did not achieve its objectives; which could lead to loss of job and withdrawal of project or development assistance from the beneficiary community. The limitations of participation still remain an issue to a number of development organisations. In a response to whether there were problems during their participatory activities with the community members, the local coordinator said,

> 'There are a lot of problems that we encounter during participatory decision-making. Some of the village people oppose our ideas and even the main programme. We sometimes take days, if not weeks or months, before a single

217

programme could be implemented. For instance, a project we implemented some few months ago in Asasetre, a farming community in the district, dragged for almost over six months before we could implement it. There were a lot of problems, because we gave them the chance to bring their views. It is very difficult to convince the rural people before we can implement a particular project. It is difficult to reach a compromise'.

He explained that, 'such problems bring conflict during our participatory meetings with the community members, yet we consider their views and implement them'. The results show that a number of development organisations consider participation a way of winning community support for development execution but it appears the rural poor does not consider participation important. The NGO also considers participation a waste of time, an ideology that retards the rate of rural development work and process. Development workers want to keep their jobs, so they enforce participation to make their agenda accomplished. In addition, it is a way to make funding agencies appreciate the good work they do which could be measured through the level of participation. Nevertheless, in reality the practice is not effective. The study indicates that because beneficiaries have different expectations from the development facilitators, participatory effectiveness remains weak.

7.8 Organisational Expectations versus Views of the Local People

Organisational expectations from participatory activities seem to differ from the way rural people view participation and what they expect from one another. The reasons behind lack of local people participation and what they really expect from participatory practice has been very enormous. Table 8.1 summarizes views of rural people and what the facilitators of CDEC expect from them in participatory practice. The views expressed were gathered from the respondents during the focus group discussions and some of the one-to-one interviews. The views were gathered from participants who were involved in the mines credit scheme.

Tab: 7.1NGO expectations versus rural people's views on participation

Characteristic Features	NGO's expectations	Rural people's views
Decision-making	Decision-making should involve all levels of people within the rural communities to ensure total support	A few people representing the community is better because most people will not participate if it is voluntary and there is no remuneration for members. Besides most people do not have time to participate
Accountability	Rural poor are not expected to know how much should be spent in their communities. Detailed accountability to rural poor will be difficult and is not necessary	Knowing how much is coming to the community for development or how much the NGO is to give will reduce embezzlement and misappropriation of funds, whether by the NGOs or community members
Empowerment	Participation make the people empowered so they can take charge of their own lives and play an active role in their communities..	Participation is important to us because that is how the rural poor can learn the skills needed to perform their duties effectively and efficiently.
Capacity building	The people at the grass-roots level do not have the know-how to build capacity though it can help improve their skills. It is NGOs that build capacity	Community members should be given the chance to build capacity but people do not respect them because they think they are illiterate

Source: Arthur

The NGOs want rural people to participate in decision-making and in activities that help empower the vulnerable, the neglected, women and children, but Mozumber and Halim see this differently. They argued that, 'community participation should include well-educated, responsible, conscious and enlightened people of the community', because 'their expertise could serve as valuable instruments to implement' development projects (Mozumber and Halim, 2006:159). Increasingly the same notion is not shared by rural people, because they feel their views must be taken seriously when formulating and implementing policy.

The rural poor want to take full control of development intervention in their communities but input of ideas from the local elite should not be over looked. But the study noted that participation of local people in financial management is heavily resisted by the NGO. During an interview the District Coordinating Director, argued that it would be difficult to involve community members in financial management or inform them how much is spent, or is needed, for development intervention. He said, 'they can participate in sharing their views as to what projects will be of great priority and benefit to them' but not take financial decisions. This shows that development organisations encourage participation but discourage it in financial management. This has weakened the trust rural community members have fin the development facilitators. There is widespread belief that some money meant for development intervention is diverted by the facilitators (diverted into/or to where?). As a result there is lack of trust in those in charge of development.

7.9 Lack of Trust and Financial Gains: Facilitators versus Community Members predicaments

Financial mismanagement is another crucial problem which has weakened the trust rural people have in development facilitators who work in their communities. Within the rural community the degree of trust is relatively low. The development workers are also not trusted by community members to be able to manage development resources. Community members do not trust development facilitators because they believe they use development money to buy things such as cars. They live in luxury accommodation and do not provide what is actually needed for development work. Development workers argue that rural people lack basic bookkeeping skills and so are unable to manage funds for development projects. They also think that because they are poor they embezzle funds earmarked for development work. Some of the interviewees argued that the facilitators inflated development project budgets so that they could benefit from the money meant for the project. Meanwhile, facilitators argued that, the rural people use local materials, which they get free and use the money provided for their purchase for their personal gain. The evidence gathered in this study showed that there is a general lack of trust among rural people towards development facilitators.

The women interviewed argued that the men use development funds to buy alcohol and do not trust them to keep the money meant for development in their communities. The men on the other hand also argue that the youth are too young and inexperienced to manage the money for development. Allowing the women to control development funds is considered, by the men, to be a shift of power too far. During focus group discussions men in Nkroful and Asenda argued that in this way they would lose not only their power but also their respect in the community. So however the funds are managed there is still financial mistrust between the beneficiaries and between the beneficiaries and the development organisations. Both sides argue the other is involved in some degree of corruption. This confirms the Afrobarometer (2008) study which showed that over 70% of Ghanaians perceive their leaders (mostly assembly men and women) to be corrupt, yet they do not want to come out publicly to demand accountability from their leaders - because this could increase social tension and damage community cohesion. This is especially true when the leaders have relatives and friends within the rural communities.

Corruption, which is gradually becoming institutionalized in Ghanaian society, is damaging trust, within the rural communities and between the rural people and their development partners. In a society where a lot of people are corrupt the truth is not told. Because there is no trust, there is the suspicion that anyone involved in financial management is likely to take advantage of the situation and amaze their own personal wealth, either through over budgeting, overpricing or diversion of funds or resources. The concept of participation has encountered some problems in its application, but it was noted during the study that rural people have their own way of applying the concept to ensure effective and sustainable development. Whether the development intervention is community driven or organisationally-instituted, the objectives remain the same – that is, to promote the social and economic development of poor people, to improve their livelihoods, to help make them self-sufficient, to economically empower them and to contribute meaningfully to rural societies.

7.10 Summary

The way and manner NGOs apply the concept of participation in their activities within the rural communities differ in many respects, but that complexities and inconsistencies still persist throughout development practice. The research findings show that, NGOs still have *a catalytic role* to play to sustain development projects in the communities within which they work. Some conflicting views were expressed during the study about how participation should be applied to achieve development objectives. For example community members want NGOs to be open and to actively involve them in financial management but the contrarily the NGO development facilitators insist financial issues should remain the sole focus of the development organisations and that there should be no community involvement in the financial management. It would be concluded that NGOs and other development institutions should learn to trust the local people they work with because this demonstrable lack of trust will not only weaken community support for NGO efforts but also reduce level of participation.

Chapter Eight

Participatory Barriers: The Dilemma of the Rural People

8.1 Introduction

In chapters six and seven, the nature of participation as applied by the NGO and NED were analysed. The paradoxes in participatory practice were critically also looked at in both chapters. The chapters, identified various ways rural community members benefit from participatory practice especially in areas that could help them identify strategies to improve their living conditions through income generating activities. This chapter will critically evaluate some of the participatory barriers which have affected and continue to affect participatory practice in rural areas and hamper development organisations efforts to achieve their goals.

The first section will look at the nature of participation in rural communities and whether the rural poor are encouraged to participate or become a passive representative in the development decision-making process. This chapter will also investigate some of the set-backs of participatory practice in the rural communities. And it will identify ways by which development facilitators could encourage the rural poor to participate so that they are empowered to manage their own development. The final section will examine some of the benefits that development organisations derive from participatory decision-making when they involve local people in their activities.

8.2 The Nature of Participation in the Rural Communities

The nature of application of the concept of participation in NED villages is not different from how it is applied in districts that similarly rely on the DACF, HPICF and the President's Millennium Development Initiative Fund (PMDIF) for development in their communities. The approach makes the UCMs as the key players involved in most development decision making within the communities. Due to the similar socio-economic activities in the various towns and villages, an approach that works in one district becomes easily applicable for other communities. However community participation has to be ideal in order to encourage rural people to play an active role in helping to meet local development objectives. The main objective of the DACF and PMDIF is to involve community members in decision-making in order to encourage better accountability, and proper implementation and monitoring of all development programmes. But what does participation mean for rural people and how are they supposed to practice it? This became the pivot questions of the investigation, because it is argued that the success of rural development depends on how participation is practised. However when this question was put to the respondents, there was overwhelming agreement that local people are only encouraged to participate when development organisations require labour for a particular intervention.

In a one-to-one interview at Nkroful a 56 year woman (see appendix I) told me that, 'to us participation is when we are doing communal labour especially when we are involved in the implementation of a particular intervention'. In most cases the people are involved only when intervention is labour intensive and such that the UCMs alone cannot provide. Another lady said 'I don't remember being invited to participate in any development planning or decision-making'. The general response was that, meetings are only organised when the UCMs want to deliver messages, either concerning communal labour, funeral announcements or that they are seeking people for a special assignment. Overall decision-making is limited to a few individuals, mostly the UCMs and elders of the village. It was observed during the investigation that community members' understanding of the term *participation* was limited to the need to perform communal labour. So to rural people participation means involvement in communal labour.

Because participation is limited to only the provisioning of labour during implementation of development intervention, it is difficult for the rural poor to be empowered through this *partial* form of participation. Decision-making is limited to a few individuals, mostly the UCMs and assembly men or women, so financial transparency of development activities is inadequate and people do not feel they are part of the development process - because some decisions are taken behind closed doors. Effective participation that embraces areas like financial management, auditing and assessment of an intervention is limited to only the UCMs. The success of participation relates to the degree of 'appropriateness and desirability of development goals and activities, the transparency of transactions and the ownership of decisions' (Francis, 2002:402), but it was also noted there is no transparency in some of the key aspects of participatory practice. Financial decision-making is non-participatory because it is limited to a few individuals. The District Coordinating Director and the Planning Officer maintained that, participation in financial management is not necessary. The District Coordinating Director explained that, 'it is inappropriate to disclose to the rural people how much is to be spent on a particular project or give them financial details if an information. As for money issues, it should remain in the assembly not to involve the general public'. The question that many people asked, during the study is, do we *really* participate? If participation is limited to provision of labour for implementation of projects and active decision-making is limited to UCMs and the few elite, then is it participation or merely representation? This was the dilemma of the rural people observed during the investigation.

8.3 Barriers to Participation: A Set Back in Community Development

Previous research in development practice has attempted to address some of the barriers to participation, yet a lot still needs to be done before participatory practice is to yields benefits to the communities in which it is applied. In their study to ascertain barriers that could affect community participation, Mozumder and Halim (2006) identified many factors that weaken participatory practice. They listed issues like women's household responsibilities, social commitments such caring for the young, elderly and the sick, and curfews imposed by husbands on their wives, as some of the factors and barriers that affect women's participation in decision-making activities. However, the constraints affecting the effectiveness of community participation in rural development activities go beyond those observed by Mozumder and Halim, because every community has its own *unique* problems and needs. These range from tribal to ethnic – and they differ remarkably.

The findings identified constraints which I call '*participation barriers*'. These are stumbling blocks or obstacles that have hindered the effectiveness of participation of rural people. Issues which raised the most serious concern during the investigation concerned spiritual attacks and the use of juju - which will be discussed in detail later in the chapter. The interviewees expressed various ways in which the nature of the participatory processes had either been affected or hindered as a result of issues beyond their control and which development organisations could not address.

8.3.1 Time as a Limiting Factor

Time is not only a limiting factor in participatory activities but it also affects a development organisation's agenda - which in effect, affect the budget of the development programmes. As development organisations work to meet their deadlines rapid inflation is also continuously affecting development budgets. Time limitation is a great concern to

226

development organisations that work in countries that experience rapid inflation or have unstable economy. Development facilitators have to work to meet the deadline of their funding agencies, so there is little time to drag out development projects over a long period of time. As the process drags along, inflation increases the budget. So to avoid this scenario, development organisations have to rush community members through a consultative and passive type of participation in order to get the programme implemented. Besides, the organisations also visit the communities at very odd times. Respondents said these visits often take place when they are busy going about their normal businesses. In an interview a fisherman from Ankobra in an interview explained that,

> 'We are fishermen and our wives are fishmongers, so if any organisation wants to visit us for any development discussion, they should come at a time that we are not fishing. If they visit us unannounced, we will not leave our fishing work and attend their meeting, because our livelihood and sources of income is from this fishing business'.

Another fisherman from the same village explained that,

> 'When the sea is *rough* like nowadays, we will participate because, we are all at home. Nobody goes to fishing when the sea is rough, because all of us depend on the sea for our livelihood. When the sea is calm and we are busy fishing, no one will attend any meeting. In fact we will not have time to attend such meetings'.

According to the interviewees, fishing at Ankobra and other villages along the coast is irregular, because it depends on the condition of the sea. Many communities along the coast experience the same problem because all of them depend on the sea for their livelihood. They go to work only when the sea is calm; but when it is rough it is very difficult to continue fishing. And if they are not fishing, the women will also be at home, - because their work depends on that of their husbands. Only a few have farms to work or market stalls to man, so most of them would be available to attend participatory meetings. However, many women have little time to add extra responsibility (Woroniuk and

227

Schalkwyk, 1998), because of their household commitments, so they are reluctant to attend meetings. Attending could also bring criticism from the men. As livelihood depends on the condition of the sea, when the sea calm and the fishermen are working they are unable to find the opportunity to attend lengthy participatory meetings.

The findings show that, the developments, facilitators do not to have the time to involve local people - because their involvement slows down the development process. When community members are not satisfied with a particular intervention it takes time to convince them to accept and implement the intervention. One interviewee, a woman in Asenda explained that,

> 'The Adventist Development and Relief Agency (ADRA) a local NGO came with a development project but they said they did not need the community members to debate over the project. They told us to accept or risk loosing it, because many communities needed the project so there was no time for such a debate. It appears the development organisations do not have time'.

Sometimes the development organisations view participation as a process that retards their agenda or slows down the process. As a result no opportunity is given to the local people to make proper decision or no avenue is created for the poor to have participatory discussions over the project. The organisations do not only rush the community members into participatory process, but also do not give them the opportunity to make well informed good decisions. This weakens the community support and trust in the process and the officials of the development organisations.

8.3.2 Social Barriers as a Hindrance to Women's Effective Participation

Besides time which has been a clear limiting factor for organisations and communities alike, social barriers have also affected women's participation in activities in the district. In NED, like other districts in Ghana, the duties of women as mothers, and carers of young children, the sick, the elderly, and the disabled and as home managers, do not permit them

228

to play their role effectively in participatory activities. This is similar to what Agarwal, (2001) noted in a rural forest management study conducted in India, and what Hirschmann's, (1991) found in rural populations in Malawi. They observed that the issue of gender relations still remains a problem in participatory activities that should involve women in the developing world. Women's responsibilities, as pointed out above, leave them with little time to attend lengthy meetings organised by development organisations or by members of their own community.

Women's responsibilities in the villages are enormous. They spend long hours on their farms or on the beach waiting for fishing boats to come in, so they can buy fish to sell in the hinterlands, in order to make a living. And that is not the end of it. Some women spend hours every night smoking the fish, which is then sent to the regional capital and other big towns to sell. They consider their livelihood activities as having a priority over participatory activities so this makes it difficult for development organisations to involve them. The in particular, said that they cannot compromise their livelihood activities with agencies' development work – mainly because they believe there is no immediate economic or material benefit for them or their families in the development work. One interviewee, a twenty eight (28) year old youth member remarked,

> 'After all participation of development activities are optional so why should one waste his or her time for something that will not give me food to eat. If I will have to participate in any decision-making process I will prefer to do so in micro credit meetings because through that I may get some money to start my business.

The rural people prefer to participate in activities that would benefit them directly, and not in programmes that would not give them any long term benefit. Besides, their social and economic commitments, gender issues have also become another cause of concern. Gender problems in participation and rural community development have been observed by a number of researchers including Helmore and Singh, seem very depressing. In their investigation into economic empowerment of women, they observed that, 'the barriers and obstacles that women experience in their lives - and in their economic activities - will have an overall depressing impact' on their household activities which could disempower them (Helmore and Singh, 2001:9).

8.3.3 Gender Bias and Power Relations

Gender bias and the issues of power relations have hampered the impact of women and youth in participatory activities. The men deliberately organise participatory meetings at times which might not be convenient for the women to attend. Most participatory meetings are organized either in the morning or in the evening when most of the women are busy. In the morning the women prepare for their day's work, for example getting children ready for school or preparing to go to the market. In the evening meetings are organised at a time when most women are completing their evening chores for their families. During the focus group discussions, the women overwhelmingly argued that the attitudes of the men hampered their efforts to participate actively in the decision-making process. One woman in Asenda reacting to the men's attitudes said,

> 'They do not want us to take part in most general meetings, especially when they will be discussing financial matters or give detailed accounts of projects. They don't want us the women to know how much they will spend on their drinks or alcohol. As husbands they should know that we are busy cooking for our families in the evenings, so how do they expect us to attend meetings at times that we might be busy cooking. The same men will end up telling us we don't cook for them. This may lead to collapse of the marriage'.

A similar observation was made in a study by Johnson and Mayoux (1998) on a participatory development. This found that when local people tried to promote participatory activities, the powerful in the communities used their positions to *sabotage* the

230

participatory networks and made participation of the women very difficult. The unfavourable times they organized the meetings also reduced the number of women who wanted to participate in decision-making.

The women and the youth explained that the attitudes of the men, in particular, have hampered participatory practice - so much so that most of the women and the youth did not want to attend participatory meetings. These kinds of problems were also observed by Agarwal (2001) who considered a similar investigation in India. He observed that the aggressive behaviour of men at meetings made it very difficult for women (who by their nature were more passive) to participate in meetings and meant they shied away from becoming leaders of committees. During a focus group discussion in Nkroful women gave similar examples of the negative attitude of the men - which made them women feel alienated during community decision-making meetings. One lady said,

> 'The meetings are normally organised at the chief's palace. During such meetings the men expect we the women to take our chairs to the meetings. Moreover, there are benches at the palace that are used by the men. If you are a woman and you live far from the chief's palace and could not bring your own chair you have to stand throughout the meeting. The women and the youth are supposed to bring their own chairs so those who cannot stand for longer period often leave. Some may stay for a short period and leave'.

They argued that, 'the men hijack the chairs so how do they expect us to stand for that long period'. In such cases women who are anyway reluctant about attending the meetings may use problems like lack of chairs as an excuse to stay away. Some may attend but without chairs, but stay for only a while and leave because they say they are tired of standing. This is a popular tactic, because if they attended for a short time at least they escape payment of fines for non-attendance. It was observed that, most people attended the community decision meetings because they did not have the money for the fines that would be imposed

231

on them if they stay away. The aggressive behaviour of the men towards the women during participatory decision-making meetings greatly reduces the women's active involvement. This makes the women and the youth shun participatory decision-making and this in turn weakens these groups active involvement in community activities in general.

8.3.4 Local Governance, Power Relations and Threats in Rural Communities

In the four villages where the investigation was carried out it was observed that the position of chiefs and their elders in local governance, the respect accorded to them by their subjects and the role they played as community leaders enhanced their *superiority* in the communities. Increasingly at locations where government peace enforcement agents such as the police, were not readily available the position of the chiefs and the elders become unique in the settling of disputes. They act as governors and councillors at the village level. However the respect accorded to the chiefs and their elders enabled them to *take advantage*, exercising their powers and exhibiting a degree of autocracy, and even intimidating or threatening their *subjects* when their authority was challenged.

Participation should be *holistic* at the community level but the attitude of the elders reduces its effectiveness. It became evident from the findings that local interest in participatory activities had waned due to excessive use of power by the elders in the villages. The youth expressed dissatisfaction about community participation which involved the elders. During one of the youth focus group discussions in Asenda a nineteen (19) year old girl explained that – (see appendix I),

> 'During participatory meetings we are even scared to talk. The boys who may be bold to talk are threatened, given all kinds of names. In some cases their parents may be informed as someone who does not respect the elders in the village. You may be reprimanded or warned. It is in fact scary to talk at such meetings'.

232

One youth member (a man) remarked that, 'the attitude of the elders makes it very difficult for us to talk during such meetings'. It was not only the youth who were intimidated or threatened during participatory meetings. Even some of the out-spoken men were attacked. This attitude was observed to be weakening the nature of participation and to be hindering the inclusion of local knowledge in development planning. The women also seemed dissatisfied with the attitude of the elders in the villages. A former UCM in Nkroful who also participated in one of the focus group discussions expressed dissatisfaction about the attitude of some of the elders. She said; 'I was once called a *witch* simply because I was not in agreement with what the elders had suggested at the meeting'. She remarked that although most of the people at the meetings were not happy with what the elders said, they could not express any sentiment about this, because they were afraid to be reprimanded after the meeting by the elders. Or as was observed by Woroniuk and Schalkwyk (1998) some of the women do not like to talk in the presence of their husbands or elder relatives. They prefer to stay quite rather than be reprimanded in front of their relatives.

To avoid demanding community cohesion, most rural people prefer to stay quiet during participatory meetings. This happens even when there are divisions, for example on issues such as religion, social classification, gender and age (Woroniuk and Schalkwyk, 1998). Some community members would prefer to avoid discussing these kinds of issues and so prefer not to take part in participatory decision-making. Excessive use of power by local leaders is weakening the level of participation and scaring some would-be participants away from active decision-making. This raises concern among organizations that work at the grassroots' level, or who try to engage local people in active participatory activities that this weakens the system of local governance. Poverty eradication which is a key agenda for development institutions and agencies, is suffering from despotism and perils from agents within the same communities which desperately need such assistance from development organisations, because the reality of participation becomes difficult to achieve.

8.3.5 Physical and Spiritual Attacks – Organisational Limit

Physical and spiritual attacks in communities are also issues of serious concern that need critical evaluation and redress if community participation is to have a significant impact on the lives of the people who are supposed to benefit from such development interventions. Unfortunately, however, it is relatively difficult to ascertain how spiritual issues affect rural development activities more especially participatory activities. Nevertheless, while it becomes very difficult to address problems affecting the effectiveness of community participation, spiritual attacks is an issue which cannot be overlooked in a traditional African society. These attacks are difficult to examine because there is little solid evidence that such things really exist? How many non-Africans will understand the concept of 'juju'[34] and the effects it can have? How can development organizations agree that such things exist, if there is no concrete evidence of the use of juju? If community members do not complain but rather shy away from active participatory practice because they know what is happening *underground* in their communities, as a result of the use of juju, how can this be criticised?

The fear of spiritual attacks is hampering not only development activities but participatory practice. A man in one of the participating villages (name with-held due to ethical reasons – see details appendix I) who was on one of the UCs in an interview, explained,

> 'The attitudes of the chiefs and the elders scare the women; they threaten. Some of them use *juju*. If you try to challenge some of their decisions or seem to be vocal during decision-making you will either get killed or *bewitched*. How can an

---

[34] Juju is a spiritual magic used by people who use witchcraft and traditional healers in West African countries to harm others. Affected people are said to have been bewitched. In some cases they use the magical powers to kill or destroy other people's activities.

innocent woman who may be single mother participate when she knows that some of these things are likely to happen? Because the women always say, I will not talk and get killed and leave my children behind'.

This is not peculiar to that village. Gwaba (2003:91)[35] studied this phenomenon in Zambia and made similar observations. In her interactions with some youth members in Zambian villages she noted that, 'it is difficult to talk in front of those men as some of them are mischievous and can work on you at night, because they 'practice witchcraft'. This practice is very common in NED, so active and outspoken individuals, usually the women, sit back and do not get involved in decision-making. This weakens active participation of the women at the community level. Among the various groups interviewed, it was acknowledged that this kind of thing not only hinders their readiness to participate, but weakens support for local their leaders and the UCMs.

Spiritualism is not a problem peculiar to the NED in Ghana. It is a common belief that leaders can exercise their authority and power over their subjects through intimidation and threats. All the interviewees acknowledged the effect of spiritual attacks which they believed is adversely affected community participation in their villages and other communities in the district. While there is awareness of the valued of participatory practice most young men and women also believe that participation must be voluntary and that it is not worth risking your life to participate in an activity that has no *direct* benefit. As one interviewee explained that,

> 'For instance the youth may agree to participate but when they realise there is no financial incentives or there is nothing to motivate them, they withdraw. The youth consider participation as a waste of time, if there is no direct benefit either in a

---

[35] Gwaba (2003) investigated community perceptions about the impact of the market liberalisation of the agricultural product on the livelihood of a community which had been limited to a centralised system of marketing their agricultural products.

form of cash or in kind, let alone the spiritual effect that may follow afterwards, if they are to be outspoken during decision-making meetings'.

When spiritual attacks, coupled with threats and intimidation are prevalent in development practice, it weakens its effectiveness and reduces community support for the development process. Overcoming such problems becomes difficult, not only for communities in which the development interventions are being executed but, more especially, for development institutions which directly work within the rural communities. This has been a challenge for NGOs, governments and development institutions when they try to engage with community members in active decision-making.

As it will observed from Figure 8.1 below that threats, intimidations, witchcraft, physical attacks and more importantly the use of juju and black magic still remain and greater setback to effective community participation and rural development management. Development organisations, donor institutions such the WB and other development partners advocate for participation, but with little knowledge of these

Fig. 8.1 Factors that Influence Rural Development Management

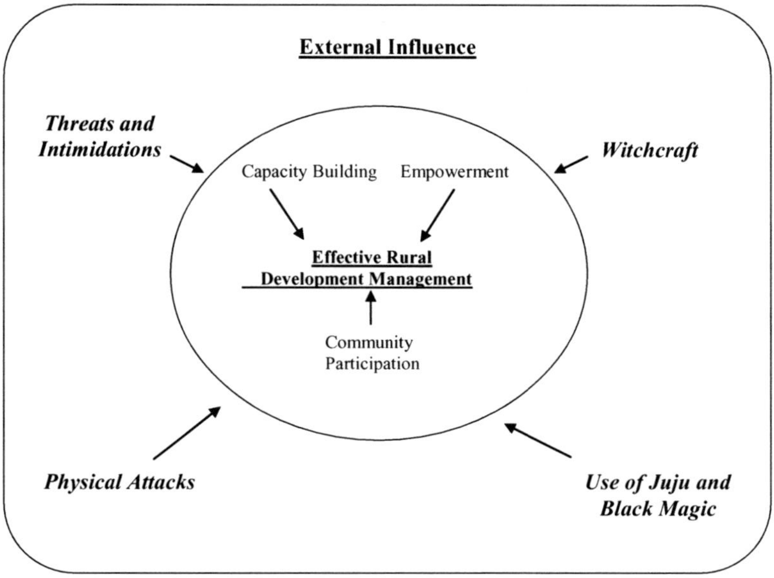

Source: Author

external influences hampering the effectiveness of community participation.

In spite of the efforts being made by NGOs to encourage participatory practice in the villages to promote effective and sustainable development, customary laws, traditional beliefs and other social factors as illustrated in Figure 8.1 above still continue to hinder their efforts to promote participation. The question which has to be answered is can NGOs and development institutions overcome these spiritual limitations? How will they address the issue of spiritualism and its effects on participatory practice? For instance, if development organisations remain in control development resources and management, how will the problem of spiritualism be addressed? This is what I call *organizational limit* or an issue that cannot be redressed by development organizations and one which therefore, becomes, a barrier to effective participation. This is perceived to be a community problem, which could be dealt with at community level - with the assistance of community knowledge and ideas. Until development facilitators, 'stand back and let others take over' Datta, (2003:56), argues the principles of participation will continue to remain in research books and on library shelves and will not have any significant effect in development practice and in people's lives.

8.4 Overcoming Barriers and Complexities: How Far Can Organisations Go?

How to overcome participatory barriers and complexities is one of the major challenges facing NGOs and development institutions that apply participatory principles in their work. *No one takes medication for the sick.* This is a common saying in Ghana, which means that no matter how difficult ones problem may be, it is the individual who has to solve his or her own problem. In other words, these barriers and complexities are community problems, and could be solve only by the community members themselves. They are problems that are *beyond* development institutions and organisations, so beneficiaries must be at the centre if such problems are to be addressed. The problems associated with community participation, which were identified earlier are not peculiar to the NED. So where do development organisations stand in regard to addressing these problems? How far can organisations go when there are societal challenges that seriously hamper the effectiveness of participation, which could be used to help desperate rural people to are in desperate need of help from development organisations and institutions to re-shape their lives? It was observed to be very difficult for rural people to address the issues confronting them in their communities, in spite of efforts being made by development organisations to help.

In chapter six I discussed, the district assembly concept which led to the formation of the unit committees (UCs) that have become such a formidable force in the campaign to tackle the problem of threats and intimidation by traditional rulers and opinion leaders in the various communities. Community leaders who are mostly chiefs, *adikros* or queen mothers, who rule the various villages and towns are supposed to settle disputes, mobilise the people for development and maintain law and order by sanctioning problematic members and using their positions to threaten and intimidate their subjects. This is expected. A member of one of the UCs during one of the focus group discussions, in Asenda, acknowledged that the work of the committee had been very effective, because they work in synergy, so it is very difficult for the elders to intimidate the members. This is because the UCM are,

> 'Very active and it is the mouth piece of the whole community. Besides, the people on the committee are many, if there is any member facing intimidation of any kind the rest of the members will be aware. So it is very difficult for the elders to single out an individual, because the other members will not agree or sit down on-concern'.

Community members are aware of what goes on in the communities and they have their own way of handling it. They live together, have community gatherings and social activities together, and attend funerals and church services together, especially in villages where there is only one church (mostly Catholic). The way they live makes their lives more harmonious and so increases the level of cohesion and reduces friction which makes it easier to address the problems that confront them.

What impact does this have on organisations working in those communities? Organisations and institutions that have development interventions in the villages locate their facilitators in the regional or national capital. They commute weekly, fortnightly or even monthly to visit the projects. Managing the projects from outside is problematic, and addressing community conflict that affects participatory activities might be impossible. Local conflict, needs to be tackled with a local approach and in with a language that is understood by the locals. Voices from outside may sound foreign to locals and making it difficult to

239

effectively intervene in development conflict. How far can development organizations go in addressing such conflicts? Development organizations should limit their influence and power, and create an enabling environment for local people to improve their own skills through participatory activities, instead of using the situation as a research tool for outsiders to acquire knowledge for use elsewhere (Chambers, 1994). Participatory practice should be revitalised in order to motivate the rural poor to contribute to effective and sustainable development. Only then would the rural poor secure influential positions and enable them to manage their own interventions, confidently and effectively.

8.5 Participation or Representation? The Real Dilemma

The dilemma of rural people with regards to participatory decision making is whether individuals from their communities must represent the whole community or the whoe, community must participate. Nevertheless, irrespective of whether development organisations expect rural people to participate themselves or to be represented by few individuals within their communities and describe it as participation, remain another issue of development debate. It became evident that, organisations consider participation as a waste of time, a deviation of their pre-plan development agenda or a neglect of already drawn development programme. In principle, participation forms part of the agenda of most development organizations that try to engage rural people but, due to the difficulties encountered when trying to do this, participation is often seen as waste of time. Observation made by Helmore and Singh, (2001:12) shows that, what 'development workers are doing in the field is not transformative and it is not participatory'. True active community participation in development decision-making makes implementation of projects difficult, results in changes to plans and could increase development budgets, because of consultations delay. This especially happens in countries where inflation is very unstable.

Participation, therefore, becomes *partial* (that is, just a few individuals are made to represent the whole community) to avoid distraction from pre-planned development programmes or deviation from development agendas. Community members also consider participation irrelevant, because as they indicated during the focus group discussions, that during participatory meetings, a few members would be able to talk. Even if you have ideas the men will not allow you to talk, more especially if you are a woman. They explained during the focus group discussions that, more often, they are represented by the UCMs in decision-making or implementation of development programmes. Their engagement is manifested more in the contribution of their labour during implementation of development projects, rather than in active decision-making process. One woman explained, during an interview in Nkroful that, 'the UCMs do very good work for us. They take decisions on our behalf, because the whole community members cannot meet always to take decisions on everything'. However, it was noted that even when the UCMs involve the whole community decision-making is either consultative or passive, because few individuals have the opportunity to talk or to really influence policy. So the dilemma of rural people remains whether to participate or to be represented?

To become economically equipped so as to harness your potential and make good use of resources available to you, requires active participation in activities that take place in your environment. However, when the respondents were asked during the investigation whether they participated or were represented during the decision-making process, the overwhelming response was that they had unit committees (UC) that represented the community members in the respective villages and towns. The whole community is involved only when the UCMs requires it to provide labour to implement an intervention. The UCMs play a very effective role in the villages and town. They plan and implement

241

development activities in the towns and villages, especially in areas where members are very proactive. Some of the UCMs liaise between the community members and NGOs and other development organisation. The interviewees reiterated that *all* the village people could not participate in all the development decision-making. This will be unmanageable, so it is appropriate that the UCMs represent village members. One of the respondents a lady explained that,

> 'There is no employment in this area. Most of us are farmers and single mothers. Even some of us do not live with our husbands, because they live outside the villages and we do not have external support. So how can we leave our livelihood activities and participate in activities that will not give us direct benefit or money. I know the development work will benefit the whole village, but we cannot risk leaving our jobs and participate in village decision-making. Besides, even if you attend the meeting, you will not have the opportunity to talk so why should we attend'?

They argued that some of the interventions are not implemented after a single meeting. Sometimes it may take several weeks if not months, before everyone agrees and it is implemented. These set-backs make it difficult for, especially the women to get directly involved in decision-making - because of their numerous commitments. The questions which remain unanswered are:

- Whether rural people are to be represented or must be made to participate?

- Do rural people really want to participate or they are enticed or coerced into participate?

- In whose interest is participation anyway?

- Are organisations coercing rural people to get involved in their development activities in order to accomplish development agenda, keep funding afloat and sustain jobs?

The continuous persistence of poverty in rural communities leaves people with no option but to continue to fight for survival and to shun participatory activities, for example, because taking part means you risk your marriage, if you are a woman. If you are a single young man or woman, who relies on by-day[36] work or street vending to earn a living, active participation could prevent you from making enough money to support yourself. So participation becomes the *duty* of those who Chambers (1997) argues have the time to spare or are free to get involved.

In chapter seven (7) it was observed that rural people are so preoccupied with their livelihoods that they prefer to be engaged in activities which could bring *direct* and *immediate* benefit, rather than participatory activities with long term goals. For example, one participatory activity that would *not* have immediate benefit would be financial assistance to enable the establishment of micro-enterprise. The youth regarded this as a waste of time. When the youth were asked why they did not play active role in participatory decision-making, they said this was because of the shortage of employment in the district and in the villages. A twenty five old man during a focus group discussion in Nkroful said,

> 'If the elders in this village are prepared to represent the whole community in every decision-making, that will be ideal for us. The elders do not have anything to do in the village and most of them do not have children. Even those who have children, they are all grown-ups so they do not need a lot of money like we the young ones'.

At Asenda the interviewees agreed with what the youth in Nkroful said, but went on further saying they appreciated the value of participation, the empowerment it offers and the opportunity it gives them to talk at some of the meetings. However, lack of employment

---

[36] A by-day job is mostly done by people who are not on government payrolls or employed in the public service and who are mostly school drop-outs or the unemployed in the communities. They do the job daily and are paid at the end of the day or after the end of the contract.

does not permit the youth to play active role in participatory activities. The big dilemma the youth faced, concerned, whether to participate, have the opportunity to voice their concerns and become empowered or to allow others to represent them, have time for their private work and remain in your employment and become less empowered. These among others are the dilemma facing the rural people and creating some set-backs to development in their communities.

8.6 Improving Decision-Making to Address Rural People's Dilemma

Improving the process of community decision-making so as to address the dilemma facing rural people, needs a comprehensive approach, involving not only the organisations that engage rural people in development but also the rural community members. Improving participation will encourage rural people to become more proactive and empower them to manage their own development. But how would the facilitators feel if they were able to transfer management responsibilities to local people who may then question their advice and knowledge? Problems associated with financial mismanagement, the lack of trust between communities and facilitators, and the ignorance of local knowledge are some of the major issues that have to be tackled if organisations are going to address the big dilemma facing rural people.

8.6.1 Building Trust through Transparent Financial Management

Lack of transparency in financial management has weakened trust between organisations, funding agencies and community members. In NED the assembly's failure to tackle corruption in development have reduced trust among individuals in the communities. Trust as Harriss (2000) argues, is the willingness of an individual to expose him/her to the risk of an opportunistic advantage of others. The exposure presupposes that individuals are not

244

taking advantage of the others in the mismanagement of resources. This is a definition also shared by Townsend et al, (2002) who believe that southern NGOs institute capacity building so that local people are empowered to demand proper accountability from their leaders in order to promote effective management.

There is general understanding that officials in control of financial resources are corrupt, so people in the local communities have a lack of trust in development workers and government officials. The respondents overwhelmingly maintained that their development officials were corrupt and so they could not be trusted to manage resources, whether financial or material. Corruption, in this regard means misuse of public authority or office for individual enrichment through embezzlement, bribery, favouritism or nepotism (United Nations Development Programme, 1999). Many local people believe that corruption has become institutionalised and a way of life (Caiden, 1997; Quah, 2002) so tackling this *social canker* has been a very difficult task for government, organisations and even individuals who become victims of corruption. Lack of effective financial management as a result of corrupt individuals, has had a negative effect on the level of support for development activities undertaken in the communities.

Financial mismanagement has been a very big stumbling block for effective participation because according to the interviewees, officials of the DA (for example the District Chief Executive, the Coordinating Director and the Planning Officer) who control development and manage development funds are so corrupt they can never be trusted. The local elite are not also trusted by their own people. And some interviewees spoke of financial mismanagement by executives on the district assembly mostly in particular, the District Chief Executive, the Coordinating Director, the Planning Officer and the Presiding Member of the Assembly and also members of the village UCMs. The elders and chiefs are also not

245

exempt from this criticism and concern about their honesty has resulted in a reduction in the degree to which they are trusted by their subjects. However, due to limited data this allegation could not be substantiated by the interviewees, and there was no solid evidence to prove the degree of corruption within the assembly and the UCMs in the villages. The perception of this corruption among the leaders has weakened support from the local people in participatory decision making and all forms of development activities.

The same sentiment was expressed by all the youth and the women in Nkroful and Asenda during the focus group discussions. The youth members pointed out that the elders accuse them of being irresponsible and consider them to be too young to be trusted with public money. But the youth and women regard the elders as being corrupt individuals who should not be trusted with development money. A lady in Nkroful explained that the men believe when women are present it is difficult for them to use money belonging to the community to buy drinks, so they do not involve the women in most activities that involve money. This is what Transparency International (TI) argues makes the poor feel alienated and makes them consider themselves to be the losers in participatory process (TI, 2008). When corruption predominates and power is entrusted in an individual who uses it for private gain the motivation for public participation weakens. The rural poor advocate for transfer of management power in other to enable them take control of development resources. But the problem of mistrust has become an issue which exists between development facilitators and community members, as well as among the community members themselves. Lack of trust is sapping the resources of the poor people, making the offer of bribes even in exchange for services which they are supposed to receive by law (TI, 2008). It is these kinds of services which corrupt officials are denying local people, which they have to get through the payment of bribes. Building trust in such an environment becomes very difficult.

8.6.2 Flexibility and Organisation's Willingness to Change

An organisations will to change or be flexible enough to integrate the ideas of the rural people has been proved a difficult challenge. To understand explicitly the concept flexibility and an organisation's willingness to change makes it necessary to ask the question what is *flexibility*? Also how can development organisations be flexible? Why and when should these organisations be flexible? The term flexible means bendable, supple, stretchy and agile, according to Oxford English Dictionary. Organisations that are flexible should be able to modify their development agenda or programme to include the views of local people. Therefore, if organisations are to be flexible, they have to be prepared to redesign their programmes to fit into beneficiaries' agenda in order to meet their aspirations or development needs. Development organisations should be able to integrate local knowledge and ideas; make room for changes in their programmes as required and redesign their strategies to accommodate the new development challenges.

The general consensus among all the participants interviewed was that the status quo has not change. Views expressed by all the interviewees indicate ways in which interventions in their communities could be managed by local people rather than the facilitators of the NGOs or the district assembly. It became evident that, the management of rural development interventions has been under the auspices of the assembly and the UCMs. However, the problems that militate against the management of such interventions still remain unresolved, because the integration of local ideas and knowledge still seem far from reality. The attitude of some development facilitators, the local authorities and community

247

members is contributing to the difficulties in managing development interventions. Development management is gradually shifting its focus from the *uppers* (that is facilitators of development institutions and organisations) towards the *lowers* (the rural poor), yet development facilitators are not compromising on what they consider to be inappropriate choices and techniques of how their interventions should be managed (Chambers, 1997; Bond, 2002).

Hitherto the management of development interventions has been the duty of facilitators while the rural poor provided labour during implementation. Development facilitators have to render accounts to the tax payer, donor agencies and other stakeholders who either directly or indirectly fund the interventions, so it was felt they were the best place to manage the projects. As facilitators have to take the blame if things go wrong rather than the beneficiaries, why should the organisations seek the views of the poor – who are less accountable? Who would be blamed if there is financial misappropriation during the execution of a particular intervention, or if an intervention was not successfully implemented? But, in spite of this, development organizations and institutions must be flexible and take into account the ideas of the rural people if they are to meet their development objectives. Because, if ideas of the local people are taken into account, they will feel part of the process, contribute to its successful implementation and improvement and even share some of the responsibility if things go wrong.

Organisation should be prepared to accept to make major changes to their own bureaucracies, to adopt a *learning approach* and be prepared to take risk (Roche in Open University, 2001). NGOs should avoid the *stiff-necked* approach to their development agendas and programmes and adopt a more flexible approach and make changes to their development agenda, where necessary. The rural poor do not seem to be satisfied with the

248

approaches currently adopted by the development organisations, but because they need the development they have no option but to accept what they are offered. Like the saying goes *'a blind person does not get angry in the forest'*. What can the rural poor do when they have to continue to rely on development organisations for assistance to improve their communities? And what can the development organisations do? Their over-reliance on external funding means their hands are tied, with regards to what they can offer, because they have their own development objectives and they control the resources. External donors make it difficult for development organisations to change the agenda, even if an alternative approach would much better suit the aspirations of the rural people.

8.6.3 Acceptance of Local Knowledge in Development Decision-Making

The integration of local people's knowledge and ideas in development decision-making seem reasonable on paper, but actually how prepared are development organisations to accept these views? On the one hand practitioners of participation have argued that local knowledge and ideas, must be integrated into development decision-making, but on the other hand participatory practice has been dominated by professionals and development facilitators (Francis, 2002). Pugh (2002) argues that, the extent to which development organisations could enhance their participatory activities depends on how the views of different groups in the community, on how rural communities could be developed are integrated into decision-making process. In other words, Pugh further pointed out that the dominance of the ideas of a few individuals may lead to unsustainable development. Pugh's view was shared by almost all the interviewees, but how feasible is it to integrate local knowledge and ideas in externally designed programme? Development organisations should embrace the views of the local people open their *doors for change* and make provision for acceptance of multiple opinions, while adapting to a culture that challenges those of development organisations (Roche in Open University, 2001).

Rural people differ in terms of their aspirations, ideas-sharing and expectations, yet strong social capital makes members work in synergy to achieve their development objectives. In one of the focus group discussions in Asenda one lady said, 'the community is ours so no matter our schedule we have to work together to develop it. Nobody will come and develop the community for us, we have to do it ourselves'. This shows that the *mobilisation spirit* in Asenda is high and has also won the support of some development organizations that work in the village. However, in spite of the strong social relations and social capital in the community there are still problems which the rural poor encounter in their interaction with NGOs and other development partners.

It became evident from the study that the development organisations find it difficult to apply participatory practice, even though they envisaged it as the *watchdog* on every development agenda – with the task of integrating local ideas and knowledge in order to encourage rural people to become empowered. Explaining some of the problems encountered with one development organisation, one of the interviewees (a lady) form Asenda explained,

> 'Some people visited our area some time ago to sink bore-holes. They did not tell us why they came or what they have come to do. They did not talk to anyone; all that we saw was some people erecting pegs. They erected the pegs and went away. We were later told the organisation was in the village to sink bore-holes. They came back a few weeks later to sink all the three bore-holes. The UCMs told us there would be a communal labour the following day, because they needed people to help them sink bore holes. Out of the three bore-holes they sunk, only one is providing water for the whole community. One was sunk at a place that the women did not want to go to fetch water, because the place is dark at night. There is no light at that place so the women are afraid to fetch water from that bore-hole.

250

The other one did not function because the water table is very low, so during the
dry season they don't get water from that bore-hole'.

This scenario was not the only incident which was highlighted by the community members
in the village. During the investigation another respondent cited a similar instance of an
uncompromising attitude of some of the organizations operating in the area. In narrating her
observation, during an interview, a lady who participated in one of the focus group
discussions in Asenda also said,

> 'We have a very good toilet fitted with water closets, but all that we needed to do
> was to pump water to supply it. Because we could afford a water tank to provide
> water for the toilet, it has been abandoned. An NGO, came to our village recently
> to construct a toilet. We requested they should provide us with a water tank, so
> that we can pump water into it and supply the toilet. They told us they wanted to
> build a new toilet, which we realised it was of low quality, compared to the old
> one that would need only a water tank to complete. They insisted that we should
> accept what they have for us or the project would be taking away'.

The women agreed that if they had been involved in a participatory way in this project, they
would have been able to say they did not need a new toilet. One of the women who had
worked on the village UC angrily said 'after all before the construction of that toilet we
were comfortable going to toilet in the bush, so we were not going to be bothered, if they
took their project away'. Development organizations always consider themselves the expert
(Chambers, 1994), when actually they lack the knowledge and know-how to fully
implement interventions within rural communities – especially when there is no local
support.

Development organisations talk about participation but they consider participation a waste
of time. They want the rural people to participate in community-driven development
interventions, but not in the activities supported by outsiders. NGOs want to *register their*

251

name in the community in relations to the projects they *claim* to have been involved in. The participation advocates, do not have enough time to practice what they preach about participatory practice. This has been the attitude of most of the development organizations operating in the communities in NED. There is no time to permit true participation and no room for inclusion of rural knowledge or ideas. Some critics have argued that facilitators of development organisations and institutions should have leaders who are 'open minded and savvy to changes in the environment and able to rally staff to shift its programme and services accordingly', so that their programmes are viable and bring real value to the beneficiaries and the development organizations (Pezzullo, cited in Roberts, et al, 2005:1853). And Fyvie and Ager, (1999) have concluded that, leaders should have the skills and technique to be innovative, adaptable and flexible, and capable of integrating local ideas into their work – in order to win support from the beneficiaries of the intervention.

8.7 Summary

This chapter has looked at participatory barriers and the dilemma that face the rural people when they are involved in participatory activities during development. It became evident that, during three decades of participatory practice, relating to development policy and practice many barriers emerged which made public participation very difficult. And there are still issues that limit development organisations' efforts to effectively practice participation - though active participation is in principle, preferred. Pressing social commitments, a shortage of time and the aggressive behaviour of men hinder women's ability to participate. Issues like spiritual attacks and the use of juju to destroy or kill active participants, are two of the major issues that scare away most rural people from participatory activities. Whether rural people should participate or be represented in development decision-making, has become a dilemma.

It can be concluded that development organisations should encourage active community involvement if they want to address the major problems that hinder community members' participatory activities. Organisations must actively eliminate the barriers that inhibit effective participation and develop a more modest and flexible approach to the development decision-making process. Over the years, 'less attention has been focused on local people's own knowledge of policy alternatives or options or relative the importance of these alternatives to other factors that influence their participation patterns' (Zanetell and Knuth, 2004:794). Helmore and Singh (2001) observed that development organizations must be made aware of the wealth of local knowledge available and that they must eliminate their preconceived notions about rural people. Without the acceptance of local people's knowledge in the development decision-making and policy formulation process, development organisations will fail to win the support of the beneficiaries for their work to achieve effective and sustainable development. If measures are not put in place to address participation barriers and paradoxes, improving the lives of the rural people will be like chasing the wind.

Chapter Nine

Conclusion, Recommendations, Policy Implications and Limitations

9.1 Introduction

The study investigated barriers in participation in rural development. It examined ways in which those intricacies could be addressed to enhance participatory practice to improve development policy formulation and practice. The theoretical perspectives that could be applied in development in different would be explained in more detailed. This section will also look at the study contribution to knowledge and some of the recommendation for future policy formulation and practice.

9.2 The Main Development Concepts and Practice

The literature search investigated various concepts in the development discourse. The concepts ranged from civil society organisations to capacity building and partnership. The literature search identified how the concepts are interpreted, understood and applied in development policy and practice. The literature indicates that the concept of participation is used by development organisations and institutions, but its interpretation and application differ. The literature never explicitly included societal norms, negative cultural practices, the use of witchcraft and juju, which have been hampering effective community participation. The interpretation is either based on the objectives of the organisation, how the organisations want to involve beneficiaries in a particular intervention, the nature of activity development they want the local people to be involved, or how and in what capacity they want the people to be involved. The literature shows that rural people's understanding of participation also differs from those of development organisations.

254

Paradoxically the rural poor understand participation as contribution of labour, provision of resources in support of a particular development intervention or few individuals representing a particular community to witness development decision making process.

One concept which was critically analysed is *forms of participation*. The literature shows that, there are various types of participation and different definitions are still coming up to increase the typology of participation, but scanty literature exists on forms of participation. The study went further to give a better understanding of the concept as a contribution to knowledge in development studies. How types of participation differ from *forms of participation* has been made very explicit by this study. Conclusively, in *narrow participation* individuals participate in some aspect of an intervention, but become very active in whichever aspect they partake. If it is participation in financial management then the individuals should know how much is spent; how the money is spent; who is spending what and where the money goes. The individuals should be able to render detailed and vivid account of what is spent on every intervention. Every participant involved in the financial management should be accountable to the beneficiaries. Narrow participation could also be referred to as deeper participation; because participants will have a deeper or detailed understanding of whatever activity they are made to partake.

Broader participation, on the other hand, is a form of participatory practice where the individuals or groups of individuals participate in various activities in the development process but not active. In other words, such individuals may participate in all, most or some of the activities, but *may not* have detailed knowledge and understanding of the process, unlike narrow participation. In some cases they could be just representatives. The participants may not be able to give details accounts of what they do and why they do what they do. Unlike narrow participation, in broader participation the participants may not be responsible of any shortcomings of the development process, because they may have little knowledge of what pertains in the process.

The literature showed the connection between participation, empowerment and capacity building. Although community participation appears to be practised in development activities, its effectiveness is being hampered by power relations. Local women feel empowered when they participate, unfortunately, gender disparity, men's aggressive attitudes and the use of power by the elite during decision-making appears to weaken participatory practice. Besides, there are other issues identified through the research findings and also hampering the effectiveness of participatory practice.

9.3 Major Findings

It became evident from the study that the application of participation in development of rural communities has been on the government's agenda ever since the government of the PNDC introduced the DA concept in the late 1980s. Although the initial idea was to involve the people in political decision making at the grass root level, the introduction of the DAC, extended the application of participatory practice to development decision-making at the grass root level. The aim was to involve the people to address the development problems they face in their communities. The government's agenda was in line with the neo-liberal development agenda which encourages the involvement of CSOs, NGOs, the private sector and beneficiaries to work in synergy to achieve development goals.

It became evident from the study that, in NED, opinion leaders' talks about community participation but active participatory activities are limited to few individuals - the UCMs, elders in the various communities and assembly members who represent the communities at the district assembly. There is little opportunity for the local people who do not fall within

256

these categories to participate in active decision making. In most cases, decisions are taken by the UCM and the whole community is informed during general meetings. Such meetings are only organised when the UCMs will need labour to implement an intervention and the committee members may find it difficult to do so without the community assistance. Or they may need resources like gravels, sand or wood which few individuals may be able to provide by virtue of the clan[37] they belong and could make them available to the community for development purposes. In this case, meetings are called to inform those individuals about what contribution they could make. This is what the rural people understand by the concept of community participation.

As indicated above it became evident that participation is *broader* in the communities in NED but never *narrow* as the study expected it to be. Narrow participation is therefore discouraged at the local level, because it could expose the negative activities of development facilitators. Development facilitators encourage participation that involve the rural people during implementation of development interventions, but discourage them in financial management and do not want to become accountable to them. Details of whatever activities they do, how they do it, who is supposed to do what, and when it is supposed to be done; how much money is supposed to be spent on development intervention, how is the money supposed to be spent, who spends what and on what and how that particular amount is spent remains the duty of UCMs or development facilitators.

The study revealed that there has been some significant improvement in most towns and villages due to the introduction of the DACF which was introduced as a result of the DAS. Besides self-help projects supported by the DACF, the DA also sponsors community development projects through income generation activities. Some of the women's groups

---

[37] A clan is a group of people in a particular family, tribe, race or relations that have the same totem and share similar believe. Clans are noted in communities in African. Properties that may belong to ancestors of such people are inherited by people in the same clan but managed by the elders of the clan.

are supported through micro credit scheme from the banks to start their own micro enterprise activities to enable them become financially active and economically empowered.

It would be noted, that since the 1970s that the concept participation became part of development policy and practice, problems that confront the youth who are engaged in participatory activities seem far from being addressed. In Ghana like many other African societies, men respect for women is still very low. This was manifested during the investigation. The power relations still hamper the youth as well as women's effective participation. Rural people feel empowered through the participatory activities but the enabling environment is not created for them to participate in every development activity. Empowerment should be an ongoing process (Johnson and Mayoux, 1998), but the local people are partially involved in decision-making, although they believe that participation form part of their development programme.

9.4 Reflection on Contributions to Knowledge

The study has made some contributions to development studies by streamlining some concepts in the development discourse while the research findings has also made suggestions that will influence participatory policy formulation and practice.

9.4.1 Contributions from Literature Search

Conceptualisation of participation in the development discourse could trace its source back into the late 1970s but there are still gaps in the practice of participation, that current and future research study could help bridge. It became clear from the literature search that *narrow* and *broad* participation are not clear enough though few writers (Burkey, 1993; Johnston and Kilby, 1995; Blackburn et al, 2002) have tried to explain it. It was not very explicit to be applied in development practice.

The study has indicated that participation should have two *forms - narrow* and *broad*. The study therefore made it clear that narrow participation could mean individuals to have deep knowledge and understanding of areas they participate, and how the individual is actively involved in all those activities. In others words, narrow participation means the individuals participate in a manner that enable them to render accurate and detailed accounts of what they do and would be able to explain how they do it, and can even take responsibilities for its failure. While broad participation means being involved or become a part of an activity or intervention, but not having deeper knowledge or understanding of what is being done? Such participants may not be able to render accurate accounts of what may happen unlike those who might be involved in deep participation. They may be just representatives or passive participation unlike narrow participation where participants could be in active involvement.

9.4.1 Research Contributions to Development Practice

Previous research has showed that women, the youth and the vulnerable do not participate because they do not have time to spare (Chambers, 1983; 1997). In NED, the social responsibilities of women as caretakers of the home, the sick, elderly and children do not allow them to participate as well. However, this investigation has made it very explicit that there are other major barriers that weaken women's willingness to participate. Some of the major problems identified by the study are *spiritual attack* and the use of *witchcraft* and *juju*. *Witchcraft* and *juju* are spiritual powers and magic that some of the rural community members more especially the elders (mostly the older men) use to intimidate, scare or kill outspoken, intelligent and very active individuals within the community. Such out-spoken individuals are either bewitched, killed, disable you spiritually or destroy your activities through magical powers. These issues were observed during the study as major difficulties

259

hampering people's readiness to participate but cannot be addressed by development organizations and institutions.

It was observed that those who are outspoken and could question their leaders or challenge their authority or demand accounts of their actions are attacked with this magical powers. The use of *witchcraft* or *juju* as known in West Africa, is used to bewitch, kill or destroy individuals who challenge the authorities' decision, is seriously affecting and hampering effective participatory practice. For example women who are very active are often called witches, while very influential youth members are considered arrogant or disrespectful.

In addition, corruption is another major problem that is also weakening trust the local people have for the development facilitators and even for the officials of the DA, because there is little accountability of development interventions they undertake in the communities. The DA officials are not prepared to render accounts to the local people and the local people are also not empowered enough to demand accountability. The study concludes that corruption is another major issues affecting effective participatory practice and is weakening community members' moral and trust for their leaders.

The study observed that, decision making at the grassroots level is mainly in the hands of UCMs, assembly members and some elders (men and few women) in the communities. Decision-making is not fully participatory, but more of a representation. Women are still discouraged to participate, and there is little support for them. The women always feel subordinated in the mix of men. In some cases, they gave all kinds of names or being ridiculed when they became very active in participatory practice. This is another issues the study identified, could be addressed only by the local people, and at the local level, because such issues are beyond the development organisations.

260

The study has therefore made it very explicit that without critically addressing those problems, women's interest in participation will continue to remain stagnant and the youth members may avoid participatory practice. While at the same time, the gender imbalance at the local level and power relations that affect participatory practice will remain unresolved. To reshape participation to accommodate beneficiaries' involvement in the management of development activities within their communities, the study identified several ways through which they could be involved in participatory practice. The rural people effective participate would enhance their level of empowerment; while effective capacity building would also enhance their level of confidence, knowledge and skills in managing development intervention effectively.

9.5 Some Recommendations and Policy Implications for Future Practice

Evidence from the study has shown that, institutions and organizations notably NGOs, donor agencies and other stakeholders have to redesign their policies and programmes in rural development, if they are to improve the lives of the rural people. The study has come out with some recommendations that if adopted would help improve participatory practice, awaken the people's moral and increase the level of motivation for them to contribute positively towards development activities in their communities. It is therefore believed that, rural community members, government institutions, NGOs and opinion leaders that either directly or indirectly work with the rural people could adopt to improve the lives of rural people. The following has therefore been put forward as some of the recommendation suggested by the study to reshape participatory practice, development policy formulation and ways in which rural development activities could be managed..

1. Participatory activities should not be limited to few individuals who might be literate, available or have time to spare as Chambers, (1997) put it, but rather should involve

everyone, no matter the age and the gender orientation of the individuals, provided they are willing and have the capability to participate. It should not be limited to few influential groups or individuals who the community thinks could perform well, can talk or are more intelligent in the society as being done in rural areas in Ghana where UCMs take development decision-making on behalf of community members. Views of such individuals should not form the basics of every decision making process in the community, but rather everyone should be encouraged to participate. The study therefore recommends that all people in the community should be made aware of when, why and how they should participate and their specific role should be made explicit to participants, irrespective of their social class, gender, age or their educational background.

Participation should not only be limited to few individuals as it is now the case in NED rural communities. In the government's decentralization programme, grassroots political participation and rural development efforts have handed over development activities into the Unit Committee Membership but rather every individual within the community should be given equal opportunity to participate on equal terms. The concept of community participation limits decision-making to few individuals UCMs, empowers them and disempowers the rest of the community members. It weakens participation rather than strengthening it. Thereby enhancing the conflict of power and limits few individuals who may use their position not to help alleviate the problems of the poor, marginalized, the vulnerable, women and children but for their selfish gains.

2. The prevalence of power and power relations within institutions, organizations and among individuals and within communities as it became evident in the study should be looked at critically and addressed. Effective participation without addressing the concept of power, who possesses it and exercise over whom; who should be disempowered and who

should be empowered need to be addressed. Ignorance of rural communities seems to block people perception on the exercise of power by few individuals over others. Allowing the poor to manage their own development, by putting them at the mainstream of affairs instead of the periphery, which hitherto has been the practice, will not enhance sustainable development as suggested by the respondents during the study. Until the conflict of power relations amongst individuals within organizations, institutions and communities are addressed effective rural development management by the poor will be far from a reality.

3. Issues hampering effectiveness of community participation as revealed in the study are threats and intimidation. This is a difficult challenge to development institutions, organizations and rural community members. It weakens and limits participation to few individuals who may have their secrete agenda in the development process. In other words, the use of witchcraft or juju to harm others and scare them away from participatory practice must be looked at critically. The objectives of such individuals or group of individuals may not be of interest to the community. It further disempowers the youth and women in particular which the study noted to be the most affected in participatory process. It has therefore been recommended that to overcome this problem there is the need for development institutions or governments to promote effective civil education programmes in their development agenda. The Civic Education Department has been working in the rural communities by sensitizing the people at grassroots on issues of development and policies, but their work should go beyond educating the people on the benefits of participation and address the causes of this intimidatory practice which is hampering the effectiveness of participation. The issue of witchcraft remain community problem and beyond development institutions and organizations. Involving the people from the communities in the development process actively and effectively would help address these

263

issues of treat, intimidation and spiritualism which weakens and scare people away from active participatory practice.

4. Rural communities cannot develop in an atmosphere of distrust. Lack of trust which is hampering the effectiveness of participation has a resultant from corrupt individuals whose attitude dampens the spirit of the rural poor in participatory practice. Addressing the issue of trust will help win support not only among rural community members involved in development, but also for agencies and development organizations that support development interventions financially. It is therefore recommended that those involved in development activities should be open in their financial management, so that there can win support either within their own organizations or among the beneficiaries, in order to improve their work. The question is how could trust be won? Trust could only be won from within the community members and between agencies and beneficiaries. If efforts are made to eliminate corrupt activities as it was identified in the study, it will win community trust. Comprehensive approach to involve people will help reduce the act of corruption which is weakening the trust among beneficiaries.

A change of attitude could mean transparency and effective accountability and cost effective way of implementing development interventions. The study further recommends that development institutions should be transparent as they expert the people at the grassroots to be, if they intend to strengthen the accountability structures. Leaders should be prepared to remain accountable and must be prepared to render account anytime they are required to so. Institutions should widen participation to involve all categories of people so that they will be empowered enough to demand accountability from their leaders. It will ensure their support from the local people and improve trust they have for the facilitator.

5. The study revealed that there has been general acknowledgement from the rural community members, development organizations and government development institutions, that capacity building is very necessary in rural development management. Nevertheless, it appears little has been done to address the shortcomings, to identify those capable of building capacity. The study recommends that beneficiaries and all stakeholders should be involved in identifying areas, which need capacity building and those to build capacity. Institutions should not neglect local knowledge when building capacity. Facilitators should not consider themselves as '*knowledgeable*' and the rural people is a '*bunch of ignorant*' who are incapable of building capacity or identifying capacity needs. Local knowledge should form the basics of capacity building and possibly by helping them to identify local ways of meeting capacity needs to achieve sustainable development goals.

6. Ensuring effective and sustainable development will only be achieved if communities work in partnership with development institutions and organizations. The continuous persistence of poverty in Ghanaian communities makes it relatively difficult for the poor to work in isolation to achieve development goals. So far rural communities in the developing world continue to rely on external support and partnership with donor's agencies, to sustain development within the communities. Working in partnership and in synergy with institutions and organizations is a way of ensuring continuous financial support from funding agencies that directly or indirectly work with rural community members or at the grassroots level. The study suggests that the indirect power and the influence being exercised over the use of resources and control of funding as Brehm (2001) argued, weakens partnership and should be avoided. Development institutions that are committed to partnership should avoid holding on to power and release control and management of

resources to the local people so as to strengthen the structures of partnership and community support.

9.5 Limitations of the study

The use of only qualitative research methodology, although considered appropriate, could limit the validity and reliability of the result, in spite of the effects to reduce them. The use of the focus group discussion was considered ideal for the study because the rural people have a common interest, live in the same area, and with common societal norm, but the difficulty in getting the people together during some of the interview schedules affected the intra-judge reliability of the study. Lack of availability of some of the respondent's could not permit them to stay throughout an interview scheduled which affected the continuous and speedy flow of the data gathering. This is what Gray (2004) argues is any issues that weakens the reliability of data due to bias on the part of the responses provided.

In some cases where the eloquent respondents were called during the interview process the remaining participants struggled to provide responses, although the participants were encouraged to talk or carry on with the discussion. All these among others, were some of the shortcomings which were anticipated but the frequency at which it occurred was a bit excessive. This could be a limiting factor in terms of provision and free flow of information during some of the discussions. Obtaining information from the government officials was very difficult. Some felt releasing information may affect their jobs though anonymity and confidentiality was guaranteed. In some cases, several visits were made though, the respondents had earlier agreed on a particular date and time for their interviews, but when it comes to the time for the interview, it became very difficult to locate them, let alone being available to be interviewed. In some cases some of the interviewees refused for the interview to be recorded. Through recording it would have been better because the tape could be played over and over to note and analyze every bit of the responses provided.

Lack of funding for the study was also a limiting factor. The continuity of the course was affected because of my financial constraints. However, in spite of the above limitations, the study would be very useful for organizations that apply participatory principles in development interventions in rural communities. It will help them to redesign their ways of engaging the rural people in participatory practice and development work with people at the grassroots level.

Another issue was interview of some of the government officials. Some of the government officials never allowed for the interviews to be recorded and also refused to be interviewed in the interview rooms, instead preferred the interviews to take place in their offices. That indicated that, the interviews had to be conducted strictly within a certain allocated time so there was little or no time for clarification of their response due to their tight schedule. In most cases such interviews were rushed through so that responses could be obtained within that short available period of time.

Language was another issue of concern. The translation of some of the key concepts into the local language (Nzema) was a bit difficult, because of the limited vocabulary of Nzema meant that the interviewees who could not speak or understand English struggled to explain things coherently and accurately in line with some the questions that were posed. Efforts were made to explain all the questions very explicitly in the local language as much as possible; however, there remains some limitation in the degree of correctness of some of the responses as far as some key concepts concerned. In addition, this study was the first experience of an interview process of that kind for most of the respondents, so some of them were somewhat nervous. Provision of straightforward answers became a problem.

Because of their inexperience, most of them were not psychologically prepared for such an interview schedule which may have weakened the accuracy of some of the responses provided.

Another area of concern was availability of secondary data gathered from the government offices. Because most NGOs are not officially registered, the data on such organisations was very patchy and in some cases officials felt reluctant to release information for reasons best known to them. However, in spite of the above, the degree of validity and reliability was not affected, because efforts were made to reduce all anticipated setbacks through triangulation of the data with a combination of focus group discussions and one-to-one informal interviews.

9.6 Reflecting Back

Rural development management which for the past three decades has been development-facilitator-centred, has now begun to change its focus toward participation of beneficiaries. However, the concept of participation been in the development discourse for almost over four decades, yet the paradox and barriers in its application still remain complex and difficult to address. Development institutions and organisations apply the concept participation in their development practice as they involve beneficiaries so that they become empowered to take full responsibility of their lives. The study observed that the task facing development organisations remain a very daunting. Some of the barriers identified during the study appear to have weakened participatory practice in most rural communities in NED. Besides the limiting factors, ways in which development organisations could involve beneficiaries in their work must also have to be looked at.

It was observed that effective participation is limited to provision of labour and the passage of information from development officials to local community members. Financial

268

management which all the respondents expressed concern, is limited to few individuals at the community level and at the district level to few officials. On the one hand, the NGO officials argue that participation of beneficiaries would be very difficult. On the other hand beneficiaries also believe that the facilitators are corrupt and take advantage and embezzle development funds. However, this sensitisation is losing focus, because the rural people's expectations of participation seem to differ from how development organisations and facilitators want participation to be practiced. Participation of the rural people has become a contribution of labour or provisioning of resources for implementation of development projects rather than proactive involvement in decision-making and implementation of development interventions. The study noted that local NGOs and the district assembly take advantage of use the local people as their source of labour to cut down their development cost and make extra cash available for embezzlement. This makes the rural poor understanding of the concept of participation to be provision of labour rather than holistic involvement of individuals in development process that agencies in development expect envisage. Notwithstanding the above, holistic involvement of rural poor in the management of their own development has not been empirically studied in the NED until this study.

The major setbacks in participatory practice are treats, intimidation and spiritualism. These are some of practices scaring away the rural people who wish to participate (more especially women and the youth). Such problems cannot be solved only by development organisations, but with direct involvement of the beneficiaries. When rural people become active players in participatory practice, they feel part of the process and contribute to its success. Rural people know their situation better; understand it very well and it is through their initiatives that solutions could be found. Without their active involvement, development organisations, mostly NGOs will achieve little to enhance participatory

269

practice. NGOs should not forget that they are 'gap fillers' and their work is not permanent. NGOs come and go but rural community development is an on-going process.

If the position of management does not change for beneficiaries to manage their own affairs with their knowledge, organisation in development will do their best but the lives of the poor in the rural communities will not register any significant changes. Efforts were made to understand the problems that weaken community participation and rural development, but a lot of work needs to be done to overcome some of the problems. This study has come up with new areas that could be investigated in the future.

9.7 Suggestions for Future Research

The study was carried out in the Nzema East District yet there are other areas in Ghana or in other countries in the developing world where similar investigation could be done to understand rural development management and community participation. The concept of participation has been investigated in different areas and many communities through academic study, projects evaluation, seminars, conferences, etc. yet a lot needs to be done in terms of research. Such investigations will help contribute to the body of knowledge in development studies and development policy and practice. This study has open doors to other areas that have to be investigated to improve development practice. The following topics have therefore been suggested for future research and investigation,

- Can Community Participation Really Improve The Lives Of The Rural Poor: A Comparative Study? In this study, an investigation has to be carried out to ascertain whether rural communities are either benefiting or improving since the concept of participation entered the development discourse about four decades ago. It will also be made explicit whether communities that apply the participatory concept can make or are making better progress that their counterparts that do not

270

apply the concept. This will provide empirical evidence which over the years have been absent in the development discourse. It will challenge practitioners of participation, agencies and donors who argue that inclusion of participation principles in every development activity is the only way through which rural communities could develop.

- Improving rural livelihood through micro-enterprise activities: Is micro-financial institutions the answer? The issue of whether micro financial institutions can improve the life of rural people is a problem facing governments in the developing world. It has been observed that financial institutions charge high interest for loans taken, so whether the local people will be able to make enough profit from their businesses and pay for the huge interest being charged and still have enough to support their families is another issue. So whether micro credit financial institutions could make a difference in people's lives in spite of the high interest being charged from the poor who take such credits has been a debate. This investigation will help to ascertain whether there is an alternative to the use of micro-credit schemes to improve the lives of the rural people.

- Managing rural development in partnership: sharing responsibilities with the poor. This study will help to identify different ways in which the rural poor could be made to play active role in the management of development within their communities, whether it is community-driven or organisationally initiated.

- Educational improvement and affordable schooling to benefit the rural poor: Encouraging participation to improve school performance to benefit the poor. To help the rural poor who would not be able to afford private education, there is the need to investigate how parents could be encouraged to participate actively in

271

school management to make them effective and affordable and also to promote quality teaching and learning to benefit the poor. It has been observed that effective monitoring of schools leads to effective teaching and learning. Private schools that have better supervision procedures perform better than public schools. Though most public schools have well qualified teachers and are better paid than private school teachers, public schools perform poorly. Parents, who can afford, prefer to send their children to private schools, instead of public schools, leaving poor children with no option that only have their education in public, though performance is low. This investigation will help to identify ways in which public schools could be improved to win parents confidence so that poor children can also enjoy effective teaching and learning.

There could be other ways in which the concept of participation could be investigated but suggestions indicated above would help future researchers and students to explore new ways of understanding participation and its application in development policy and practice in rural communities.

References

Abacci Atlas (2005) *A Short Ghanaian History: Facts, Maps, Flags and Pictures from Countries around the World.* Accessed at http://www.abacci.com/atlas/history3.asp?countryID=204, on 05/07/2005

Abrokwa, M. (2005) *A Swot Analysis of the PRSP: A Civil Society Perspective.* Accessed at http://www.cspr.org.zm/Reports&Updates/GhanaPresentation.doc on 06/07/2005

Afrobarometer (2008) *Popular Opinions on Local Government in Ghana*, Briefing Paper Prepared by CDD-Ghana, No. 52 Accessed at http://www.cddghana.org on 14/05/2010

Agarwal, B. (2001) Participatory Exclusion, Community Forestry and Gender: An Analysis for South Asia and a Conceptual Framework. In *World Development Journal*, Vol. 29, No. 10, pp 1623-1648.

Akyeampong, K. (2007) *50 Years of Educational Progress and Challenges in Ghana*, A paper presented at the Centre for International Education, University of Sussex, UK

Alsop, R. and Norton, A. (2004) Power, Rights and Poverty Reduction. In Alsop, R. (ed) *Power, Rights and Poverty: Concepts and Connections*, The World Bank and DFID pp3-14.

Anwar, Q. (2003) Six Experiences With PRA. In Cornwall, A. and Pratt, G. (eds) *Pathways to Participation: Reflections on PRA*, London: ITDG Publishing pp 25-31.

Arnstein, S. R. (1969) A Ladder of Citizen Participation, *Journal of American Institute of Planners,* Vol 35, pp216-225.

Baikie, N. (2003) *Analyzing Qualitative Data: From Description to explanation*, London: Sage Publication.

Bakewell, O., Brehm, V., Mebrahtu, E., Methven, S. and Sorgenfrei, M. (2004) *Institutional Co-operation between Africa NGOs and External Partners: "Current Constraints and Ways Ahead".* Background paper prepared by INTRAC. International Symposium on Building the Capacity and Resources of African Non-Governmental Organisations, African Union Conference Centre, Addis Ababa

BancoSol (1997) *'An Overview of BancoSol' and 'Controlling Fraud'*, Presentation by Pancho Otero to Workshop in Zimbabwe, January, pp 52-69

Barrientos, S. (1998) How to Do a Literature Study. In Thomas, A., Chataway, J. and Wuyts, M. *Finding Out Fast: Investigative Skills for Policy and Development.* London: Sage Publications Ltd pp87-106.

Bashyam, L. (2002) The Role of the Northern Development NGOs (Christian Aid). In Desai, V. and Potter, R. B. T. *The Companion to Development, Studies.* London: Arnold, pp514-519.

Bates, R. H. (1995) Governments and Agricultural Markets in Africa. In Corbridge, S. (ed) *Development Studies: A Reader.* London : Arnold pp147-164.

Batley, R. (2002). The Changing Role of the State in Development. In Desai, V and Potter, R. B. (eds) *The Companion to Development Studies*, London: Arnold pp135-139.

Becker, S. H. and Geer, B. (2004) Participant Observation and Interviewing: A Comparison. In Seale, C. (ed) *Social Research Methods: A Reader*, London: Routledge pp. 246-251

Bergdall, T. D. (1993) *Methods for Active Participation: Experiences in Rural Development from East and Central Africa*, Oxford University Press, Nairobi, Kenya.

Blackburn, J. and Holland, J. (1998) General Introduction. In Blackburn, J. and Holland, J. (eds) *Who Changes? Institutionalising Participation in Development,* London: Intermediate Technology Publications Ltd pp1-8.

Blackburn, J., Chambers, R. and Gaventa, J. (2002) Mainstreaming Participation in Development. In Hanna, N. and Picciotto, R.(eds) *Making Development Work: Development Learning in a World of Poverty and Wealth.* World Bank Series on Evaluation and Development. Vol.4

Blaikie, N. (1993) *Approaches to Social Enquiry,* Cambridge: Polity Press

Blaikie, N. (2003) *Designing Social Research: The Logic of Anticipation*, Cambridge: Polity Press,

Blunt, P. and Jones, M. L. (1992) *Managing Organisations in Africa*, Berlin: Walter de Gruyter & Co

Blurr, V. (1995) *An Introduction to Social Construction.* London: Routledge

Bond, R. (2002) Planning and Managing Development Projects in Kirkpatrict, K., Clarke, R., and Polidano, C. (eds) *Handbook on Development Policy and Management,* Cheltenham, UK: Edward Elgar pp421-433

Brehm, V. (2001*) NGO and Partnership*, Policy Briefing Paper for the NGO Sector Analysis Programme presented to INTRAC, No. 4

Brett, T. (2000) Understanding Organisation and Institutions In Robinson, D., Hewitt, T. and Harriss, J. (eds) *Managing Development: Understanding Inter-organisational Relationships,* London: Sage Publications pp19-48.

Bryman, A. and Burgess, R.G. (1994) Reflections on Qualitative data analysis. In Bryman, A. and Burgess, R. G. *Analyzing Qualitative Data*, London: Routledge pp 216-226.

Burkey S. (1993) People *First: A Guide to Self-Reliant Participatory Rural Development,* London: Zed Books Ltd

Cammack, P. (2002) Neoliberalism, the World Bank and the New Politics of Development. In Kothari, U. and Minogue, M. (eds) *Development Theory and Practice: Critical Perspectives*, Basingstoke: Palgrave pp157-178.

Chambers, R. (1983) *Rural Development: Putting the First Last,* Essex: Pearson Education Limited

Chambers, R. (1994a) *All Powers Deceives*, IDS Bulletin, Vol. 25, No 2, pp14-26

Chambers, R. (1994b) Participatory Rural Appraisal (PRA): Challenges Potential and Paradigm, *World Development*, Vol. 22, No 10, pp1347-1454

Chambers, R. (1995) Paradigm Shifts and the Practice of Participatory Research and Development. In Nelson, N. and Wright, S. (eds) *Power and Participatory Development: Theory and Practice,* London: ITDG Publishing pp30-42.

Chambers, R. (1995) Rural Poverty Unobserved: The Six Biases. In Corbridge, S. (ed) *Development Studies: A Reader*, London: Arnold. pp.164-173

Chambers, R. (1997) *Whose Reality Counts: Putting The First Last*, London: ITDG Publication

Chambers, R. (1998) Beyond ''Whose Reality Counts?'' New Methods We Now Need. In Borda, O. F. (ed) *People's Participation: Challenges Ahead*, London: Intermediate Technology Publication pp 105-130

Clark, D.J. (2002) NGOs and the State. In Desai, V and Potter, R.B. *The Companion to Development Studies,* London: Arnold, pp504-508.

Clarke, C. (2002) The Latin American Structuralists In Desai, V. and Potter, R. B. (eds) *The Companion to Development Studies*, London: Arnold pp92-96.

276

Clarke, R (2002) Civil Society and its Role in Development. In Kirkpatrick, C., Clarke, R. and Polidano, C. (eds) *Handbook on Development Policy and Management*, Cheltenham, UK: Edward Elgar Publishing Ltd pp363-371.

Clayman, S.E. and Gill, V.T. (2004) Analysing Qualitative Data. In Hardy, M. and Bryman, A. (eds) *Handbook of Data Analysis*, London: Sage Publication pp589-606.

Cleaver, F. (2001) Institutions, Agency and the Limitations of Participatory Approaches to Development. In Cooke, B. and Kothari, V. (eds) *Participation: The New Tyranny?* London: Zed Books Ltd pp36-55.

Clemente, R.D. From Participatory Appraisal to Participation in Governance in the Philippines. In Cornwall, A. and Pratt, G. (eds) *Pathways to Participation: Reflections of PRA,* London: ITDG Publications pp 41-46.

Colen, L., Manin, L. and Morrison, K. (2007) *Research Methods in Education*, London: Routledge

Colman, D. (2002) Agricultural Development Policy. In Kirkpatrick, C., Clarke, R. and Polidano, C. (eds) *Handbook on Development Policy and Management*, Cheltenham, UK: Edward Elgar pp78-85.

Contreras, D., Puentes, E. and Bravo, D. (2005) Female Labour Force Participation in Greater Santiago, Chile: 1957-1997, A Synthetic Cohort Analysis. *Journal of International Development,* Vol. 17, No 2 pp169-186.

Conway, D. and Heynen, N. (2002) Classical Dependency Theories: From ECLA to Andre Gunder Frank. In Desai, V. and Potter, R. B. (eds) *The Companion to Development Studies*, London: Arnold pp 97-101.

Cook, T.D. and Campbell, D.T. (2004) Validity. In Seale, C. (ed) *Social Research Methods: A Reader*, London: Routledge pp 48-53.

Cornwall, A. (1995) 'Towards Participatory Practice: PRA and the Participatory Process'. In de Koning, K. and Martin, M. (eds) *Participatory Research in Health,* London: Zed Books pp 94-107.

Cosway, N. and Anankum, S. A.(1996) Traditional Leadership and Community Management in Northern Ghana. In Blunt, P. and Warren, M. D. (eds) *Indigenous Organisation and Development,* London: Intermediate Technology Publications Limited pp 88-96.

Country Profile: Ghana (2005) *The Local Government System in Ghana* accessed on www.clgf.org.uk Accessed on 22, February, 2005

Cresswell, T. (1997) Participatory Appraisal in the UK Urban Health Sector: Keeping Faith with Perceived Needs. In Hill, E. (ed) *Development for Health*, Oxford: Oxfam Publication pp 31-39.

Cusworth, J. W. (1994) Rural Development Project Management: Changing Prioties in Management Styles. In Analoui, F. (ed) *The Realities of Managing Development Projects*, England: Avebury

Datta, C. (2003) Participation of the People. In Cornwall, A. and Pratt, G. (eds) *Pathways to Participation: Reflections on PRA*, London: ITDG Publishing pp 54-59.

Desai, V. (2002a) Community Participation in Development in Desai, V. and Potter, R. B. (eds) *The Companion to Development Studies*, London: Arnold pp117-121.

Desai, V. (2002b) The Role of Non-Governmental Organisation (NGOs) in Desai, V and Potter, R. B. (eds) *The Companion to Development Studies*, London: Arnold pp 495-499.

278

Director of the External Aid Coordinating Committee (1993) *Difference between Government and Donor Perceptions of Sustainability,* Presentation made at the Regional Directors' Conference, Ministry of Health, Ghana

District News (2005) The Local Government Act, http://www.ghanadistricts.com Accessed on 03/03/2006

Dixon, C. (1990) *Rural Development in the Third World*, London: Routldge

Drinkwater, M. (2003) Reflection on Participation and Empowerment. In Cornwall, A. and Pratt, G. (eds) *Pathways to Participation: Reflections on PRA*, London: ITDG Publishing pp 60-67.

Dugan, M. A. (2003) *Empowerment*: A knowledge Base Essay. Accesses at http://www.beyondintractability.org/m/empowerment.jsp on 09/10/2005

Dunne, M., Akyeampong, K. and Humphreys, S. (2007) *School Processes, Local Governance and Community Participation: Understanding Access*, Consortium for Research on Educational Access, Transitions and Equity, Create Pathways to Access, Research Monograph, No. 6, Accessed at www.http://www.create-rpc.org on 14/08/2010

Dwyer, D (2002) Ethnicity and Development in Desai, V and Potter, R. B. (eds) *The Companion to Development Studies*, London: Arnold pp 459-461

Dzorgbo, D.B.S. (2001) *Ghana in Search of Development: The Challenge of Governance, Economic Management and Institution Building*, Aldershot, Hampshire: Ashgate

Ellis, F. (2000) *Rural Livelihoods and Diversity in Developing Countries*, Oxford: Oxford University Press

Esman, M. J. (1991) *Management Dimensions of Development: Perspectives and Strategies*, Connecticut: Kumarian Press

Eyben, R. (2004). Linking Power and Poverty Reduction. In Alsop, R. (ed) *Power, Rights and Poverty: Concepts and Connections,* The World Bank and DFID pp15-28.

Farrington, J., Bebbington, A., Wellard, K. and Lewis, J. D. (1993) *Reluctant Partners? NGOs, The State and Sustainable Agriculture Development*, New York: Routledge

Fay, B. (2004) *Contemporary Philosophy of Social Science,* Oxford: Blackwell Publishing

Feeney, P. (1998) *Accountable Aid: Local Participation in Majors Projects.* Oxford: Oxfam, Great Britain

Flick, U. (2004) Constructivism. In Flick, U., Kardorff, von, E, and Steinke, I. (eds) A *Companion to Qualiative Research,* London: Sag e Publications pp 88-94.

Fowler, A. (1995) Assessing NGOs Performance, Difficulties, Dilemmas and a Way Ahead. In TU870 *Capacities for Managing Development*, A Study Guide Milton Keynes, The Open University

Fowler, A. (2002) NGDO-Donor Relationships: The Use of Abuse of Partnership. In Desai, V. and Potter, B. R. (eds) *The Companion to Development Studies*, London: Arnold pp 508-514.

Francis, P. (2002) Social Capital, Civil Society and Social Exclusion. In Kothari, U. and Minogue, M. (eds), *Development Theory and Practice: Critical Perspectives.* Hampshire: Palgrave pp 71-91.

Francis, P. (2002).Community Participation and Decision Making, In Kirkpatrick, C., Clarke, R. and Polidano, C. (ed) *Handbook on Development Policy and Management.* Cheltenhan: Edward Elgar Publishing Ltd pp400-407.

Fulop, L. and Linstead, S. (2004) Power and Politics in Organisations. In Linstead, S, Fulop, L. and Lilley, S. (eds) *Management and Organisation: A Critical Text*, Hampshire: Palgrave Macmillan pp182-209.

Gajanayake, S. and Gajanayake, J. (1993) *Community Empowerment: A Participatory Training Manual on Community Project Development*, Illinois: Office of International Training and Consultation

Gariba, S. (2005) *Partnership for Participatory Development: Defining New Paradigms in West Africa*. PD Forum Abstract/Paper, G.A.S. Development Associates, Ghana.

Gaventa, J. and Valderrama, C. (1999) *Strengthening Participation in Local Governance*. Background note prepared for workshop at the Institute of Development Studies, June, 21-24. In Cornwall, A. and Pratt, G. (eds) *Pathways to Participation: Reflections on PRA*, London: ITDG Publishing pp 54-59.

Georgiou, S.N. and Tourva, A. (2007) Parental Attributions and Parental Involvement: Social Psychology of Education, *An International Journal*, Vol. 10, No 4, pp473-482

Gershberg, A. I. (1999). Fostering Effective Parental Participation in Education: Lessons from a Comparison of Reform Process in Nicaragua and Mexico. *In World Development Journal*, Vol. 27, No. 4. pp 753-771.

Ghana (2005) *The National Redemption Council Years, 1972-79*. Accessed at http://lcweb2.loc.gov/cgi-bin/query/r?frd/csty:@field(DOCID+gh0028) on 14/04/2005

Ghana (2006) The District Assemblies. Accessed at www.country-data.com/cgi-bin/query/r-5214.html on 03/03/2006

Ghanaweb (2005) *Rawlings Runs Away*. General News Accessed at http://www.ghanaweb.com/GhanaHomePage/NewsArchive/printnews.php?ID=951 15 on 28/11/2005

Gill, R (2006) *Theory and Practice of Leadership*, London: Sage Publication Ltd

Gray, D. E. (2004) *Doing Research in the Real World*, London: Sage Publications

Guijt, I and Shah, M. K (1998) Walking up to Power, Conflict and Process. In Guijt, I. and Shah, K. M. *The Myth of Community: Gender Issues in Participating Development*. London: ITDG, Publishing, pp1-23.

Gwaba, R.M. (2003) Reflecting of PRA, Participation and Gender In Cornwall, A. and Pratt, G. (eds) *Pathways to Participation: Reflections on PRA*, London: ITDG Publishing, pp 88-93

Hall, J. A. and Trentmann, F. (2005) Contests Over Civil Society: Introductory Perspectives. In Hall, J. A. and Trentmann, F. (eds) *Civil Society: A Reader in History, Theory and Global Politics*, Hampshire, New York: Palgrave Macmillan, pp1-25.

Hall, S. (2004) Foucault and Discourse. In Seale, C. (ed) *Social Research Method: A Reader*, London: Routledge pp345-349.

Hammersley, M. (1992) *What's Wrong With Ethnography? Methodological Explorations*, London: Routledge

Hammersley, M. (2004) Some Reflections on Ethnography and Validity. In Seale, C. (ed) *Social Research Methods: A Reader*, London: Routledge pp. 241-245

Haque, M.S. (1999) *The Fate of Sustainable Development Under Neo-liberal Regimes in Developing Countries*, International Political Science Review, Vol. 20, No 2 pp197-218

Harrison, G. (2005) Economic Faith, Social Project and a Misreading of African Society: The Travails of Neo-liberalism in Africa, *Third World Quarterly*, Vol. 26, No 8, pp1303-1320

Harriss, J. (2000) Working Together: The Principles and Practice of Co-operation and Partnership. In Robinson, D., Hewitt, T. and Harriss, J. (eds) *Managing Development: Understanding Inter-organisational Relationships,* London: Sage Publications pp 225-242.

Hart, C. (1998) *Doing a Literature Review: Releasing the Social Science Research Imagination*, London: Sage Publications Ltd

Hettne, B. (2002) Currents Trends and Future Options in Development Studies In Desai, V. and Potter, R. B. (eds) *The Companion to Development Studies*, London: Arnold pp7-12.

Hewitt, T. (2000). Half a Century of Development. In Allen, T. and Thomas, A. (eds) *Poverty and Development into the 21st Century*. UK: The Open University in association with Oxford University Press pp 289-308.

Hickney, S. and Mohan, G. (2004) Towards Participation as Transformation Critical Themes and Challenges. In Hickney, S. and Mohan, G. (eds) *Participation: From Tyranny to Transformation? Exploring New Approaches to Participation in Development*, London: Zed Books pp3-24

Hilderbrand, M.E. (2002) Capacity Building. In Kirkpatrict, C., Clarke, R. and Polidano, C. (ed) Handbook on Development Policy and Management, Edward Cheltenham, UK: Elgar Publishing Ltd pp 323-332.

Hildyard, N., Hegde, P., Wolverkamp, P. and Reddy, S. (2001) Pluralism, Participation and Power: Joint Forest Management in India. In Cooke, B. and Kothari, V. (eds) *Participation: The New Tyranny?* London: Zed Books pp 56-71

Hilhorst, D. (2003) *The Real World of NGOs Discourses, Diversity and Development,* London: Zed Books Ltd

283

Hill, E. (1997) *Development for Health*. Oxford: Oxfam Publications

Hirschmann, D. (1991) Women and Political Participation in Africa: Broadening the Scope of Research. *World Development* Vol. 19, No. 12 pp 1679-1694.

Hitchcock, G. and Hughes, D. (1995) *Research and the Teacher: A Qualitative to School Based Research,* London: Routledge

Holland, J. and Brook, S. (2004). Measuring Empowerment: Country Indictors. In Alsop, R. (ed) *Power, Rights and Poverty: Concepts and Connections*, The World Bank and DFID pp93-110.

Hooker, R. (2005) Civil Society as Political Society. In Hall, J. A. and Trentmann, F. (eds) *Civil Society: A Reader in History, Theory and Global Politics*, Hampshire, New York: Palgrave Macmillan pp 26-39

Hopf, C. (2004) Research Ethics and Qualitative Research. In Flick, U., Kardorff, von E., Steinke, I (eds) *A Companion to Qualitative Research*, London: Sage Publications pp334-339

Hudock, A. C. (1999) *NGOs and Civil Society: Democracy by Proxy?* Cambridge: Polity Press

ISSER (2001) *The State of the Ghanaian Economy in 2000.* The Institute pf Statistical, Social and Economic Research (ISSER) University of Ghana, Legon

Jain, G., L. (1997) *Rural Development*. India: Mangal Deep Publications,

James, R. (2001) Power and Partnership. In James, R. (ed) *Power and Partnership? Experiences of NGOs Capacity Building,* Oxford: INTRAC, Publications pp123-141.

Johnson, H. and Mayoux, L. (1998) Investigation as Emowerment: Using Participatory Methods In Thomas, A., Chataway, J. and Wuyts, M. (eds) *Finding Out Fast: Investigative Skills For Policy and Development,* London: Sage Publications in Association with the Open University pp147-171

Johnston, B. and Kilby, P. (1995) 'Unimodal' and 'Bimodal' Strategies of Agrarian Changes. In Corbridge, S (ed) *Development Studies: A Reader*, London: Arnold pp109-120.

Jorgensen, L. (1996). What are NGOs Doing in Civil Society? In Clayton, A (ed) *NGOs, Civil Society and the State: Building Democracy in Transitional Society*, Oxford: INTRAC Publication pp36-54.

Kamat, S. (2002) *Development Hegenomy, NGOs and the India New Delhi*, Oxford: Oxford University Press

Kellerman, G.E.J. (1997) Implementation of Development Projects and Programmes. In Kotze, D. A. (ed) Development Administration and Management, Pretoria: J. L. van Schaik Publishers pp49-60.

Kessey, C.B. (2004) *Participatory Implementation: The Gender Dimension in the Implementation of Community Level Project in Ghana.* Unpublished PhD Thesis, University of Helsinki, Finland

Kihika, M. (2009) Development or Underdevelopment: The Case of Non-Governmental Organisations in Neo-liberal Sub-Saharan Africa, *Journal of Alternative Perspectives in the Social Sciences,* Vol. 1, No 3, pp783-795

Killick, T. (2002) Aid Conditionality, In Desai, V and Potter, R. B (eds) *The Companion to Development Studies,* London: Arnold pp480-484

Kitzinger, J. (2004) The Methodology of Focus Group: The Importance of Interaction between Research Participants In Seale, C. (ed) *Social Research Methods: A Reader*, London: Routledge pp. 269-272.

Kontinen, T. (2005) *Producing A Project- Power Relations In Negotiating A Shared Object In NGO-Development Co-Operation*, Stream 18: Postcolonial Stream Proposal, University of Helsinki, Finland.

Korten, D. (1992) Rural Development Programming: The Learning Process Approach in Lynton, R. and Pareek, U. (eds) *Facilitating Development: Reading for Trainers, Consultants and Policy-Makers*. London: Sage pp338-344.

Kothari, U. and Minogue, M. (2002) Critical Perspectives on Development: An Introdution. In Kothari, U. and Minogue, M. (eds) *Development Theory and Practice: Crirical Perspectives*, Basingstoke: Palgrave pp1-15.

Kotze, D.A. and Kellerman, G.E.J. (1997) Participation and Managerial Approaches to Development. In Kotze, D. A. (ed) *Development Administration and Management* Pretoria: J. L. van Schaik Publishers pp35-48.

Kumar, R. (1996) *Research Methodology: A Step-By-Step Guide for Beginners*. London: Sage Publications

Lane, J. (1995) Non-Governmental Organisations and Participatory Development: The Concept in Theory Versus the Concept in Practice. In Nelson, N. and Wright, S. (eds) *Power and Participatory Development: Theory and Practice*, London: ITDG Publishing pp181-191.

Lawani, B. (1999) *Non-Governmental Organizations in Development: Case Study in Solapor District*, New Delhi: Rawat Publication

Laws, S., Harper, C. and Marcus, R. (2003). *Research for Development: A Practical Guide*, London: Sage Publication Ltd

Lee, R. M. and Feilding, N. G. (2004) Tools for Qualitative Data Analysis. In Hardy, M. and Bryman, A. (eds) Handbook of Data Analysis, London: Sage Publication pp 529-546.

Leftwich, A. (1995) Governance, Democracy and Development in the Third World in Gorbridge, S. (ed) *Development Studies: A Reader*. London: Arnold pp427-438.

Leurs, R. (1998) Current Challenges Facing Participatory Rural Appraisal. In Blackburn, J. and Holland, J. (eds) *Who Changes? Institutionalising Participation in Development,* London: Intermediate Technology Publications Ltd, pp124-134.

Lewis, D. (2002) The Rise of Non-Governmental Organisation: Issues in Development Management. In Kirkpatrick, C., Clarke, R. and Polidano, C. (eds) *Handbook on Development Policy and Management*, Cheltenham, UK: Edward Elgar Publications Ltd, pp373-380.

Ling, T. (2000) Unpacking Partnership: The Case of Health Care. In Clarke, J., Gewirtz, S., and McLaughlin, E. (eds) *Now Managerialism New Welfare?* London: The Open University, in Association with Sgae Publication pp 82-101.

Long, C. (2001) *Participation of the Poor in Development Initiatives: Taking Their Rightful Place*, London: Earthscan Publications Ltd

Lorenz, E. (1989)'Neither Friends Nor Strangers: Informal Networks of Sub-Contracting in French Industry'. In Gambetta, D. (ed) *Trust: Making and Breaking of Co-operative Relationships*, Oxford: Blackwell pp194-210.

Lukes, S. (2005) *Power: A Radical View* (Second Edition), Hampshire: Palgrave Macmillan in association with British Sociological Association

Mabogunji, A.L. (1989). *The Development Process: A Spatial Perspective*. London: Unwin Hyman Ltd

Makumbe, J. and Mayo, S. (2000) NGOs and Development. In Mayo, S., Makumbe, J. and Raftopoulos, B. (eds) *NGOs the State and Polities in Zimbabwe*, Harare: SAPES Books pp1-6.

Malik, H. (2003) Sharing my Dilemmas: Mixed Messages on PRA and Participation. In Cornwall, A. and Pratt, G. (eds) *Pathways to Participation: Reflections on PRA*, London: ITDG Publishing, pp 105-113.

Marshall, C. and Rossman, G. (1995) *Designing Qualitative Research (Second Edition)* Thousands Oaks, California: Sage Publication Inc

Mawdsley, E., Townsend, J., Porter, G. and Oakley, P. (2002). *Knowledge, Power and Development Agenda: NGOs, North and South*, UK: INTRAC

May, T. (2001) *Social Research: Issues, Methods and Process*, Buckingham: Open University Press

Mbaku, J. (2004) NEPAD and Prospects for Development in Africa, *International Studies Journal*, Vol. 41, No 4, pp388-408

McAslan, E. (2002) Social Capital and Development. In Desai, V. and Potter, R. B.(eds) *The Companion to Development Studies*, London: Arnold pp139-143.

McEwan, C. (2002) Postcolonialism in Desai, V. and Potter, R. B. (eds) *The Companion to Development Studies*, London: Arnold pp127-131.

McGrew, A. (2000) Sustainable Globalisation? The Global Politics of Development and Exclusion in the New World Order. In Allen, T. and Thomas, A. (eds) *Poverty and Development into the 21st Century*. UK: The Open University in association with Oxford University Press pp3-22.

Michener, V.T. (1998) The Participatory Approach: Contradiction and Co-option in Burkina Faso. In *World Development Journal* Vol. 26, No. 12 pp 2105-2118.

Ministry of Employment and Social Welfare (2006) *Registration Procedure of Non Governmental Organisations in Ghana*, Accra: Department of Social Welfare

Ministry of Social Welfare (2005) List of NGOs operating within the Western Region of Ghana; Introductory Note from the Regional Coordinating Director

Minogue, M. and Kothari, U. (2002) Conclusion: Orthodoxy and its Alternatives in Contemporary Development. In Kothari, U. and Minogue, M. (eds) *Development Theory and Practice: Critical Perspectives*, Basingstoke: Palgrave pp 179-190.

Miraftab, F. (2004) Making Neo-liberal Governance: The Disempowering Work of Empowerment, *International Planning Studies Journal*, Vol. 9, No. 4, pp239-259

MLGRD (2005). *The Mission Statement.* Ghanaweb document. Accessed at, http://www.ghana.gov.gh/governing/ministries/governance/localgov.php on 06/07/2005

Mohan, G. (2002) Participatory Development in Desai, V. and Potter, R. B. (eds) *The Companion to Development Studies*, London: Arnold pp 49-54.

Morse, J. M. (1994) Designing Funded Qualitative Research. In Denzin N.K and Lincoln, Y. S. (eds) *Handbook of Qualitative Research*, Thousand Oaks: Sage Publications pp 220-235

Moser, C. and Kalton, G. (2004). Questionnaire In Seale, C. (ed) *Social Research Methods: A Reader*, London: Routledge pp73-87

Mosse, D. (2004) Power Relations and Poverty Reduction. In Alsop, R. (ed) *Power, Rights and Poverty: Concepts and Connections,* The World Bank and DFID pp 51-67

Mosse, D. (2007) *Power and the Durability of Poverty: A Critical Exploration of the Links*

289

between Culture, Marginality and Chronic Poverty. CPRC Working Paper, 107.

Moyo, S. (2000). The Structure and Characteristics of NGOs. In Moyo, S., Makumbe, J. and Raftopoulos, B. (eds) *NGOs, the State and Politics in Zimbabwe*, Harare: SAPES Books, pp 47-61.

Neefjes, K. (2003) PRA, poverty and livelihoods: reflections from inside the bowels of an international NGO. In Cornwell, A. and Pratt, G. (eds) *Pathways to Participation: Reflections on PRA*, London: ITDG Publishing, pp128-134.

Nelson, N. and Wright, S. (1995) 'Participation and Power', In Nelson, N. and Wright, S. (eds) *Power and Participatory Development: Theory and Practice*, London: Intermediate Technology Publications:, pp1-18.

North, D. (1990) *Institutions, Institutional Change and Economic Performance*, Cambridge: Cambridge Press

One World Action (2008) *Citizen's Participation and Local Governance in South East Asia*, London, Accessed at www.oneworldaction.org on 14/08/2010

Open University (2001) *Capacities for Managing Development* Course Material for the Open University Development Management Course Unit TU870

Panday, D.R. (2002) Technical Cooperation and Institutional Capacity Building for Development: Back to the Basics. In Fukuda-Parr, S., Lopes, C. and Malik, K. (eds) *Capacity for New Development: New Solutions to Old Problems*, UK: Earthscan Publications Ltd pp61-83.

Parfitt, T. (2002). *The End of Development Modernity, Post-Modernity and Development*, London: Pluto Press

Parkes, M. and Panelli, R. (2001) 'Integrating Catchments Ecosystems and Community Health: The Value of Participatory Action Research' *Ecosystem Health*, Vol. 7 No. 2 pp 85-106.

Pawson, R. and Tilley, N. (2004) Go Forth and Experiment In Seale, C. (ed) *Social Research Methods: A Reader*, London: Routledge pp.54-58

Pearce, J. (2000) Development, NGOs, and Civil Society: The Debate and its Future. In Pearce, J. (ed) *Development, NGOs, and Civil Society*, Oxford: Oxfam Publication, pp15-43.

Pearce, J. (2004) *Development, NGOs and Civil Society: The Debate and its Future*. Book Series, Accessed at www.developmentinpractice.org/readers/NGOs/intro.htm on 20/04/2008

Pearson, R. (2000). Rethinking Gender Matters in Development in Thomas, A. and Allen, T (eds) *Poverty and Development into the 21st Century*, Milton Keynes: Open University pp 383-402.

Pedler, M., Burgoyne, J. and Boydell, T. (2004) *A Manager's Guide to Leadership*, Maidenhead: McGraw-Hill

Penrose, A. (2000) Partnership In Robinson, D., Hewitt, T. and Harriss, J. (eds) *Managing Development: Understanding Inter-organisational Relationships*, London: Sage Publications in association with Open University pp 243-260.

Perakyla, A. (2004) Reliability and Validity in Research Based on Tapes and Transcripts. In Seale, C. (ed) *Social Research Methods: A Reader*, London: Routledge, pp325-330

Pickford, J. (1991) *The Worth of Water*, London: Intermediate Technology Publications

Potter, D. (2000). The Power of Colonial State. In Thomas, A. and Allen, T. (eds) *Poverty and Development into the 21st Century*, Milton Keynes: Open University pp271-288.

Potter, J. (1996) Discourse Analysis and Constructionist Approaches: Theoretical Background. In Richardson, J.T.E. (ed)*Handbook of Qualitative Research Method for Psychology and the Social Science*, London: Blackwell, pp125-140.

Potter, R.B. (2002) Theories, Strategies and Ideologies of Development In Desai, V and Potter, R. B. (eds) *The Companion to Development Studies*, London: Arnold pp61-65.

Pretty, J. (2003) What Have We Learned about Participatory Methods? Some Thoughts on the Personal and Professional. In Cornwall, A. and Pratt, G. (eds) *Pathways to Participation: Reflections on PRA*, London: ITDG Publishing pp170-176

Pretty, J. N. (1995) Participatory Learning for Sustainable Agriculture. In *World Development Journal*, Vol. 23, No. 8 pp1247-1263.

Pugh, J. (2002) Local Agenda 21 and the Third World in Desai, V. and Potter, R. B. (eds) *The Companion to Development Studies*, London: Arnold pp 289-293

Quah, J.S.T. (2002) Controlling Corruption in Kirkpatrict, K., Clarke, R., and Polidano, C. (eds) *Handbook on Development Policy and Management,* Cheltenham, UK: Edward Elgar pp 333-341

Redclift, M. (2002) Discourses of Sustainable Development in Desai, V. and Potter, R. B. (eds) *The Companion to Development Studies*, London: Arnold pp 275-278

Rieger, F. and Wong-Rieger, D. (1990) Organisation and Culture in Developing Countries: A. Configurational Model. In Jaeger, A. and Kanunga, R.N. (eds) *Management in Developing Countries*, London: Routledge pp101-127

Robinson, D., Hewitt, T. and Harriss, J. (2000). Why Inter-organizational Relationships Matter. In Robinson, D., Hewitt, T. and Harriss, J. (eds) *Managing Development: Understanding Inter-organizational Relationships,* London: The Open University in Association with Sage Publications pp1-16.

Robson, C. (1999) *Real World Research: A Resource for Social Scientists and Practitioner-Researchers*, Oxford: Blackwell Publishers Ltd

Robson, C. (2003) *Real World Research: A Resource for Social Scientists and Practitioner-Researchers,* Oxford: Blackwell

Rondinelli, D. (2002) Public-Private Partnerships. In Kirkpatrick, C., Clarke, R. and Polidano, C. (eds), *Handbook on Development Policy and Management*, Cheltenham, UK: Edward Elgar, pp381-388.

Rooy, V. A. (1998a) Civil Society as Idea: An Analytical Hatstand? In Rooy, V. A. (ed) *Civil Society and the Aid Industry*, London: Earthscan Publications Ltd pp8-30.

Rooy, V. A. (1998b) The Art of Strengthening Civil Soceity. In Rooy, V. A. (ed) *Civil Society and the Aid Industry*, London: Earthscan Publications Ltd pp1997-220.

Sahley, C. and Pratt, B. (2003) *NGOs Responses to Urban Poverty: Services Providers or Partners in Planning?* Oxford: INTRAC

Sayer, A.(2000) Realism *and Social Science*. London: Sage Publications Ltd

Schneider, H. and Libercier, M.H. (1995) Towards a New Participation. In Schneider, H. and Libercier, M.H. (eds) *Participatory Development from Advocacy to Action,* Paris, France: Organisation for Economic Co-operation and Development

Scholte, J.A. (1999). *Global Civil Society: Changing the World. Centre for the Study of Globalization and Regionalisation (CSGR)* University of Warwick.

293

Sedlacek, G. and Hunte, P. (2000) Evaluating the Impacts of Decentralization and Community Participation on Educational Quality and the Participation of Girls in Pakistan. In Bamberger, M. (ed) *World Bank Report*, Washington: World Bank

Siddle, D. J. (1978). Rural Development and Rural Change. In Mountjoy, A, B. (ed) *The Third World: Problems and Perspectives*, The Macmillan Press in Association with The Geography Magazine, pp112-120.

Silverman, D. (2000) *Doing Qualitative Research*, Sage Publications, London.

Simon, D. (2002) Neo-liberalism, Structural Adjustment and Poverty Reduction Strategies, In Desai, V. and Potter, R. B. (eds) *The Companion to Development Studies,* London: Arnold pp86-92

Smith, M. (2003) *Social Science in Question*, London: Sage Publications

Songorwa, A. N. (1999) Community-Based Wildlife Management (CWM) in Tanzania: Are the Communities Interested? In *World Development Journal* Vol. 27 No 12 pp

Stevenson, J. (2002) *The Complete Idiot's Guide to Philosophy*. USA: Alpha Books

Strauss, A. and Corbin, J. (1990). *Basic of Qualitative Research: Grounded Theory Procedures and Techniques*, London: Sage Publications

Strauss, A.L. and Corbin, J. (2004). Open Coding. In Seale, C. (ed) *Social Research Methods: A Reader*, London: Routledge pp 3003-306

Structure of Local Government (1994) *Local Government Information Digest*, 4, No. 6, Accra, November- December 1991, 42 Accessed at www.photius.com/countries/ghana/government/ghana_government_regional_an Accessed on 04/04/2005

Tellegen, E. and Wolsink, M. (1998) *Society and its Environment: An Introduction*, Gordon and Breach Science Publishers, The Netherlands

The library of Congress Country Studies (2005) *Ghana: The District Assemblies*. Accessed at http://workmall.com/wfb2001/ghana/ghana_history_the_district_assemblies.html Accessed on 05/07/2005

The Local Government System in Ghana (2006) assessed at www.clgf.org.uk on 03/03/2006

Thomas, A. (2000a) Poverty and the End of Development. In Allen, T. and Thomas, A. (eds) *Poverty and Development into the 21st Century*, Oxford: The Open University in association with Oxford University Press pp3-22.

Thomas, A. (2000b) Meaning and Views of Development. In Allen, T. and Thomas, A. (eds) *Poverty and Development into the 21st Century*, Oxford: The Open University in association with Oxford University Press pp 23-48.

Townsend, J.G., Mawdsley, E. and Porter, G. (2002) Challenges for NGOs, in Desai, V. and Potter, R. B. (eds) *The Companion to Development Studies*, London: Arnold pp 534-538

Trivedy, R. and Acharya, J. (1996) Constructing the Case for an Alternative Frame for Understanding Civil Society, the State and the Role of NGOs. In Clayton, A. (ed) *NGOs, Civil Society and the State: Building Society in Transitional Societies*. Oxford: INTRAC pp 55-64.

Verwey, L. (2005) *Nepad and Civil Society Participation in the APRM*. An Occasional Papers, IDASA-Budget Information Service- Africa Budget Project. Accessed at http://www.idasa.org.za on 23/07/2005

Walton, J. and Seddon, D. (1994) *Free Market and Food Riots: The Politics of Global Adjustment,* Cambridge, MA: Blackwell Publishers

Wanmali, S. and Islam, Y. (2002) Food Security in Desai, V. and Potter, R. B. (eds) *The Companion to Development Studies*, London: Arnold pp 159-165.

Warwick, D. P. (1993) The Politics and Ethics of Field Research. In Bulmer, M., and Warwick, D. P. (eds) *Social Research in Developing Countries: Surveys and Censuses in the Third World,* London: UCL Press pp315-330.

Weinberger, K. (2000) *Women's Participation: An Economic Analysis in Rural Chad and Pakistan,* Peter Lang, Frankfurt am Main.

Weinberger, K. (2001) Women's Participation in Local Organisations: Conditions and Constraints. In *World Development Journal.* Vol. 29. No. 8. pp1391-1404.

Whaites, A. (2000) Let's Get Civil Society Straight: NGOs the State and Political Theory. In Pearce, J. (ed) *Development, NGOs and Civil Society,* Oxford: Oxford Publication pp124-141.

White, S.C. (2000) Depoliticising Development: The Uses and Abuses of Participation. In Pearce, J. (ed) *Development, NGOs, and Civil Society,* Oxford: Oxfam Publication pp142-155.

Whitehead, A. (2004) *Persistent Poverty in Upper East Ghana. Basis Brief, Collaborative Research Support Program*, No. 28. Accessed at www.eldis.org on the 12/10/2008

Whyte, F.,W., Richardson, L. and Denzin, N. K. (2004) Qualitative Sociology and Desconstructionism: An Exchange, In Seale, C. (ed) *Social Research Method: A Reader*, London: Routledge pp491-498.

Winter, P. (2000). Glossary for New Samaritans. In Barrow, O. and Jennings, M. (eds) *The Charitable Impluse, NGOs and Development in East and North-East Africa*, Oxford: James Currey Ltd pp 31-44.

World Bank (2001) *Attacking Poverty*, New York: Oxford University Press

World Bank (2004) *Participation (PRSP) Poverty Reduction Strategy Formulation* www.worldbank.org/participation/PRSP/technotes/tn18.htm.

World Bank (2005) *World Bank-Civil Society Collaboration-Progress Report for Fiscal Years 2000 and 2001*, The World Bank, Washington DC accessed on http://www.worldbank.org/ngos

Woroniuk, B. and Schalkwyk, J. (1998) *Participation, Governance, Political Systems*, Stockholm, SIDA, Accessed at www.sida.se on 14/05/2010

Yunus, M. (1997 'The Grameen Bank Story: Rural Credit in Bangladesh'. In Krishna, A., Uphoff, N. and Esman, M. (eds). *Reasons for Hope: Instructive Experience in Rural Development,* Connecticut, USA: West Hartford Kumarian Press pp 9-24.

Zelenev, S. (2005) *Forging Partnership for Social Protection in South and East Asia*, United Nations Secretariat/DESA.

BREIF ON THE DEPARTMENT OF COMMUNITY DEVELOPMENT

1.0 INTRODUCTION

On September 19th 1949, the Gold Coast Government issued a Memorandum on "Community Development and Local Government". The Colonial Secretary's covering letter to this Memorandum was explicit with regards to Community Development as follows:

> "The acceleration of the economic and social development of the community in every part of the Gold Coast by harnessing the community's own energies in the settled policy of the Government".

> By 1951 an experiment in Community Development, which was started in 1949 by means of a mobile teams, composed of literates drawn from various organisations covered Trans-Volta (now Volta Region) Ashanti and Fante area. This experiment proved the depth and quality of Social Services that educated people were prepared to render to their less unfortunate countrymen, at least in Mass Education and the beginning of the Department of Community Development.

> It was established to assist rural and disadvantaged urban poor communities to improve upon heir socio-economic well being by building upon their initiatives and with their active participation.

The Department operates in all the 110 districts (now 134 districts an observation made during the field work of the researchers PhD work) in the country and has stationed majority of its field staff at the sub district levels to promote a more a more interactive relationship with the communities. The Ministry of Local Government, Rural Development and Environment exercises ministerial responsibility for the Department.

2.0 VISION

Our vision is to facilitate the attainment of total development socially, culturally, economically and politically - for the vulnerable and disadvantaged by the year 2020.

3.0 MISSION

The Department of Community Development exists to mobilise and work in partnership with communities by using all available resources to improve the living standard and social well being of the people in an effective decentralised system through adult education and extension services.

4.0 AIMS AND OBJECTIVES

Within the broad objectives of seeking an improvement in the socio-economic well being of rural and deprived urban communities the Department pursues the under-listed specific objectives:-

> To assist in the eradication of illiteracy and ignorance among the adult population

> To facilitate the dissemination of development related information to the people at the grass roots

To relay back o the government the views and opinions of the people about national policies and development programmes thereby creating a two way communication channel between government and the people

To provide technical services towards the construction of essential socio-economic infrastructure for needy communities using self-help methods

To transfer employable skills to the youth through training in mass education institutions like Rural Development College, Women Training Institutes and Technical Institutes

To extend support services in community animation, mass mobilisation and grass roots organisation to sister development agencies.

To expose women to opportunities for enhancing their socio-economic status

To provide counselling, guidance, conflict resolution and other services to unit communities and other local organisations

To undertake socio-economic surveys on needy communities to enable them assess their situation and proceed to initiate economic projects

To ensure an enhanced community participation in local development efforts and national reconstruction processes

5.1   MASS EDUCATION DIVISION
It undertakes the identification and registration of learners and the teaching of adult illiterates in the art of reading, writing and reckoning in basic English and Vernacular. The organisation of discussion session with chiefs, opinion leaders, economic groupings and community residents on relevant issues which are of interest to them. Such discussions lead to the initiation of community and group action for improved living conditions. The Department's Audio Visual Aids (AVA) Unit and Rural Development College located at Kwaso in Ashanti Region are under the Mass Education Division.

5.2   AUDIO VISUAL AIDS UNIT
The Department has an Audio Visual Aids (AVA) Unit, which is the support wing of the Department providing printing services for the production of development communication materials and other needs. It is made of four components sections namely, the Video/Electronics, Printing, Photography and Graphics

a. Each of the ten (10) regions of the Department has a video van with a coloured television set, video deck, electricity generators, video films and other accessories for undertaking video film shows on development issues. There is one video camera at the Head Office for recording development activities.
The electronic section undertakes the repair and maintenance of the of the equipment and all other electronic equipment

b. The Printing Press at the Head Office is engaged in printing of educational materials, headed letter forms, files covers, certificates for the training institutes and other materials required by the Department.

c. The Photographic section is responsible for the provision of Photographic coverage of all departmental activities. The Department has professional photographers in 7 out of the ten regions hence some photographers cover more than one region.

The Graphic section prepares illustrations for exhibitions and other adult education programmes, banners printing of "T" shirts and other activities.

5.3 RURAL DEVELOPMENT COLLEGE – KWASO-ASHANTI

The Department established the Rural Development College on June 18, 1983 to offer training in community development approaches and rural development over a two-year period, leading to the award of a Diploma in Community Development.

Apart from departmental staff, the college admits staff members of non-governmental organisations, District Assemblies and private persons who persons who desire skills upgrading prior to engaging in grass roots development work.

Admission requirements include four credits at GCE 'O' Level/WASSCE including English, a pass at entrance examination and successful interview.

Courses offered include Research Methods, Communication, Social Structure of Ghana, Project Planning, Population Studies and Community Development. Students prepare a long essay as a requirement for the award of the diploma.

Over 800 students have successfully completed the course.

5.4 TECHNICAL SERVICES DIVISION

The Department's Technical Services Division has four sections. These are:-
   a. Works Section
   b. Survey Section
   c. Drawing Section
   d. Mechanical Section

Technical advice and support are provided for self-help projects being undertaken in communities. Training workshops are held while on the job training is provided to local artisans to enable them acquire improved constructional skills.

Type plans of school buildings; KVIP latrines and health posts are prepared for communities. Surveying and the preparation of site plans and village layouts are also undertaken.

The construction of self-help projects is supported with equipment like de-watering pump, vehicles and materials. The Division also provides supervision for departmental projects being executed through private contract.

6.0 FUNCTIONS OF THE DEPARTMENT

The Department undertakes six (6) main development programmes. These are Adult/Community Education and animation, Functional Adult Literacy, Home Science Education, Self-help Construction Projects, Youth Skills Transfer and Extension Services.

6.1 ADULT/COMMUNITY ANIMATON AND EDUCATION

The department organises the adult population into adult study groups comprising between 20 and 30 adult members. The groups are used as channels for conducting group.

Discussions on national programmes, developmental issues and other subjects or topic of interest to them. This discussions serve as opportunity for acquiring in-depth knowledge and to express their opinion on such subjects.

In addition mass meetings which are community durbars attended by majority of community residents are held for lectures, video film shows, drama and other activities to be undertaken to create awareness and educate the communities on relevant issues.

6.2 FUNCTIONAL ADULT LITERATCY

In collaboration with the Non-Formal Education Division of the Ministry of Education (NFED), the Department implements the functional adult literacy programme under which illiterate adults are organised into literacy classes to learn how to read and write first in their own local languages and then in English using a functional approach. The Department assists in creating awareness about the benefits of a literate adult, identify literate adults who can be facilitators, provides supervision and assists in the training of facilitators.

6.3 WOMEN'S WORK PROGRAMME

The programme involves the formation of women groups through which women are given skills training for income generating ventures, micro credit support, and product marketing. Exhibitions/demonstrations are organised to expose women to rich Ghana food table. Various children's wear are made. Women are also exposed to appropriate technology equipment and home products. Home visits are undertaken to impart home management techniques to women.

Discussions on nutrition, safe motherhood, environmental sanitation and other vital subjects are held to broaden the understanding of women. Current activities are:

Establishing women groups with 15 to 30 members as channels fro routing development assistance to the women members and their households

Training women in income generating schemes such as soap making, cassava processing and shea butter processing

Sources funds from NGOs, like ENOWID Foundation, Africa 2000, WHO Functional Literacy/Health Project and Womankind Worldwide for women as micro credit to enable them expand their income generating projects

Holding exhibitions/demonstrations on home products, improved food types and labour saving devices for women groups and other community members. Undertake home visits to impart skills in home management, nutrition and other subject areas.

6.4 YOUTH VOCATIONAL SKILLS PROGRAMME

The youth vocational skills programme seeks to provide the youth with employable skills and thereby stem the rural to urban migration while making young men and women productive, self-reliant citizens. A total of twenty (25) youth training institutions have been established out of which eighteen (18) are Women Training Institutes (WTIs) which offer 2 to 3 year course for young women in Catering, Dressmaking, Hairdressing, Home Management, Needle Work and English. The remaining 5 are Technical Institutes, which train young men in Carpentry, Masonry, Auto Mechanics, Draughtsmanship and English.

These institues admit SSS dropouts, JSS graduates, semi-literates and utilise training methodologies that are suitable to each group.

The WTIs are located at Madina Accra, Prampram, Suhum, Ho, Tamale, Bolgatanga, Navrongo, Bongo, Wa, Sunyani, Agona, Bekwai, Axim, Tarkwa, Takoradi, Panfokrom, Nsoatre, Bechem and West Kpong.
The Technical Institutes are in Ho, Sunyani, Kibi, Kwamo and Kintampo.

6.5 SELF-HELP CONSTRUCTION PRODUCTS (COMMUNITY INITIATIVE PROJECTS

Under this programme communities which generate interest in the acquisition of basic socio-economic infrastructure after adult education sessions are assisted to embark on the construction of primary schools, junior secondary schools, health posts, KVIP AND VIP latrines, community centres and other projects using self-help methods.

The programme also involves the training of local artisans in new constructional techniques to enable them construct facilities in their communities.

6.6 EXTENSION SERVICES

Support is extended to government agencies, non-governmental organisations and international agencies through collaborative programmes in areas like community animation and public education to enhance the implementation of various development programmes. Focus group discussions, village drama, puppet shows, cinema/video films, role-plays and other methods are used during the programme.

Animation and public education campaigns undertaken in recent years include Road safety campaign AIDS Prevention and Control, Anti-Bush Fire, The Value Added Tax (VAT), Family Planning, Payment of Water User fees and the recent Populations Census exercise.

Appendix B

WOMEN IN RURAL AREAS IN GHANA
THE MINISTRY OF LOCAL GOVERNMENT AND RURAL EVELOPMENT
ACTIVITIES GRADED TOWARDS THEIR PROGRESS
THE DEPARTMENT OF COMMUNITY DEVELOPMENT

1.0 Background

Women constitute 51% of the Ghana's population (2000 census) and majority live in the rural areas. The Ministry of Local Government and Rural Development (now called Ministry of Local Government, Rural Development and the Environment) has therefore developed programmes principally through the Department of Community Development to support rural women.

2.0 Programmes

The Department of Community Development is one of the Decentralised Department under the Ministry of Local Government and Rural Development.

It has a Women's Work programme that supports rural women. Its main objectives are to improve the socio-economic status of women to make them economically independent to contribute meaningfully to their families and national progress. The programme therefore supports rural and urban poor women through the following activities.

2.1 Group Development

Women are organised into groups to enable them collectively achieve objectives which individually cannot be achieve. Currently there are 1'625 Women's Groups countries wide with 32,500 members. These groups are empowered through training on group development skills (group dynamics, relationship, resource mobilization, leadership, etc). Furthermore, the groups are used as entry point for all public education on topical issues like HIV/AIDS, Family Planning, Civic responsibilities, etc.

2.2 Income Generating Activities

Currently, all the groups are involved in income generating activities depending on resources available in the communities. Group members are provided with skills in income generating activities food processing, garment construction, batik, etc). Rural women undertake these activities to raise household incomes and improve on household nutrition and basic needs.

2.3 Home management

Women are taught basic home management practices, reproductive health, child care, nutrition and good sanitation practices.

2.4 Micro finance

The groups are linked to micro-financial institutions for financial support for income generating activities. The institutions supporting them include District Assemblies (Poverty Alleviation Fund (PAF). Rural Banks, Social Investment Fund (SIF) AARDDO Credit, etc. the Financial Institutions are mainly located in urban settings and access to credit is difficult and insufficient for the women.

Most groups have cultivated saving habit and are using their savings as revolving fund to support their activities.

2.5 Water facilities

Women collect water for domestic use and which takes much of their time. They are therefore empowered to form water and sanitation. Committees at the community level as part of decision making process in the provision of water and sanitation facilities.

2.6 Reproductive Health and HIV/AIDS

Reproductive health and HIV/AIDS education is undertaken under the District Response Initiative. Community and District Level Planning for control of STI and HIV/AIDS.

Although the Department of Community Development engages in the above programmes to support women, it has been facing problems such as:-
-   Lack of transportation to enable field staff reach every women in the field.
-   Inadequate logistic support for effective fieldwork.
-   Difficulty to access credit by most groups to support expands their businesses.
-   Inadequate training packages for fieldworkers.

DEPARTMENT OF COMMUNITY DEVELOPMENT (DCD)

1.0 Mandate

The DCD is one of the key Departments under the Ministry of Local Government and Rural Development (MLGRD). Its primary mandate is to promote and ensure improvement in the living standards of the rural areas and disadvantaged sections of urban communities through their own initiatives and with their active participation. The Department therefore promotes the socio-economic well being of rural communities, the disadvantaged and urban poor within a decentralised administrative system. Its primary focus is on helping the vulnerable and socially excluded to improve upon their situation by building on their own initiatives and assets (mostly time and talent).

Objectives and Functions
Objectives

The objectives of the department are;

- ❖ To increase social and economic growth in the rural communities through activities of poverty reduction, employment creation and illiteracy eradication among the adult and youth population of the country.
- ❖ To improve the status of women through their participation and involvement in socio-economic activities in the country
- ❖ To decrease the total dependence of communities on the Central Government in the provision of social infrastructure and amenities by encouraging self-help spirit in the communities
- ❖ To facilitate the participation of specialised Governmental and Non Governmental Organisations (NGOs) in integrated rural development programmes and projects
- ❖ To decrease and curb migration of the youth from rural to urban areas by transferring appropriate technology and vocational skills to enable the youth achieve and maintain a meaningful life while remaining in their local communities.

Functions

In order to achieve the above objectives the Department performs the following functions:

- ❖ Stimulates, mobilises and organise adults and youth into viable groups for establishing, saving and credit opportunities, especially in the rural areas of the country.
- ❖ Mobilises and organises trade-training groups for the transfer of appropriate technical and vocational skills for both the youth and other adults in the socio-economically deprived areas of the country.
- ❖ Implement the National Functional Literacy Programme, especially among the rural population
- ❖ Stimulates, mobilises and organises women with focus on the under privileged of the rural areas through women's empowerment programmes
- ❖ Organises self-help groups, self-help projects and provides technical expertise to ensure adherence to policies and efficient use of resources by local community entities such as District Assemblies and Units Committees
- ❖ Extend Community Development Services to assist specialised Governmental and Non Governmental Organisations engaged in countrywide rural development

Administrative coverage

The Department has administrative offices in all the 10 regions and 134 district capitals in Ghana. it also has 545 mass education teams, 25 youth training institutes (including 20 women's training institutes offering vocational training, hair dressing, catering, computer training, home management and entrepreneurship training) and staff strength of 1063 countrywide as at December 2003.

2.0 Key Programmes for the Vulnerable and Exclusion

The Department's primary mandate is to improve the general living conditions of the rural and urban poor through empowerment and community action. This thinking has influenced the Departments key programmes and activities. The key programmes of the department that impact directly on the vulnerable and the poor include the following;

> **Traditional Skills and Vocational Training**

These actives focus on equipping participants with the skills required for self-employment and self-sufficiency. It aims at creating opportunities for the poor, vulnerable and socially excluded to increase their incomes and asset bases in order to enhance their coping mechanism. This is also borne out of the Department's believe in the strength of the link between low and unreliable incomes and vulnerability and also that empowering women is perhaps the most important tool to fight intergenerational poverty, which also tends to perpetuate vulnerability and social exclusion.

The DCD's skills and vocational skills training activities are conducted at its National Women's Training Centre and at various Women's Training Institutes located in the regions. DCD trains women in basic skills such as catering, dressmaking, needlework and craft as well as home management.

> **Rural Industrial Skills Training**

This training is primarily aimed at youth residing in the rural areas of the country. It is conducted at centres for rural industries situated strategically to serve all the regions. Here the DCD trains and equips youth with useful vocational skills for rural industries, self-employment and improvement of their communities.

> **Non Formal Education activities**

These activities are targeted primarily at the vulnerable groups such as rural women, children and youth who are illiterate and focus on adult education and extension services using visual aids and other mass education skills and techniques such as poetry, singing, puppetry and drama. Adult education activities are provided through group meetings periodically combined with lectures and discussions and other experimental learning methods.

> **Adult Literacy**

This activity is designed by DCD to give another opportunity to school dropouts, adults and other youth who have no access to formal education. Literacy classes are conducted in English and local languages. There is also a fair attempt at introducing basic numerical activities. Through these activities DCD emphasises a functional approach to problem solving and attaining functional literacy.

> **Extension service**

This activity is directed at increasing rural women's involvement and participation in the socio-economic and political uplifting of the communities and the country as whole. This activity, also known as rural women's fieldwork is pivotal to DCD's community development projects as it includes training in home management skills, income generation skills, business management, improved child-care, health and nutrition. DCD is the pioneer and the most experienced agency in organising and implementing projects in mass communication and information sharing countrywide. DCD has the capacity to assist other Ministries and community organisations involved in rural development activities by preparing members of the communities for the intended social actions of these organisations. In recent times DCD has played a key role in mobilising communities in support of campaigns to stimulate payment of tax, voting wisely, guinea worm eradication, family planning methods and practices, preventing teenage pregnancies, environmental sanitation and hygiene, drug abuse and addiction, and aids education and prevention which all constitute risks for the chronic poor, vulnerable and socially excluded.

In recent times DCD has focused its attention and dwindling resources on improving skills and creating opportunities in rural areas in order to stem the menace of street children. The department is also involved in providing skills training to the street children in vocational employable skills to assist, rehabilitate and resettle in the home communities. In addition the department is also mobilising support and care to People Living With Aids (PLWA) one of the most vulnerable and socially excluded groups in Ghana. DCD is also organising training programmes for organised groups of vulnerable women and also assists them to have access to micro finance. Provide technical skills and services for community self-imitated projects.

Areas of concentrated of DCD work

The deprived communities and areas that have attracted the most attention of the DCD include the following given the extent of poverty, deprivation of these communities and their ability to slide into extreme and chronic poverty at the least shock in the society. The areas include:

- The Savannah areas
- The three Northern Regions
- Parts of the Central Region
- Parts of the Volta Region
- Afram Plains
- Parts of the Brong Ahafo Region
- Some urban communities, for example Sodom and Gomorrah in Accra
- Western Region

3.0 Views on Vulnerability and Exclusion

The Department of Community Development has no official definition of vulnerability and social exclusion. They have thus adopted a pragmatic approach to identifying vulnerable and socially excluded people as well as communities. In that regard they focus on a combination of the following indicators in the choice of programmes and targeted beneficiaries. They include:

- Nature of the community
- Appearance of the people in the community, their looks way of dressing, the way they speak and comport themselves among others.
- Health of children in the communities
- Mothers whose children still die from the six killer diseases
- Those who will be affected first if there is any problem (famine, civil conflicts)
- Access to good drinking water
- Access to toilet facilities

307

- Energy sources of the people (fire wood, millet stock, gas stove, etc)
- Access to food and nutrition
- The extent of disaster periods
- Seasonal variations in vulnerability, for example the north is vulnerable during the planting season (April-June)
- General levels of income
- Households who are the first to remove their children from school

4.0 Role of V&E in Selection of Programmes

The V&E themselves have a limited role in the selection of programmes intended by the DCD to impact their lives. This stems from 1) lack of a working definition of the vulnerable and socially excluded 2) the community-based approach to the work of DCD and 3) lack of resources for a proper stakeholder engagement. In a limited number of instances, however, there are broad based community consultations depending on the nature of the programme and the community in question. The department normally uses community entry strategies that allow them to solicit community buy-in into their pre-determined programmes and interventions. In other cases the DCD determines the programmes with key opinion leaders who may not necessary be vulnerable and excluded.

5.0 Measurement Indicators

DCD has no officially established indicators for measuring vulnerability and social exclusion. This also stems from the lack of proper and comprehensive definition and focus on vulnerability and social exclusion.

6.0 Impact of Programme on Targeted Beneficiaries

DCD has been implementing general community-based programmes whose impact has not been properly assessed because of lack of quantifiable objectives, baseline data and clear-cut input, output, outcome and impact indicators at the inception of the projects. Judging by the DCD's overall objective of community empowerment and improvement in the lives of rural and urban areas the increases in rural and urban poverty means the overall impact of the DCD's activities has been minimal. Specific DCD interventions in specific communities have achieved tremendous success. These include education on guinea eradication and non-formal adult education and acquisition of vocational skills.

7.0 Institutional/Capacity Challenges

The DCD is faced with serious institutional capacity challenges that have rendered it almost moribund. Like most MDAs, low salaries and lack of adequate logistics have greatly undermined the capacity of the highly qualified and well-trained human resource within the DCD to function professionally and to achieve the desired results.

Staffing

Out of the staff establishment of 1500 DCD currently has 1063 workers. This has reduced from 1071 in 2002. A request for staff in the categories defined below since November 2003 is still outstanding.

Category	Qualification	Number
Community Development	University Degree	50

Officers		
Assistant Community Development Officers	Diploma in Community Development	60
Technical Instructors	Higher National Diploma (HND)	72
Technical Staff (Masons, Carpenters)		30
Total		212

Low Budgetary allocation

Budgetary allocation to the DCD has dwindled rendering it incapable of implementing programmes. The Table below shows budget allocation to the Department in the last three years:

Year	Nominal Budget Allocation (cedis)	Real Budget Allocation (2001 Base Year cedis)
2001	6,975,004,492	5,387,271,123
2002	9,084,085,536	7,352,399,497.16
2003	12,899,327,994	12,506,599,979.17
2004	14,759,751,480	

(Bennet I already asked Willie to get these figures, could you please asked him again
I'll also remained him)

8.0 Key Policy Message

Policy should focus on empowering old institutions rather that creating new ones to ensure fuller utilisation of existing capacity with the public and private sectors.

9.0 Key Findings & Conclusions

1. The DCD has very good national coverage and experience to provide technical support to the District Assemblies in the design and implementation of programmes aimed at the vulnerable and socially excluded. It needs however to be well resourced with additional staff and logistics to provide this critical missing link in the planning of most District Assemblies.

2. Most MDAs (for example MLGRD itself) are implementing programmes for which the DCD has experienced technical expertise. This duplication of functions also results in inefficient resource use. A better coordinated approach to tackling vulnerability and social exclusion will result in a more efficient utilisation of capacity within key state and private institutions.

3. the department has virtually no project funds. Most of the budgetary allocations pay staff salaries and emoluments and some minimal level of capital expenditure.

4. DCD has a good focus on community development and social mobilisation that can be tapped to tackle vulnerability and social exclusion. They are already at the front line of development in deprived communities, where in most cases the truly vulnerable and socially excluded can be found.

5. The lack of clear definition on vulnerability and social exclusion by a key rural and community development focused state institution is a challenge to the attempts at tackling vulnerability and social exclusion.

10. Names and Positions of Staff Consulted

Name	Position
Mr. P. I. Ayanaba	Acting Director
Mr. J. A. Asakanyigarigo	Deputy Deputy Director
Mr Paul Avorkah	Assistant Director
Service Opare	Assistant Director
Ms Faustina Essandoh	Principal Community Development Officer (Women's Needs)

MAPS OF GHANA AND WESTERN REGION OF GHANA

Map of Ghana

Source: http://www.mapsofworld.com/ghana/ghana-political-map.html (July, 2005)

Map of the Western Region of Ghana Showing Nzema East District

Lightning Source UK Ltd.
Milton Keynes UK
UKOW04f1836250714

235794UK00001B/51/P

9 783659 281631